# FOREVER BOY

# FOREVER BOY

## A Mother's Memoir of Autism and Finding Joy

### KATE SWENSON

PARK
ROW
BOOKS

PARK
ROW ™
BOOKS ™

Recycling programs
for this product may
not exist in your area.

ISBN-13: 978-0-7783-1199-7

Forever Boy: A Mother's Memoir of Autism and Finding Joy

Park Row Books
22 Adelaide St. West, 41st Floor
Toronto, Ontario M5H 4E3, Canada
ParkRowBooks.com
BookClubbish.com

Printed in U.S.A.

To the boy who smells like the wind, the boy who saved me, the boy who healed our family, the girl who completed us and my husband for never giving up on me, thank you.

# FOREVER BOY

# INTRODUCTION

I dreamed of being a mother from an incredibly young age. While some little girls daydream about being a ballerina or becoming president, I wanted a family. I would fantasize about it often with my Barbies and baby dolls, playing house well into my tweens.

When I moved into my first home with my fiancé, my mother dropped off numerous tubs of my childhood belongings in my kitchen. It appeared she had saved everything. In the first tub, I found awkward photos of me in thick glasses with a bowl cut (my mother called it the Dorothy Hamill and said it was darling...it was not), faded second- and third-place ribbons from elementary school track meets, handwritten notes to friends, and countless diaries with little keys. The secrets of my life inside.

"Brody and I are going to get married and have five babies and dogs and horses and live in a big, beautiful house. We will have three girls and two boys. I will be a veterinarian. He will play professional basketball and we will be in love forever. Our life will be perfect."

I was seven, and it was obvious I had my whole life planned

out. But not once did it occur to me that one of my babies could have a disorder that would prevent him from communicating even the simplest need. Or that his body would grow, but his understanding of safety and independence might not. Nobody thinks it could happen to their child.

But the thought nagged me for years after we learned the diagnosis. What if I had known? What if someone had whispered the secrets of my future in my ear during my pregnancy, as if they had a crystal ball?

*"You and your baby are destined for a world different than most. You will call him Cooper, yet the world will call him disabled.*

*"It will be hard at first. You will experience suffering, struggle, and sadness, but eventually you will overcome it, and catch a glimpse of the unbelievable joy he brings to your world. You will come to understand that in fact, you are the lucky one.*

*"But the beginning, well, it will nearly break you."*

If I had been warned about autism and all it would change, would I have run away crying? Or laughed out loud? I guess I'll never know. I do know that nothing prepared me for the way stress and worry would overshadow a large part of my life for years to come. And I don't know if anything truly could have. It was something that I had to experience for myself.

You may read the first chapters of this book and think it's a sad story. Please keep going. You'll see it is not.

You may also think it's a story about a boy with autism. And while yes, Cooper is certainly the star, it is also the story of me as a mother, finding my way down an unexpected path.

It is the story of mistakes and triumphs—of altered dreams and agonizing hope.

A story of a marital compromise, and sibling rivalry, and the shifting perspective of advocacy, as I tirelessly find new ways to give my nonverbal boy a voice in this world.

In the end, it's about discovering exactly who I was meant to be.

And I owe it all to my son.

# ONE

Jamie and I met right after I graduated from college, during an internship I took at a large bank. I had no desire to work in banking, none whatsoever, but I wanted to make money and get my foot in the door somewhere. Spending my time with professional men and women seemed like a logical next step toward adulthood.

I was just coming out of a relationship and not really looking to date anyone. As a woman who always had a boyfriend, for the first time in my life I had the freedom to do whatever I wanted, whenever I wanted. I spent my summer working two jobs and having fun with friends.

Then I met Jamie, five years my senior, and far too serious for me. He was working on a promotion from banker to branch manager and had no time for me. In fact, many years later he would tell me he nicknamed me the "flouncy intern in the short skirt" and ratted me out to our boss for taking long lunches. We were at different places in life, or so I thought. But midway through the summer, we found ourselves together at a softball tournament, the rest of our coworkers canceling last minute. We decided to make the best of it and ordered a pitcher of beer on the patio of the bar.

He spoke of his future plans, his dreams of owning a little house and a fishing boat, and his close relationship with his family. When he got up after a bit to go catch for his softball team, I was a goner. I don't know if it was the tight white baseball pants, the fact that he was a real grown-up man and different than everyone else I had dated prior, or a combination. I spent the night daydreaming about a future with Jamie.

A year later, on a beautiful fall night, he proposed on one knee. I said yes before he could even finish the words, "Will you marry me?" The next year flew by. We purchased a two-bedroom home in Two Harbors, Minnesota, a tiny city located on Lake Superior, where the average high temperature in the summer was sixty degrees. Neither of us knew anyone there, but Jamie had been promoted to manage two smaller banks up the North Shore, so we decided to make it home. I had said goodbye to my career in banking when I found out how much direct sales was involved and took a position as a marketing co-ordinator for an assisted-living facility. We spent our time living a rather simple life. Just starting out in our careers, neither of us really made any money, but we didn't know any different. We bought that old fishing boat Jamie had told me about on our first date and spent most of our time outdoors and fixing up our old house. And we planned our wedding.

During this period, I very distinctly remember attending a weekend of premarital counseling at the church we had chosen. The class was centered around topics that a couple might encounter throughout their marriage. The class was led by two pastors, a husband and wife. It seemed completely unnecessary because we were madly in love; our relationship could handle anything, and certainly we didn't need help from some counselor.

We sat around the table, munching on cookies and drinking

punch, while the pastors threw out different scenarios. How would you handle a partner with an addiction? Or a partner who lies. A partner who gambles.

They told stories that seemed ridiculous. One included a wife racking up hundreds of thousands of dollars of credit card debt in secret. In another, a husband drank a case of beer every night on his drive home from work, only to tell his wife he was sober. Jamie and I giggled at some of the stories and gave a side-eye to the rest. We spent much of the time doodling and planning our honeymoon.

It's not that we were rude. We just couldn't believe that we would ever end up like that. We were best friends, young and in love. I was twenty-four and he was twenty-nine. We had planned our life together and wanted the exact same things. A house full of kids, country living, success in our careers, and eventually a cabin on a lake to retire to. It was simple. It was planned and therefore it would happen. Oh, the arrogance of twentysomething kids.

The day dragged on. The final question at the end of the session was, "How would the two of you handle having a child with special needs?" I can still remember one of the pastors asking that question. I can even see him—what he was wearing and how he said it so casually, so matter-of-factly. Like it was a common thing. It is burned in my brain now. The foreshadowing is not lost on me.

I remember thinking, *What a silly question.* That would not happen to us. He went on to briefly talk about the stress of having children, and how a child with special needs intensifies it. I remember not being jarred by the question, not in the slightest. I mean, we were healthy and invincible. We had no special-needs children in our families. In fact, I didn't even know a person with special needs. I also didn't plan to do drugs or drink during my pregnancies, so obviously our babies would be fine. Perfect.

I think we scribbled down on the paper that we'd love that

baby just like any other baby. Because that's what you are supposed to say. Right? We were both good people with huge hearts. And that was that. The class was done, and we were off to live our fairy-tale life, the thought of special needs never crossing our minds again until much later.

On September 13, 2008, Jamie and I were married on the wettest day the North Shore had ever seen in a tiny church on a river. The day started with sunshine and a marching band at 6:00 a.m. Like the rain, the musical serenade was not expected either. But it happened to be the morning of an annual Rollerblade marathon, so we danced our way to breakfast to "The Ants Go Marching" and pretended it was for us.

Hours later it was downpouring. The rain came down sideways and in sheets. One would think as I stood in the window of the church, watching our guests run in under giant umbrellas, that I would have been devastated. But I wasn't. I didn't care at all.

Sweating the small stuff that was out of our control was not in my character. I didn't care that one of my family members stole money out of the card basket I made, or that a member of our wedding party passed out before the ceremony was over, or that my new groom had hit a skunk on the way to the church and smelled a bit funky.

I cared that I was getting married to my best friend, the man who made me laugh like no other and rubbed my feet while we binge-watched seasons of 24 and drank 7 and 7's. While Jamie and I were quite different people, and I have the love language compatibility quiz results to prove it, we had one thing in common. We chose joy and simplicity.

Our wedding was a huge success. I loved every second of it. We danced the night away until 2:00 a.m. with our friends and family and went to bed happy and married. But the next morning, after our friends and family were gone and we were alone in our living room, surrounded by gifts, I burst into tears. My new husband didn't know what to do. Instead of feeling happy, I felt depressed. There had been so much buildup, from the parties to the showers to the constant planning, and then it was just over. I felt like a whole phase of my life had just ended.

As I sat there, I thought back to holidays and big events with my mom over the years, and how she always cried when they were over, and how I never understood why. In that moment I did. She loved the anticipation, the planning, and the buildup. Just like I did.

I turned my excitement to babies after our wedding. We had gone off birth control the month before, neither of us knowing how fast it would happen. We got pregnant the first time we tried, shortly after our wedding. We were surprised by how easy it was. We saw a heartbeat at eight weeks. A little flicker on the screen. We told everyone and immediately announced it on Facebook.

At thirteen weeks, I started to get the feeling that something was wrong. It was the Sunday of Christmas weekend, and the day before a routine doctor's appointment and an ultrasound. We spent the day at my father's house. I was a wreck, sensing that something was just a bit off. I couldn't put my finger on anything specific, just that I no longer felt pregnant. A friend told me that was normal and that symptoms can fade in the second trimester. Google told me it was not really all that normal. The word that came up was *miscarriage*. A word that hadn't crossed my mind.

That evening, Jamie and I went for a walk in the woods with our dogs, a normal evening pastime for our little family. I broke down and cried about halfway through. I told my husband my fear. I was fairly sure something was wrong with the baby. He told me it would be fine. But to Jamie, everything always was fine. He was unshakable.

The next morning, we were crammed into a tiny little room at my OB's office for my twelve-week ultrasound, one week late. This was a big appointment, and Jamie's first time being

in an ultrasound room. I was in a crinkly gown, legs up in stir-
rups, with Jamie standing next to me, holding my hand. The
tech first put the sticky gel on my stomach, moving the device
in a slow circular motion.

After just a second, the tech turned the screen away from us,
excused herself, and left the room. In her absence, Jamie and I
waited in silence. She came back minutes later and said she was
going to do a transvaginal ultrasound. As she pulled the big
wand out, rolling the condom-like sheath down the shaft, Jamie
burst out laughing. "Where is THAT going?" I was thankful
for his humor.

After a minute she removed herself from the room again. In
that instant I knew. I had read enough horror stories the night
before to know what was coming. Our doctor entered after what
felt like an eternity and said there was no heartbeat. The baby
was gone. Just like that. No real niceties. No small talk first.
He did not beat around the bush. My worry was confirmed. I
had my answer.

He too called it a miscarriage. He said it is the body's way
of discarding pregnancies that are not viable and attempted to
provide comfort to me by telling me that something was wrong
with our baby and this was the body's way of telling us that.
"You are not alone. Ten to twenty percent of pregnancies end
in miscarriage. It's quite common." I'm not sure if that was supposed to make me feel less alone, but it didn't.

The doctor went on to scribble a picture on a prescription pad.
It looked like chicken scratch when he turned it around for us to
see. Side by side, drawn close together, were two large circles.
Each large circle had a different size smaller circle inside, one
visibly larger. Jamie and I still to this day talk about that picture.

"See." He pointed to the picture and said, "Your baby looks
like this one, but it should look like this one at twelve weeks."

I viewed it through tear-filled eyes. I didn't see it. I immediately thought of that episode of *Friends*, when Jennifer Aniston

doesn't see her baby on the ultrasound but nods in agreement anyways. He patted me on the shoulder and told us we could try again in a few months, almost like a coach pats his player. He also told us we could have the drawing.

But that wasn't the worst memory of that day. Jamie had to leave. He had to get to a loan closing at one of the banks he managed. He couldn't miss it, and while it was not his fault, I was crushed. I had to wait by myself and schedule the appointment that would remove from my body the baby I had wanted so badly.

As I sat with the scheduler, going over the details of what a D&C was and how the surgery was performed, my tears fell fast and hot. She said I would need to report to the surgery center at five o'clock the next morning and to make sure not to eat after midnight that night. My head snapped up.

"Wait. What? Tomorrow morning? Shouldn't we wait to see if this is wrong?" It was all happening too fast. Shouldn't I get a second opinion? What if the dates were wrong?

She didn't say anything, just made a sad little sound. She then handed me the card with the appointment date and time written on it. Her face said it all.

I had to drive myself home. I left a sobbing message for my boss and for my mom and then turned my phone off. I didn't want to hear that miscarriage was common. I didn't want to hear that we could try again in a few months. I wanted to be sad. I spent the rest of the day trying to figure out how I was going to tell people that I was no longer pregnant, angry at myself for announcing so early. Every scenario felt sad and awkward.

When Jamie returned from work that evening, he found me curled up on the couch. He repeated what our doctor had said. "We could try again. This was a good thing. Something must have been wrong with our baby. Next time it will be perfect."

We arrived at the hospital the next morning for the procedure. The surgery itself was fast. When I woke up in recovery, still groggy from anesthesia, I asked the nurse if my baby was gone. I drifted back to my anesthesia haze before she could answer, but I do have this memory of her saying out loud, maybe to another nurse, that it was one of the saddest questions she'd ever been asked post-surgery.

I cried for weeks after losing that baby. For the first time I felt a huge loss of control over my own life. I turned to diet, exercise, running mostly, and figuring out why my body had failed me. I dove into research and read about other women who suffered from a miscarriage. I needed to educate myself, but even more than that, I needed to make a connection to others who understood what I was going through. The women I virtually met after my miscarriage would go on to become lifelong friends, that loss bonding us. Finding others who understood was life-changing.

Jamie didn't grieve like I did, and after talking to other women, I guess that's normal for husbands. My body went through something monumental and I wanted to talk about it, but he did not. I was angry that he wasn't sad enough over the loss of our baby, and I suppose he would have said I was too sad. We did not have many fights during our first year of marriage, but we fought hard about our grief over losing that child.

I became hyperfocused on getting pregnant again, almost as if it was a job. Sex became planned and not at all fun. I peed on ovulation sticks in a bathroom stall at work, crying when I didn't get the smiley face. A coworker said to me, "Travel, enjoy this time together. You'll have babies before you know it." She wasn't wrong, but her brazen attitude offended me.

Some time later, after dramatically convincing myself we would never have children, I got a positive pregnancy test. Yet instead of excitement, I felt fear. I didn't want to fall in love with another baby, only to lose him or her.

I left the test on the bathroom sink before hopping on the treadmill in the basement to run. When Jamie got home shortly after, I asked him to grab me a hair tie in the bathroom. He came downstairs carrying the test, with the biggest grin on his face. "Is this real?" He was so excited. We didn't say a word to anyone until we were twenty weeks along. Not even to our parents.

Around six months, I finally calmed down and let myself enjoy my pregnancy, and I found out that once I relaxed, I loved being pregnant. Jamie was excited too and even purchased a baseball bat and glove for his first son. When they arrived in the mail, I cried. Jamie's relationship with his dad was unlike any I had ever known before. They were best friends, speaking daily on the phone. His dad had coached him through many years of sports and was his biggest fan. I had no doubt that Jamie would have the same relationship with our son.

Cooper was born on December 6, after what felt like the longest pregnancy ever. When you have a child diagnosed with special needs, you will forever be asked about your pregnancy and birth. Every therapy center, school, even county you live in will want to know about those nine months. I always found it to be invasive, checking boxes about my vaginal birth on a school form. But the answers stayed the same. Besides gaining way too much weight, my pregnancy was perfect. No issues whatsoever.

The beginning of the birthing process was rather uneventful and slow-moving as well, although the excitement over meeting Cooper and becoming a mother was almost more than I could handle. Because of the baby's potential size, and lack of movement as I neared forty weeks, my doctor scheduled me for an induction. Jamie and I arrived at the hospital on a Sunday night, and the process was started with Cervidil. No progress. The next morning, I was hooked up to Pitocin. No progress. After hours of walking up and down the hallways, finally there was progress but not enough. While we were ready to meet our baby, he was not ready to meet us. It appeared that we were on his timeline, which was excellent foreshadowing, if you ask me. He wasn't going to budge for any of us.

Finally, after being in the hospital for twenty-four hours, it was time to push. I felt excitement as the nurse modified the bed, dimmed the lights, and instructed my husband to grab a leg. His face turned white as he looked down. If he could have run away in that moment, he might have. I don't think he was prepared for such an up-close and personal experience.

During the birthing class about labor, I had foolishly assumed pushing came natural to a first-time mother. Like it would be instinctual. It was not for me. I felt awkward and exposed. And after a rather uncomfortable fecal situation, which my husband assured me was nothing, but would tease me about for years to come, I felt discouraged.

Two hours later we had progress. His head had crowned but he was stuck. I was exhausted and didn't know how much more I could take. After all that work, I was nervous my doctor was going to mention the word *C-section*, but instead he used the word *episiotomy*. That did the trick, and I felt immediate relief.

Cooper was born seconds later.

I thought for sure the doctor would place him on my chest right away so I could bond with him immediately like I had seen in the movies, but instead he was passed backward to a waiting nurse without even a glimpse for me. Within seconds, multiple people surrounded him.

I kept waiting for the cry. Everyone talks about that first cry, how it pierces the room. But our room was silent beyond the murmurs from the group surrounding Cooper.

The doctor kept repeating, "He's okay." But I was thinking, how did he know? He was working on me, stitching me up. He was not even looking at the baby on the table behind him. I reminded myself of the old airplane, flight attendant scenario. When you are on a plane, going through turbulence, there is no reason to panic until the flight attendants do. If they sit down and buckle up, well, hang on. The doctor was my flight attendant. He wasn't panicking.

I kept wiggling my butt around, trying to see what the nurses were doing. My doctor told me to hold still, but I couldn't. Finally, I heard a few words and phrases coming from the whispering nurses.

*"Intubate. Not breathing right. Come on, baby. Breathe."*

It felt like an eternity. In reality it was probably minutes.

*"I want my baby. I want my mom. Jamie, get my mom."*

And then the piercing, angry cry filled the room. It was Cooper. He was here. Just a little late to the party. And with that I collapsed back against the bed, my arms exhausted from holding myself up, trying to get to my baby. I let out the breath I didn't know I had been holding.

As the nurse set the bundle in my arms, she said, "Congratulations, mama. He's beautiful. And big! You have a nine-pounder here."

I looked down, and finally saw my baby. After all that hard work, and the scare, I had him, and I wasn't letting go. One of my girlfriends had told me the second you have your baby in your arms, the pain of childbirth disappears. She told me the beautiful stories of her daughters' births, claiming she didn't feel an ounce of pain after. I was the opposite. The second I had him, I felt every ounce of pain. He had put me through the wringer. But I didn't care. It didn't matter anymore. I had never loved something more.

The nurse informed us that his Apgar score was exceptionally low, but he seemed to be perking up, so they would just monitor him closely and he wouldn't have to visit the NICU. He did look a little bit like he'd been through hell. His head was cone-shaped and bruised, his blond hair matted down with blood. But what I remember the most were his eyes. I always assumed babies come out sleepy. Not our Cooper. He was wide-awake, eyes open, looking around the room. They seemed to be darting, almost, as if he was trying to make sense of what had just happened. He looked confused. Lost.

Finally, the room cleared out, and as the nurse closed the door behind her, I heard my mom say, "Is everything okay?" She responded with, "Yes, they just need a minute." She was right. We did.

Silence filled the room. Jamie and I finally looked at each other. "Were you scared? Oh my God, I was so scared."

"Naw, I knew it would be alright."

Once again, his calmness amazed me. He seemed unrattled, even unfazed by what had just happened. I, on the other hand, was still shaking.

I looked down again, unwrapping the blanket from the baby in my arms. We counted his fingers and toes. I giggled at the softness of his skin. Jamie kneeled at the side of the bed and placed his finger in our son's hand.

"Hey, Cooper, it's your mama and daddy!" Suddenly I felt my peace. I had my baby. I fell in love immediately and all at once. I was a goner. Images of baseball games and a little boy catching his first fish flashed before my eyes.

People ask me all the time when I realized something was different about my baby. Typically, the questions come from moms of toddlers who have concerns about their own child's development, and they want to be reassured that their child is fine. That it is not autism. I remind them that every story is unique, no two the same.

Some parents speak of a perfectly developing baby and then the flip of a switch at twelve months, the light seeming to dull. Or their toddler is speaking full sentences only to stop overnight. I've had countless videos shared with me…toddlers saying *mama* and *truck* and *ball*, the parents heartbroken over what used to be and is no more. Some parents claim they knew it was autism from day one, while some never saw it coming.

For me, I don't remember a time it wasn't autism. I might not have known the definition of the word yet, or the seriousness of the diagnosis, but looking back, I knew that my baby was autistic from the second I held him in my arms when he was just minutes old. Autism was woven through him, completing him, like an intricate quilt, unable to be separated out. Even though over the years to come I would desperately pray for it to be. I would try to determine what parts were my little boy and what parts were autism until I eventually realized they were one and the same. Removing the diagnosis would mean removing all of him, a realization that would take me years to accept.

There was a time in our lives when Jamie and I found the very question of raising a special-needs child unimaginable—ridiculous, even. Yet here we were, thrust into a life we were both wholly unprepared for, one that would challenge us, and change us, as a couple and as parents.

Tan pants and a denim shirt. That's what the pastor wore.

# TWO

While most parents pray for a healthy baby, I know a lovely woman, a mother, who told me that she and her husband prayed for their son to have Down syndrome. I met her when I was many years into autism but hadn't quite come to acceptance yet. She radiated joy, and I was drawn to her energy. I told her the story of Cooper, and she told me the story of her son.

At her thirty-fourth-week OB appointment, the doctor noted that her belly was measuring far too big and immediately did an ultrasound. She said at forty years old, ultrasounds are bittersweet because while they offer a much-anticipated glimpse of the baby, they also prompt anxiety about issues that come with advanced maternal age. The doctor confirmed it was a boy and then explained that there were irregularities.

A level two ultrasound confirmed that the baby's brain was deformed and if born, there was a high probability that he would be unable to walk, talk, move, or breathe. But there was another possibility too. The doctor told them the baby could be born with Down syndrome. Suddenly, a diagnosis where their baby lived was something they hoped for. He was born a week later with a head full of red hair. He had Down syndrome and a few other complications but was otherwise healthy. They were thrilled. She said the support they received from friends, family, even the medical community was immediate. And because they knew about the syndrome during the pregnancy, there was never a question that their son would be different once he was born.

It wasn't like that for Jamie and me. Instead, it was three years of searching for answers, most of them turning up more questions, the world denying Cooper's delays and differences at first. I sometimes wonder if it would have been different for us if we knew our son had autism all along, if it had been black and white. Definitive. Maybe if an ultrasound had detected it at twenty weeks, and we knew about it when the nurse placed Cooper in my arms for the first time, then we would have understood why it seemed like he was born into a world he didn't understand.

But a diagnosis of autism does not work like that. There is no blood test. There are no common physical markers. Instead, the signs vary from person to person, presenting in different ways. It can take years to diagnose and even longer for parents and family to accept. And that support she referred to—well, we didn't find that for many years to come.

We had nine months to ready our lives for Cooper—longer if you consider that I had been planning for him since my own childhood—but nothing prepared me for the disruption I felt that first week. The months leading up to his birth were all excitement. We both could not wait to be parents and spent many nights imagining who he would be. Would he be creative like me? Athletic like Jamie? We had so many things we wanted to teach him. How to catch a fish, hit a baseball, and ride a bike being a few. Jamie even dug out photos from his childhood and beamed as he showed me a picture of an athletic, blond-haired boy, riding a bike. I felt like I was looking at my future son.

"It's my Schwinn Predator. God, I loved that bike. It was so cool. My dad and I already talked about restoring the Predator for Cooper."

When I entered my third trimester, I printed a list off the *What to Expect When You're Expecting* website and made sure to check every box. I decorated the nursery in blue sailboats and stocked the changing table with diapers and onesies. We interviewed pediatricians. We visited countless day cares. We bought a baby doll to help acclimate our two puppies. We had not one but three beautiful baby showers. And we attended birth classes at the hospital where we planned to deliver. The class consisted of four one-hour sessions once a week and a hospital tour. We learned about the birthing process in graphic detail, a C-section versus vaginal delivery, possible medical interventions, how challenging breastfeeding can be, and the importance of sleeping when the baby sleeps. My biggest worry was the pain of childbirth. Beyond that, I wasn't afraid at all. Many of my friends had recently had babies, and none of them seemed to be struggling with motherhood, so I felt confident that I would be fine too.

Upon completion of the course, they gave us a certificate, and Jamie gave himself the official title of Certified Birthing Coach. He joked he wanted a T-shirt with his professional title to wear to the delivery. Or a hat. I told him not to add it to his résumé quite yet. As December neared, we were ready. We had checked all the boxes to have a baby.

I believe most newborns come into this life knowing what to do. It is instinctual. I know this because after Cooper, I had two more babies who effortlessly eased into life, seeming to know full well how to eat, sleep, and grow. But my beautiful Cooper, he seemed a bit lost at his newfound life. The life of a newborn didn't seem to come naturally to him.

Within hours of birth, we tried nursing. A sweet older nurse showed me how to position him in different ways, how to bring him to me instead of hunching over to him, how to cup my breast into a C shape, and how to gently pull down his bottom lip to help with latching. Only it didn't work like it was supposed to. His mouth couldn't quite figure it out. My baby could not latch. I think I pressed that call button for help a dozen times. As my frustration grew, so did his. I cried more tears than I could count trying to figure out how to breastfeed my baby those first few days. I adamantly refused to give up. I was not a quitter.

After three visits to the lactation consultant and finding out Cooper had lost well over a pound of weight, I switched to exclusive pumping. I felt instant relief as I watched him suck down a full bottle of breast milk. I knew I had made the right decision.

Sleeping didn't come naturally for him either. Newborn babies are supposed to sleep eighteen hours a day. That is what Google told me. My mother-in-law seconded it. Not my newborn. Instead, he slept eight hours in a twenty-four-hour period. In the hospital, he seemed to stockpile all the sleep he needed, and decided once home, he was done with all that nonsense. The rest of the time he was awake, wide-eyed and looking around, or crying.

We tried snuggling skin to skin. We tried taking a warm bath together. At that time, I couldn't figure out why my touch didn't seem to provide him comfort. The newborns I had known in the past loved cuddling up in the crook of my neck, making little squeaks. My baby wanted to be upright, facing outward, looking at the world. He loved lights and movement on the television. Most people have sleeping newborn pictures... I have pictures of Jamie sleeping in the recliner, head to the side, mouth open, and a wide-eyed baby, fully awake, studying the ceiling fan intently.

At the end of week one, I told my husband that they must have given us the wrong baby. There must have been a mix-up, because my mom said I slept all the time as a baby. And Jamie's mom said the same thing about him. We joked about going back

to the baby store and asking for an exchange. I felt pressure in
those early days to act like life was perfect. The pressure placed
on new mothers is no joke, autism or not.

Before Cooper, the curtains in my home were always open.
I loved sunshine and light. I loved sound, too, and my quirky
old house with the groaning furnace and squeaky floor. I always had country radio playing in the background or HGTV
on the television. And my husband would admit that I talked
a lot. We had frequent visitors too. Friends stopping by for a
drink or family visiting from out of town. Our home was alive.

That all changed drastically during the first week after Cooper was born. Once we realized that sleep was precious, and that
we had one goal and one goal only, to get that baby to sleep,
we became focused. We pulled the curtains in the living room
making it completely dark, even during the day. The music was
replaced with a white noise machine. The illuminated television
was muted. The ringers turned off on our phones. We communicated in whispers. Life became an endless cycle, and I couldn't
tell you if it was morning or night. I felt like a zombie.

Jamie was handling it all way better than I was, which is sur-
prising because he had no experience with babies at all. Maybe
it was because he only needed six or so hours of sleep a night
while I needed a solid nine. He also wasn't attached to a breast
pump every three hours with cracked nipples. He quickly perfected the supertight swaddle, how to change a diaper, how to
warm a bottle, and how to calm an overly emotional Kate. He
took turns with me pacing the floor and rocking in the old blue
recliner. He even put down masking tape on the floor to remind
us where the creaks were. He cooked and cleaned too. Many
years later he would tell me that the only memory he retained
from those first few weeks was the time he spent in the basement, pacing the cold cement floor, while Cooper wailed in
his arms, just so I could get some precious sleep. Without him
I would have been lost. Caring for Cooper was a two-person

job, but he was about to go back to work. His paternity time was ending, which scared me.

The night before Jamie was supposed to go back to work, I found myself standing in my kitchen, nursing tank top wide open, shoving Christmas cookies into my mouth, one after another. Tears were streaming down my face almost as if someone had flipped a switch on me. Jamie walked in, took one look and said, "I think you should call your mother. Or my mother."

That only made me wail harder. I couldn't stop crying, which felt weird because I wasn't much of a crier before becoming a mother. To combat the crying, I laughed maniacally at myself for crying about nothing.

"I'm not sad, Jamie. I'm just tired and overwhelmed. There is a difference."

I never thought the beginning of motherhood would be easy, but I didn't necessarily think it would be quite so hard either. I felt like a failure. Like I didn't know how to help my baby. This was not what I had pictured.

Jamie dialed the phone and handed it to me. I could hear the worry in my mother's voice as I told her about her grandson. That conversation was the first time I said, "I think something is wrong." But instead of saying it about my son, I said it about me. "I can't figure this out, Mom. He does not sleep."

She told me that there was nothing wrong with me, that it was mild postpartum. She told me to give the baby to Jamie, take a warm bath. Give myself a break. I knew in my heart she was right. That night I gave myself a little pep talk. I reminded myself that what I was feeling was totally normal. Being a first-time mother is hard, and this wouldn't last forever. I would make it through. We would make it through.

The next day I brought up my concerns with Cooper's pediatrician. I felt like a traitor as I told her how hard it was, almost whispering. I explained how Cooper never slept—at all.

But the doctor insisted it was normal. "Some newborns don't

sleep, Katie. Some are just more challenging than others. They get mad and upset and that's just normal. You don't get to pick what you get, and you, dear, got a challenging one. Go easy on yourself. You're a first-time mom. You'll figure it out."

"But why does he cry so much? He's just so angry all the time."

She went on to tell me it could be colic and that I could try removing certain foods from my diet in hopes that would help. Coffee, dairy, spicy foods, and anything tomato-based. Or even switch to formula.

She asked me if I had a support system and if I was having suicidal thoughts. I told her yes and no, but that I felt turned inside out. Like I couldn't get my bearings.

"This is just so different than I imagined..." I let my voice trail off.

While I spoke, she looked Cooper over from top to bottom and declared him perfect. With that she hugged me and whispered, "You are doing a great job, mama. Hang in there." Her advice as she walked out the door was, "Take him for a car ride. That worked for all three of my kids."

The next week, a friend of mine invited me to a mommy-and-me class at a bookstore in Duluth, which happened to be a thirty-minute drive from our home. I thought back to what the doctor had said, *Take him for a drive, it worked for my kids,* so I quickly said yes. Plus, I was desperate for socialization.

The second I buckled Cooper in his car seat, he started screaming, and he didn't stop until I pulled into the mall parking lot half an hour later. I felt frazzled and stressed as I drove, my fingers gripping the steering wheel so tightly my knuckles were white. I became so worried by his screams that I pulled over on the side of the expressway halfway through and climbed in the back seat of my car to check on him. As trucks whizzed by, I looked to see if he was being pinched or squished. Maybe he was cold or too warm. Nothing appeared wrong with him, yet he was inconsolable. I tried offering him a bottle and then a pacifier. He wanted neither. Since I was halfway between home and the mall, I had a choice. I could have turned back, but I chose to keep going. I would enjoy my first outing as a mother if it killed me.

When I walked into the bookstore, I felt good. Cooper was finally exhausted and sleeping in his stroller, and I saw friendly faces. The instructor told us all to grab a carpet square and sit down with our babies. Some of the moms had little babies like mine, and some had toddlers wiggling around. The instructor played soft music and advised us all to close our eyes and sway with our babies to the music. I was hesitant to wake my sleeping son but did as the instructor advised us. I gently pulled my son out of his carrier, sat down with the other moms and started swaying. His eyes darted open, not content to stay in that in-between sleepy place that most newborns are accustomed to. I could tell that he wasn't going to sleep through this like most newborns would. Cooper started thrashing. I swayed harder. He thrashed harder. I felt the sweat start to pool on my back and on my neck. *Come on, buddy, you got this*, I thought to myself.

While Cooper and I were still in the honeymoon phase of his life, I'd learned enough about him to know that he was about to really start screaming. I started to panic internally. It wasn't that I thought any of the women would care that I had a crying baby. It was that I felt like a failure because I couldn't figure him out. And no other babies were crying.

As the swaying turned to baby massage, Cooper started crying so hard I had to get up and walk the perimeter of the room with him. I tried bouncing him, feeding him, burping him, all the things I was supposed to do. But he wouldn't stop crying. The other mothers tried to assist with ideas to help calm him down, but nothing worked. I eventually left. I didn't like how out of control I felt with my own baby. But even more, I didn't like that feeling of other people thinking something was wrong with my baby.

Once buckled back in his car seat, Cooper passed out immediately, exhausted from our adventure into the real world. Only after I clicked my seat belt in place did I let the tears silently fall from my eyes. As I drove home, I tried to convince myself that what I was feeling was postpartum sadness and that I wasn't the worst mother.

As Cooper approached twelve weeks, it was nearing time for me to go back to work. In a way I was relieved. Maternity leave had been different than what I originally pictured. I had hoped to do a few Pinterest-type projects around the house, visit Jamie for lunch at his office, and travel to visit my parents and friends back in Wisconsin. But none of that happened. I was happy if I survived the day, if I got a shower and dinner on the table by 6:00 p.m. Cooper and I never once got into a routine with sleep. While most babies settle into a nap schedule by three months old, Cooper did not. I still spent much of my time trying to get him to sleep and sleep longer than forty-five minutes at a time.

Before I could return to work, I had to visit my OB for my postpartum checkup. The purpose of the appointment is to make sure the mother is physically and emotionally settling into a life with baby. My doctor asked me questions about my body. Was I experiencing any pain? He asked me questions about my emotions. Was I experiencing any sadness? How was breastfeeding going? I answered every question truthfully and honestly.

When he asked me about our method of birth control, I burst out laughing. "Are people having sex already?" I was shocked. Not only did I still not want to be touched, I could not think of a single time Jamie and I could have had sex in the last three months if we'd wanted to. Intimacy would require a sleeping baby.

After my doctor checked all his boxes, he said to me, "You

are good for ten thousand more miles." I sure hoped he was right because I didn't feel that way. While my body had physically healed, nothing had prepared me for how grueling the demands of motherhood would be on me. I felt like I didn't know who I was anymore.

The morning I had to return to work, I was surprised to find that my pre-pregnancy work pants were so big they wouldn't stay up. I dug the scale out and the number read 135. No wonder I didn't recognize myself. I hadn't been this weight since I was a teenager. I glanced in the mirror, something I hadn't been doing a lot of lately, and I saw that my cheekbones were sunken and there were dark bags under my eyes. I looked like a ghost. I barely recognized myself.

As I dropped Cooper off for his first day of day care, I was anxious to say the least. We had picked a small facility run by a nice woman who had a daughter of her own. Cooper was the youngest of a small group of children, and I was concerned with how she was going to manage his needs along with six other kids. She wasn't concerned in the slightest and waved me out the front door, saying she dealt with fussy babies all the time. On the way to work I called my mom, feeling worried. "Day care is great for babies, Katie; it puts them on a schedule. This is a good thing." I had been awake since 3:00 a.m., so a schedule sounded divine.

I settled back into work effortlessly. I loved my job and was proud of the position I held at a large nonprofit specializing in families and children. I enjoyed going to work and feeling like an adult. I enjoyed leading meetings and problem-solving. I was exhausted but rejuvenated after one day. Throughout the day, text messages arrived, bringing me updates of a happy baby enjoying his first day of day care. I was slightly confused but so relieved. When I arrived to pick him up, I practically ran to hold him. Being away from him all day felt as if a part of me was missing. She told me he didn't sleep much, which made me chuckle, but was content watching the other children play. He enjoyed the stimulation.

Over the summer Jamie and I seemed to find our parenting groove. I wouldn't say Cooper got easier. I'd say we adapted to him. We slept in shifts. We shuffled and juggled and took turns. We knew our life with our baby was different than that of our friends with their kids, but we also knew it wouldn't be challenging forever. We spent much of our time walking around the neighborhood, pushing him in a stroller. As long as we were moving, he was happy. There was only one rule: we couldn't stop walking.

On a whim, we decided to list our house for sale and search for land to buy in Duluth. When Jamie and I spoke of our future, the story always involved wild children running around in the woods, climbing trees, and building forts. That is how we both grew up, and we wanted the same for our children. Plus, we wanted to get closer to the city where I worked. We moved four weeks later. Because our home sold so fast, and we hadn't found a place to buy yet, we were forced to move into a rental property a few miles from the home we sold while we searched for the perfect home to raise our family.

When I look back on the time spent there, I refer to it as the dark days of my life. The rental was six hundred square feet, and I felt lonely. I did my best to make a home out of it, but it never felt like one. Jamie had recently transferred banks to Duluth in our anticipation for our move, which equaled longer days with a longer commute. With him being the primary breadwinner and working so much more, most of Cooper's care fell to me when I wasn't working. I hadn't made many friends where we lived since I worked thirty minutes away and grew up even farther away, and we spent a lot of weekends alone, just the two of us. I wanted so desperately to go places, like my friends did with their kids—zoos, parks—but it never worked out for us. Every trip seemed to be too overstimulating for Cooper, and resulted in us leaving early, often both of us in tears.

So most of our time was spent close to home, around our neighborhood, and visiting the shores of Lake Superior. I would bring a blanket and snacks, and we would sit together, watching the waves come in. We would sit there in silence, the fact that he wasn't babbling never crossing my mind. He was mesmerized by the bright-colored stones that covered the beach. He would always choose two after careful inspection, one for each hand, and hold them in his tightly closed fists. I would study him as he gazed at his hands and wonder what he was thinking about. His focus was unwavering. Many times, other children would come running up, sand shovels and buckets in hand, bending down to his level, and asking him to play. He never even glanced in their direction though. He just opened and closed his hands and stared at the water.

Often other families would set up blankets next to ours, their toddlers close enough for me to observe. I'll never forget those first feelings of something being off with Cooper. How they crept in, so sneaky-like, causing me to double take the differences. I would compare Cooper to other children, as most parents do, watching them shovel sand into a bucket or vroom a truck through a pile. My brain would take note, my heart denying what I was seeing. Some days I would pack up early, relieved to get away from those differences and leave them behind at the beach.

Some mothers say they fall in love with their babies the second they are placed in their arms. Others say it's from the second they saw that positive pregnancy test. But some claim it takes a while to settle into the love. Like two people getting to know each other.

For me, I fell in love with Cooper the second I saw him, but my love grew by a million in those early, lonely, confusing days, just the two of us. I knew he was challenging. I knew he wasn't like other babies his age. I wasn't blind, even though I wasn't ready to admit it out loud. But I think it made me work harder to be his mom because it was so challenging to connect with him. I knew his sounds, his expressions, and his cries. We didn't have words, and even though I longed for them desperately, I credit the lack of verbal communication for bringing us close. I became his person and he became mine.

The first time I heard the word *autism*, I was sitting in a lunch-and-learn at work eating a ham and cheese sandwich. Cooper was eleven months old. The presenter spoke about the most common signs of the disorder. Delayed communication. Doesn't smile. Repetitive behaviors. Rigidity. Lack of eye contact and imaginative play. As she spoke, I started to have an out-of-body experience. I thought, *Autism?* A boy I babysat in college had every sign this person was describing to me. But his parents never mentioned autism so he must have been undiagnosed at that point. I spent my time chasing him and trying to prevent him from killing their dog. I lost seven pounds that summer, and my hair may have turned gray. I was thankful when the summer was over. But that boy was nothing like my Cooper. As the presenter spoke about aggressive behaviors, I suddenly felt suffocated, like the walls were closing in on me. The autism she described sounded very scary, very dark. Were people staring at me? Did they know? I stood up, but did so too forcefully, and my chair hit the wall behind me, causing everyone in the room to look at me.

Once out of the conference room I leaned my body up against the cool wall to collect myself. I took a few deep breaths and then made my way to my office. I closed my door and entered the word *autism* into Google. I spent the rest of the afternoon reading everything I could about the disorder. Everything I read said not to worry until age two, and that diagnosis doesn't even happen until age three.

On a piece of paper, I scribbled down different signs and then next to each one wrote yes or no. By 3:30 I had myself convinced it was not autism. My son wasn't babbling, yes, there was no denying that, but autism, no way. I felt confident that this would all be fine as I drove to Cooper's day care to pick him up.

As I pulled into her driveway, I saw a gaggle of children jumping in and out of a snow pile. I smiled, knowing how much Cooper loved snow. Only I did not see his white-blond hair or bright red hat in the group. I looked around the yard, searching for my boy. My heart dropped as I saw him in the far corner, next to the fence, staring out. He looked like a little prisoner trying to escape, his face pressed up against the metal of the fence. His teacher quickly came up and told me he was having a rough day today and didn't want to play. I could tell she felt bad. Maybe even nervous that I might be angry.

I tried to get his attention, yelling his name. He barely gave a glance back. Meanwhile, other children's parents had arrived, the little girls and boys screaming *mama* and *dada* and running arms open to their parents. I made my way to the back of the yard, scooping him up in a huge squeeze, putting on my all-too-familiar armor, shielding our differences from people. On the ride home I called my mother. "Mom, Cooper should know I'm his mom by now? Right? I get the feeling that sometimes he doesn't know who I am…"

"That's ridiculous, Katie. He knows you're his mom. All babies know their mothers." I changed the subject, almost embarrassed by my self-doubt. She was right, I thought. She had to be right. But what if she wasn't? In a way, Cooper felt like a little ghost to me. I knew he was there, of course, but he didn't seek me out or really seem to care where I was in the house. Instead, he ran from room to room, doing nothing really, yet purposefully moving. I could see him and hear him. But I could rarely reach him. I would follow behind him, trying to engage him, stealing hugs and kisses when I could. I was desperate to play with him. Desperate to feel love from him. But he was more content being by himself.

At his twelve-month well child visit, I was supposed to fill out the evaluation that the nurse gives you at every well child visit. You tell them if you have smoke alarms and guns in your house, enough food to eat, and concerns about your baby. In the past, I raced through them because Cooper was meeting all of his physical milestones. He rolled over, sat, crawled, and walked all on schedule. But this time, I had concerns. Only, my toddler wouldn't let me fill out the form. Waiting rooms turned him into the Tasmanian Devil. He would run in circles around the room, throwing crayons and climbing on chairs. I would follow, my only goal being to keep him from going behind the reception area, or escaping out the front door, which humorously seemed to be his only goals. His movement never subsided, not even for a second, and he was just so fast. Even though it was the dead of a Minnesota winter, I didn't wear a coat, a T-shirt often sufficing. I was always covered in sweat from chasing, my hair thrown up in a bun, a picture of the busy mom.

When we finally made it to the exam room, I was exhausted and frazzled. But I told her my concerns anyway, as I tried to keep Cooper out of the garbage can, or stop him from ripping the paper off the examination bed. As he flipped the lights on and off, I explained that he wasn't cooing or babbling or pointing or waving. He wouldn't mimic and had zero interest in toys. As I neared the end of my list, I braced myself for what was coming. Only, she wasn't concerned.

"He makes great eye contact, Kate. The speech will come. Boys are lazy. Let's wait until he's closer to two before we worry."

I was shocked but relieved in a way. She had given me a free pass not to worry. But I couldn't help but think back to the lunch-and-learn about autism. I had to ask.

"Do you think something is wrong with him?"

Her answer was not at all what I expected to hear and would haunt me for years to come.

"At this age, we would be looking for signs of mental retardation." I reeled back as if I had been slapped.

I knew we lived in a rural area and were possibly behind the times in our political correctness, but the words *mental retardation* sounded incredibly negative to me. I was speechless. I didn't ask any more questions. Before I left, the nurse gave me a list of things a twelve-month-old baby "should" be doing. I looked it over and felt relief. My son wasn't that delayed, and most of these things, I could work with him on. I felt motivated.

Shortly after that appointment, I made the decision to cut my hours at my job to have more time with Cooper, a decision I agonized over. I wanted the best of both worlds, to have a successful career and be mother of the year, but something in my mommy gut told me Cooper needed more of me. This wasn't an easy decision. My income was vital but we ultimately decided that if we modified our lifestyle we could make it work. This was the best way to help our son be successful. I know not every person can relate, but my self-identity was very much tied to my job, and losing a part of that, even though it was just mere hours, made me feel a bit ashamed. Maybe even a bit resentful.

In those early years, before we had answers, I diagnosed Cooper constantly in my head. I became obsessed with Dr. Google, and I would spend time learning about speech delays, developmental delays, and autism. The signs and differences. And I would keep score in a way, convincing myself that it was or wasn't. I was exhausted and motivated at the same time. We lived in a constant place of looking for answers, but for many years there didn't seem to be any. Just signs that pointed us in one direction or another, autism or not.

One of the most impactful signs came in the form of a purple dinosaur.

I can still see Cooper the day he found the television. It was incredibly early on a Saturday morning, well before 6:00 a.m., the sun just waking up. We were living in that awful rental house, waiting to close on the hobby farm we had purchased. He was wearing white fuzzy footie pajamas with bright-colored stars on them. His hair was long, much longer than we would have liked. But he refused to sit for a haircut, and we didn't have the energy to force it.

I was watching the local weather and chugging coffee, the caffeine vital to my survival. As it turned 6:00 a.m., the TV came alive with a loud, silly sound, and then a purple dinosaur was dancing on my screen. We often speak of defining moments in life. This was one of them.

Cooper snapped his head up, and a change happened in him. It was like life came to his eyes. A slow smile spread across his face as he made his way to the entertainment center, pulling himself up to get closer. He even looked back at me to see if I was seeing what he was seeing. I stood there, mouth open, watching him take it all in. He squealed in delight, even clapped his hands. It was the first time I had seen my son truly happy.

His cartoon friends did wonderful things at first for him. They taught him to wave and point and clap. He danced to their songs and learned to identify trucks, tractors, and trains. They gave Jamie and me a break too. Finally, Cooper had something to do instead of wandering around the house anxiously, unsure of how to spend his time. We were thankful at first for his newfound hobby. That is, until it turned to an obsession.

We found ourselves controlled and walking on eggshells by his need for his shows. Because the cartoons he preferred were not on one after another, one of us would have to sit at the TV, rewinding and fast-forwarding his programs. If we pulled him away or turned the television off, he would rage uncontrollably. We tried hiding the remotes, unplugging the TV from the wall, even removing it from the room entirely. While technology brought life to him, it seemed to at the same time take him from our world. I will admit we were a little embarrassed by the tight grip the television held over him. Well-meaning friends and grandparents would make comments, telling us to simply turn the television off, reminding us that we were the parents and kids didn't need TV all the time. And while we understood that, even agreed with it, we didn't seem to have a choice in the matter.

Trips outside were met with screams and meltdowns. We tried hiking, boating, even picnicking, activities we both loved. Cooper would thrash and refuse to be there. His rigidity, a telltale sign of autism, could be seen a mile away, although at the time we just assumed he was a challenging toddler. All the signs were there, but no one to put them together and tell us the answers.

Most children can be diagnosed with autism by age three. But some, like Cooper, can be diagnosed much younger. Looking back, it was black and white, or classic autism, as they call it, but like many of the stories I hear from other parents, it took years of concerns being dismissed, even ignored, until it couldn't be denied any longer. A complicated dance of sorts, back and forth. When all was said and done, it would take nearly four years for us to get a diagnosis, valuable time wasted, in my opinion.

While many people probably assume that knowing is devastating, I felt the opposite. There is a peace that comes with knowing and having answers. Because once you know, you can begin fixing and helping. You can begin accepting. It was the not knowing, the in-between place, and the worry that I wasn't doing enough or the right things that was devastating.

Today, I tell parents to push as hard as they possibly can to get answers, whether it's autism, a developmental delay, even a speech delay. A typical first reaction will be to shield their children from something so heavy and so lifelong, but they need to move past that, because a diagnosis means help. It means services. It's the golden ticket.

I hear stories all the time of parents running from the diagnosis, not returning phone calls, or even lying on evaluations. Grandparents, aunts and uncles, even friends have reached out to me on behalf of a child that isn't getting the help they need. The person reaching out wants to know if they should say something. I shy away from that question every single time because I can remember the very real anguish of being in a place of denial. And what I felt when people pointed out my son's differences.

If your child has autism, it's not going away, parents. No matter what box you check. You can't outrun it and you can't hide it. Their autism is woven through them, it's who they are, and pretending, lying, avoiding, will only cause you anguish, and eventually your child too. Remember, a diagnosis doesn't change your child or the love you have for them. In fact, for me, it made it stronger.

I once interviewed an adult woman for my website who wasn't diagnosed with autism until she was in her mid-twenties, just days before she planned to take her own life. She spoke of never being accepted by her parents or peers and spending much of her life feeling broken and hating herself for being different. Her advice to me was, "Embrace your son for who he is and love him through his hardest moments." She is estranged from her parents now. In her words, "My diagnosis didn't fit into their picture-perfect life." I never want my son to feel that way, not ever.

For me, realizing my son was different happened slowly over time and then eventually all at once, consuming me from head to toe, a transformation so subtle at first that most around me missed it. Some days I could be blissfully unaware in that in-between place, convincing myself he was just a little behind or different in his own beautiful, stubborn way. Eventually, as he aged, there was no possible way to pretend anymore. But one thing stood true from the very beginning: Cooper was exactly who he was supposed to be. The person who needed to change was me.

# THREE

Motherhood is like an exclusive club. And if a positive pregnancy test or dried ink on adoption papers secures your membership, then it is the experiences that we encounter as our children grow and develop that keep our membership valid.

Never was there a club I wanted to be in more, and I made sure that everyone knew it. I shared stories of my very typical pregnancy, my traumatic delivery, and those first few exhausting months of life with a newborn with anyone who would listen. In the beginning, I was speaking the same language as other mothers. My stories resembled those of so many other women I knew. But then something changed. Subtly at first. Playgroups turned to therapy sessions. Preschool turned to special education. Missed milestones turned to worry. With each realization that my son was different, something pulled, or maybe even pushed us out of the exclusive club.

I tried, desperately at first, to blend in with our peers. Probably longer than I should have. I would watch other mothers sip coffee, sitting or standing together at a park or a playdate, sharing stories. They would laugh about the darnedest things their kids did or said. Meanwhile, I would be chasing my toddler, sweating, climbing through tunnels or sliding down slides, watching those seemingly perfect mothers with the seemingly perfect children, longing to be one of them.

Of course, like life, it was not all perfect. Many times, the other mothers would commiserate about the hard parts of motherhood too. But even their struggles I could not relate to. They'd vent about their kid's nonstop chatter, hearing *mommy* a hundred times a day or the never-ending demands to play ball or ride their trikes.

I tried fitting in. I tried telling my stories. But when I spoke about milestones missed, the worry that was eating me alive, I could see the confusion on their faces. They didn't know how to respond to me, so they were either silent or they downplayed my worry because that's what friends do. I felt like an imposter, eventually staying silent myself, trying to blend in so I could stay longer.

I could not figure out what I was feeling. Anger, jealousy, sadness, desperation to fit in. I mean, these women were my friends, our kids the same age. The dreams of our babies growing up side by side were still fresh in my mind. We were never excluded, Cooper and I, never once. But we were not necessarily included either.

As I cycled through the emotions of being different, I eventually realized it was me, not them. They didn't push me out. I left on my own.

Years later, I would go on to form my own club. One with other mothers like me who watched their babies grow up in therapy waiting rooms and strapped on armor every morning ready for battle. These mothers so full of hope that if you stripped it all away, the clothes, skin and bones, there would be nothing left but love for a child. These mothers saved me countless times over the years. They got me up off the floor, they dried my tears, and they reminded me that being different is not a death sentence. We get to keep living. It's just a different life than the one we originally imagined.

If I were to describe Cooper's toddler years with one word, it would be *lonely*, a word that I didn't know before having a baby could be associated with motherhood. One I felt guilty for even thinking.

I would share that feeling with girlfriends who had babies the same age and they would quickly agree. They would tell me how they missed their lives before kids and the friendships and the fun. They would nod their heads in solidarity, but what I was feeling was different. And I was too scared to admit it to them.

This was the kind of lonely that comes from knowing in your heart that your child is different and there is nothing you can do to change it. It's a loneliness that creeps in at 3:00 a.m. after being awake for hours with a screaming child, wondering why they won't sleep, or being in the same room as your child but knowing you can't communicate with them. Or even standing in a crowded room full of children the same age as yours and seeing the differences firsthand.

I was lonely for my son. I had this beautiful boy. The boy that I prayed for and loved so much it consumed me.

In a way he felt like a stranger to me, almost as if I wasn't his mother, but more like a caregiver. Or someone who worked for him. I did all the things mothers do. I changed his diaper. I wiped his nose. I got him snacks. I bathed him. And I waited, for the good parts. I waited for him to play a game with me. I waited for him to show me trucks and planes and trains with excitement and joy. I waited for him to say *mama*. I waited for hugs and kisses. And while I waited, I loved him enough for the both of us.

It was a very confusing time for me. I knew every mole on his body, the curve of his fat toes, and the hazel in his eyes. I knew his sounds, his cries, and when meltdowns were coming.

In a way, I felt like a bridge between two worlds, his and ours, the bridge allowing him into this world as much as he could be. But anything more than that was a mystery. I did not know why he loved watching children dance and play on television but refused to dance and play himself. I did not know why he slept with seven blankets, surrounding his body like a nest, or what he was trying to tell me when he touched my face or hit his own head in frustration. He did not invite me into his world. It was not at all what I pictured motherhood to be like. I kept on pretending.

We would go places for a long weekend, friends' houses for playdates, parks, all the places families go. But it would never work out. Cooper would scream in the car to and from. He would refuse to sit in shopping carts or at a restaurant. If I needed him to walk, he would flop down in protest. If I needed him to sit, he would run. If I tried to carry him, he would wiggle out of my arms and down my body. The list of places we could go successfully was shrinking by the day. I wondered if he was purposefully sabotaging our outings. I continued to make excuses. Saying he was teething or not feeling well, because I truly didn't know why it was all so hard for him. I couldn't figure it out. It was almost like he didn't know how to "just be" present. Every situation seemed to send him into hysterics.

During one visit to a friend's house for her daughter's second birthday, I watched my friends' kids gather around the presents and cake while Cooper sat feet away, glued to his ten-inch TV/VCR combo that had to now travel with us. He was nearly two years old himself. I saw the ridiculousness in our child having his own television that traveled with us. I tried shutting it off for the birthday song, feeling pressure to have my son join the party, but he screamed so loud, banging his head on their wooden floor, that everyone just stared at us, mouths open, until the old crabby grandpa said, "Turn it back on so I can enjoy my granddaughter's birthday." I was mortified. I made an excuse to leave early, ashamed of what had happened and vowing to never go anywhere again. While I drove, angry thoughts screamed in my head. Some at that awful man. Some at myself for taking his rudeness. I even felt anger toward my own son. I needed to know why this was all so hard, and for a brief second, I blamed Cooper. Immediately, waves of guilt washed over me for thinking such a terrible thought.

I spent a lot of time that year privately looking for answers on Google and at the local library during my lunch breaks. While I knew in my heart something was different about Cooper, I didn't feel comfortable talking about it yet with many people. I also had this fear that saying it out loud would make it real. I had all these emotions, and while some made sense, like worry and confusion, others were puzzling. I was angry that my son was struggling so much. I was frustrated that our life was so different. I was even jealous of other mothers, a feeling that was entirely foreign to me. I wanted my son to be fine. It was that simple. So it was easier to keep it all locked inside.

During Cooper's first two years of life, I brought him to the doctor constantly. My mommy instinct was telling me that something was wrong. He wasn't sleeping or playing or talking, and I thought he was sick, but I couldn't put my finger on what was wrong. The signs and symptoms were there though. He would bang his head on the ground or against his high chair as if his head hurt. He had a chronic runny nose. He was irritable, whined constantly, and never slept.

But at every appointment, I would hit roadblocks. Cooper rarely had a fever, a required symptom for most illnesses. And examining him was like examining a bear. He wasn't an easy patient, and he screamed when touched. There would be running and kicking if anyone went near him.

The only thing our doctor ever seemed to truly take note of was his ears. No matter when she looked in them, they were hot, swollen, and red, which she was quick to say could be from his tantrum or an ear infection. She always erred on the side of ear infection, I think sensing my desperation for sleep and help, and prescribed antibiotics. But they never seemed to fix the problem. After ten days we would be back again.

I was exhausted. Exhausted from missing work to bring him to the doctor, exhausted from having a sick kid all the time, and exhausted from fighting for someone to listen to me. I felt like I was standing in a room screaming for someone to take me seriously and help my kid, but no one would listen. What we were experiencing wasn't normal.

Other times, if I was really worked up, I'd demand answers as to why he wasn't talking or playing, only to be met with opposition. In children under the age of two, doctors are looking for certain red flags before they refer a parent for help.

Does the child make eye contact and respond to their name? Does the child line up objects and/or spin wheels? Cooper always made eye contact and he always responded to his name. He didn't line objects up and he didn't spin wheels, but still I would get, "he's a boy," "he's a late bloomer," and "wait until he's two to worry." I was even told I was just a first-time mom worrying. People have asked me if I was offended by those responses from a doctor who was supposed to help us. That answer is no, because I wanted her to be right. There is nothing I wanted more in my life than for her to be right.

A few months after Cooper's first birthday, we finally moved into an idyllic hobby farm on five acres in Duluth. The house was old, and needed a lot of improvements, but the property more than made up for the ugly wallpaper and cracked beige laminate flooring. The listing told us about the apple trees peppering the property, nearby ponds and streams. A simple trail went around the acreage and led to three different outbuildings, a dog kennel, a chicken coop, and an old pole barn, perfect for exploring. It was exactly what we'd wanted.

After a showing late one night, Jamie convinced me it was

the one. The house needed a lot of work—and I mean *a lot*—but in our mind it was a steal. We immediately made an offer, right there, from our car. And on the drive home we spoke about how the hobby farm was the perfect place to raise boys. This would be our forever home.

Thirty days later it was moving day. An oversize truck backed up to the front door of our rental, and Jamie, his parents, our friends, and I moved load after load, filling the truck. All the while, Cooper stood with his nose pressed to the television, watching his purple dinosaur friend. I kept waiting for him to notice the room emptying out or even acknowledge the chatter of the people surrounding him. The green couch went first. Then the recliner, kitchen table, and end tables. Each load had to go directly by him and out through the front door. He was oblivious.

Jamie's buddy said to me, "Cooper is such a good kid! My son would be out the front door and in that moving truck so fast." Comments like that stung because what he was praising wasn't really something to be praised. It was a huge red flag.

Eventually the house was empty except for the large television, the entertainment stand it sat on, and the little boy glued to the screen. The adults and I gathered behind him, happy that we were on the last load. As we stood there, we chatted about how much stuff we had and how much Cooper loved Barney. My mother-in-law, who worked as a nurse, questioned his hearing. She knew of his chronic ear infections, and after seeing how oblivious he was firsthand to his surroundings, her question was not off base. But I told her we had no concerns about his hearing. He could hear a train whistle three counties over.

Jamie unplugged the television and I studied Cooper's face, waiting for some acknowledgment of his grandparents or the empty room. He just stared blankly at us. It was only when Jamie and his dad picked up the TV and started maneuvering it out the front door that Cooper reacted. His screams echoed throughout the empty house.

As I drove Cooper to our new home, while Jamie followed behind in the moving truck, I had a chilling realization. Would Cooper have noticed, or even cared, if we had locked up the house and driven away without him?

Two months after we moved in, I found out I was pregnant. If the test had not flashed positive before I finished peeing on it, I probably would not have believed it. Being pregnant requires one act, an act that I could not remember doing in ages. Cooper still was not sleeping through the night, sometimes waking ten or more times a night. We were awake more hours of the night than we actually slept. Jamie and I worked in shifts, and we had not gone to bed or woken up together in months. We were like two ships in the night. And it was not like I was throwing on sexy lingerie while he opened a bottle of wine.

Once I caught my breath, and tried to remember when my last period was, I called Jamie sobbing. I'm not even sure how he understood what I was saying, but eventually the word *pregnant* must have come through. I expected him to be mad or sad or even confused like I was, only, he wasn't. He was excited.

When he arrived home from work that day, he brought me a bouquet of pink flowers for the little girl he knew I wanted. We spent the rest of the day talking about bringing another baby into our lives, when we were already stretched too thin. He let me list all my fears without saying a word. "How are we going to afford two in day care? What if Cooper never starts sleeping? Or talking? How am I going to be pregnant and not sleep?"

I am often asked if I was scared to have another baby when we still hadn't figured out what was going on with Cooper. The answer is no. As far as I knew, I just had a challenging baby, and he would eventually grow out of it. I thought he would wake up one day talking and Jamie and I would laugh at how worried we had been.

So no, I wasn't worried that something would be wrong with my second baby. But I was scared about not being enough. I was already feeling like there wasn't enough of me to go around. When I was at work, I worried about Cooper. When I was with Cooper, I thought about work and what had to be done. I wasn't even sure where Jamie fit in, and now there would be even less of me to go around.

That night I jumped headfirst into the rabbit hole of worry. My husband did not join me there—he never did—but he did listen. He reassured me that there was nothing wrong with Cooper and that he would catch up. He promised me our son would start sleeping and talking before this new baby was born and that we would figure out the money part. He told me it would be great that they would be close in age and play together.

I let myself relax with his reassurance. He was right. Babies are the best, and I had originally wanted half a dozen all close together. This was the first step toward that. I convinced myself then and there it was going to be great. And when I found out the baby was a boy, I knew Cooper would have a best friend for life. My friend Ashley reassured me how wonderful two kids close together would be. Her own two daughters entertained each other endlessly.

During my pregnancy, I asked Cooper's pediatrician for a referral to Early Intervention Services through the school district. I had learned from a woman through work that there is help available. You just have to ask for it. Although I felt like I had been asking for nearly two years now, I asked again. She agreed to put in the referral and at the same time recommended that Cooper have tubes placed in his ears and a hearing test done. She noted that he had seven ear infections in the last few months, and the next logical step was tubes. For me that was a light-bulb moment. The ear infections must have been the reason he wasn't sleeping.

She was quick to tell me that she didn't necessarily know if tubes would help, but with kids who can't communicate, it's important to mitigate any pain they may be having. She used the words *quality of life*. Three words that would pop up many times over the years to come. Three words that no parent ever wants to hear in relation to their child.

The idea of surgery when Cooper was so little was terrifying, but both Jamie and I were excited at the possibility of a happier and healthier Cooper. The ENT had made a grandiose statement that almost all children start talking once ear tubes are placed. Some even overnight. He also made promises of improved sleeping and ability to sit and focus. To say we put all our hope into one surgery is an understatement.

We arrived at the surgery center at 6:00 a.m. happy but were quickly taken down a notch. When we checked in, I informed the nurse that our son was nonverbal and may have a hard time with all of this. I emphasized the word *may*. Her response was not at all what I expected.

"What's wrong with him? Why can't he talk?"

I explained that nothing was wrong with him. He just had no words yet. She seemed to dislike Cooper from the start, and the feeling was mutual. He refused to wear the gown she provided. He would not sit in the bed or ride in the red plastic wagon used to calm children down. He kicked at her when she held his face and inserted calming medicine into his mouth and scolded him for his behavior. "We do not kick the nurses." Of course, she wasn't wrong, but he was also a very scared little boy who had never had medicine forcefully injected into his mouth before.

Jamie and I both breathed a sigh of relief when the anesthesia finally took over and his body went calm. We felt like we had run a marathon, and we collapsed in our chairs after he left the room.

The way that nurse treated Cooper, like he was a monster, bothered me for years to come. I had wanted to speak up and say something, but instead I kept quiet to be polite. I learned a valuable lesson that day…challenging kids, the ones who can't communicate, the ones who don't readily obey, who do not listen or even understand, are treated differently. Not always, but often. And as parents, we need to voice our concerns whenever possible. It's a skill that did not come naturally to me at first, and I would eventually have to learn.

We were advised that the ear tube procedure would be fast, thirty minutes or so, from start to finish, but the hearing test could take longer. They told us not to panic. As Jamie and I waited, we spoke about what our son's voice would sound like and what word he would say first. Jamie thought *dada*, of course. I said it better be *mama*. I noted the desperation in both our voices.

As the time dragged on, I started getting nervous. Two hours seemed long, but the nurse assured us that all was fine. Finally, after another thirty minutes, a woman made her way into our room, introducing herself as the audiologist who performed our son's sedated hearing test. She stood as she spoke.

She informed us that Cooper had a significant hearing loss. When she said "fitted for hearing aids," I stopped listening to her. I felt like I was Charlie Brown tuning out his teacher. I just shut down.

She left abruptly before we could ask any questions, advising us to make an appointment as soon as possible. Jamie and I sat there stunned, both of us silent. I had been looking for an answer, and I guess I had found one. My son couldn't hear.

Once we were alone in the room, I broke down crying. Jamie sat stoically, showing very little emotion, each of us processing the news in our own way.

When they wheeled Cooper back in the room, he was wrapped up in his fuzzy red blanket with snowflakes on it. He was sleeping, unmoving. It was the first time I had seen him motionless during the daytime hours in ages. He looked so small. His long blond hair was parted to the side. I sat by him, waiting for him to wake, and let the guilt flood me. How had I not known my son was deaf?

I spent the evening googling and crying and trying to figure out how I had missed this. Never once did I have any concerns over my son's hearing. The next day, while Jamie was at work, I spent the day performing my own hearing tests on my son. Any parent out there who suspects a hearing loss in their child knows exactly what I am talking about.

I whispered his name from behind the couch and from the kitchen. I shook musical instruments to startle him. I banged pots and pans together. I blew whistles. I made an annoying humming sound. I covered my mouth when I spoke to him to see if he could hear me.

He passed all my tests. Every single one. Without a doubt in my mind, my son could hear, but maybe I was crazy. I wanted to trust my gut, but how could a doctor be wrong?

When Jamie returned home from work, I met him at the door, ecstatic. "Cooper can hear! He can hear everything!"

I was waiting for a high five or an *atta girl* for figuring out that our son could hear, but instead he looked at me and shook his head. "Kate, Cooper is deaf. The doctor told us so. Why do you do this to yourself?"

"Dear God, Jamie, doctors make mistakes. They aren't right one hundred percent of the time. What if someone told you that you had cancer? Or needed to have a limb removed? Would you just do it? Or would you get a second opinion? Should I just dig your damn grave?"

He looked squarely at me and said, "Kate, this would explain why he doesn't talk to us or play with his cousins. This could be a good thing. Why can't you see that?"

That shut me right up. While I didn't necessarily believe that our son was deaf, I understood what he was saying and where he was coming from. This would be an answer to why our son was different and would mean we could stop searching and start helping him. But it didn't sit right with me.

The next day I brought Cooper to the audiologist to discuss his test results. I did not want to go, especially alone, but Jamie had to work. I was determined to hear her out, share my "at-home" test results and then ask for another hearing test just to be sure. I wanted to observe his hearing loss with my own two eyes.

As Cooper sat and watched Thomas the Train on my phone, she pulled out a graph and explained that while Cooper was sedated, she performed an Auditory Brainstem Response Test, or ABR. She put electrodes on his head and ears, played sounds through earphones, and then measured his brain response to the sounds.

"We determined that your son cannot hear most speech sounds, birds chirping, wind in the trees, the ticking of a clock, or even an airplane overhead."

I sat there, staring at her, stunned and confused. What she was saying didn't make any sense.

"Has he heard my voice? Because he seems to respond to my voice one hundred percent of the time."

"We can't be certain," she said.

I looked at Cooper next to me on a stiff chair, sitting still for once, eyes glued to my phone. Every few seconds he would giggle. The volume on the phone was at a whisper, but he seemed to hear it fine. Or maybe he was laughing at the video itself. I was not sure.

I felt like I was in the bizarro world.

She went on to explain that he would need to wear hearing aids for the rest of his life, but even then, he most likely would never have fully functional hearing.

"Children learn speech from modeling. Meaning, they learn from listening to their parents speak. Cooper has possibly never heard you or anyone else, so he would have no reason to start speaking."

I kept shifting my eyes between her and Cooper, noting that every time his name was said out loud, he would lift his eyes up, away from his program, and look to us.

"Hearing aids are the best thing for him. We can do the molds here tomorrow and have them ready in two weeks." She also informed me that our insurance was not the best and the out-of-pocket price would be $2,000, an amount that we did not have.

I felt like this was going too fast. I was losing control.

"I want a second opinion," I said. "I think he can hear everything. This feels drastic."

She said that extra testing would just be a waste of money and time and our insurance most likely wouldn't cover that either. She was positive our son had a hearing loss and that what I was feeling was grief and denial.

I felt like a little girl who had been scolded.

She handed me a packet of information and told me that the school district would be contacting us. All children with significant hearing loss are reported to the school and county so additional services and resources can be provided to families. And just like that it was done.

That night I googled hearing loss in children. As I studied the outdated pictures of small children with clunky hearing aids, I let myself play the "what-if" game.

*What if he gets teased or bullied? What if he can't learn because he cannot hear? What if he can't play sports? How will he wear a bike helmet? Or a baseball helmet? Will he be able to drive a car?*

*But what if he learns to talk? That would be amazing. But what if he sounds funny?* I was up and down.

The next week a lady from the school came to our house to explain to us how the deaf program worked in the district. This was our first experience having someone in our home to discuss our son. It's a very strange feeling, one that I'm not sure I've ever gotten used to. When you enter the world of special needs, your child becomes a statistic. And on top of that, you will most definitely need additional help to navigate it all at some point. And before you know it, you will have someone in your living room telling you how to care for your child. It's a very vulnerable feeling.

"It's important that you stop speaking to Cooper and switch completely to sign language so he can learn his primary language. Speaking to him will only confuse him."

I repeated her words back to her.

"You want me to stop speaking to my own son? In my own home?"

That sounded so ridiculous to me. As if we should shut him out even more?

She explained that Cooper's hearing loss, his disability, qualified him for special-needs services. She said it was a good thing.

The words *disability* and *special-needs services* screamed at me.

Suddenly I was incredibly angry. This woman did not know my son. She had a piece of paper with a checked box for hearing loss. I felt defensive, an emotion that maybe was wrong, but I didn't agree with the diagnosis.

Jamie and I fought for hours that night. I did not think our son had a hearing loss and wanted a second opinion. Jamie disagreed and thought I was putting myself through hell for no reason. I wasn't sure how two people could see one situation so differently. He thought I was in denial. I thought the same about him.

Two weeks later we picked up Cooper's hearing aids. I couldn't fight anymore. Not with myself or with my husband. I allowed myself to accept the fact that my son was deaf and that it was a good thing we were getting him help. His audiologist told us that once he could hear, he might start talking. And just like that, hope bubbled up.

The first week with hearing aids was challenging to say the least. For most children, autistic or not, getting them to actually wear the hearing aids is the hardest part, so our audiologist recommended having Cooper practice wearing them first before even turning them on.

At first, he refused to wear them. I mean, our child refused to wear hats, gloves, even sandals. Hearing aids were a long shot. Once they were inserted in his ears, he would violently rip them out and chuck them across the room, as if they burned his skin. But after a few days, he seemed to build up his tolerance, and by the end of the week, he was wearing them from morning until night.

We were pleasantly surprised. Once Cooper had success, the audiologist turned them on and up. Jamie and I were practically giddy as we inserted the now functioning hearing aids into his ears. We were waiting for that light-bulb moment of joy you see on TV when a child hears their parents' voices for the first time. I even had my cell phone out to record a video to send to his grandparents.

"Hi, baby," I whispered.

The look in his eyes was pure terror. He reached for his head, clawing at his ears while screaming. He took off running down the hallway.

Jamie and I both stood there for a split second, shocked, but then we quickly chased after him and removed the hearing aids from his ears. Both Jamie and I dropped to the ground to console him, me holding him and Jamie rubbing his back. He was visibly shaken and continued to scream for a few minutes. We didn't know if we should try putting in the hearing aids again or not.

A fellow mom of a child with a hearing loss told me that this was all normal. Cooper had most likely never heard sounds before and was scared. But that didn't sit right with me. He acted as if everything was too loud suddenly. My mother's intuition told me one final time that this was all wrong. With that I vowed to get a second opinion. And I vowed to do it with or without Jamie.

Looking back, this was a monumental time for me as a mom. I

had always believed that the professionals in our lives were right, and yes, most of the time they are. But nothing was, or ever will be, textbook with Cooper. The rules that seem to apply to most people, don't to him. Up is not up and down is not down. I knew I had to find my voice and I had to do it alone.

I researched and found out that our school district had an audiologist who could work with us free of charge. After a few of my desperate emails and frantic phone calls, she agreed to visit our home and review Cooper's records. Jamie wanted no part of it, a point of contention between us. I think it was just all too much for him. Nothing was simple.

After she arrived, she told me that she reviewed Cooper's hearing results from his tube surgery, and something didn't seem right to her. During the surgery he failed the ABR but passed the hearing screening. She said that a person with a hearing loss would fail both of these if they truly had a hearing loss. She set up a hearing test for the following week at a local clinic.

I took Cooper alone to the appointment, and in secret. I knew I would be crushed if I was wrong and I didn't want the immediate "I told you so" from Jamie. I just wanted to go and find out if my kid could hear. The kind audiologist met me in the waiting room and told me that she would test Cooper's hearing and test for all of the language sounds, pitches, etc. She was wonderful and patient and kind, like a grandmother. Just what I needed. Just what Cooper needed. She also told me not to get my hopes up. An ABR is rarely wrong.

She led Cooper and me to a dark, cool, soundproof booth, the size of a closet. The only thing inside was a chair. I sat down and pulled him up on my lap and rubbed my nose into his coarse hair. I gave him a little squeeze and whispered in his ear, "Come on, buddy, you can do this." I said a silent prayer begging for him to cooperate, just once. He giggled at the tickle of my breath on his neck. I wondered if he could sense my desperation.

The audiologist positioned herself in front of us on the other side of the glass just outside of the booth. I stared forward the entire time, giving no reaction as different pitches and sounds came out of the speakers. When Cooper heard a sound, he would turn his head to whichever side it came from, and a creepy old-fashioned clown and monkey would clap, rewarding him for looking. Then she would "woo-hoo" to get him to look forward again before playing another sound.

I studied her face as the sounds went on. She gave no reaction.

I tried to stay calm, but I felt my excitement rising. *Am I imagining this?* I thought. He was most definitely hearing every sound. After the longest five minutes of my life, the lady opened the booth and engulfed me in a big hug.

She looked right at me and said, "He heard every single sound and pitch I could test for. Your son can hear fine. He heard it all."

I burst into tears, overwhelmed by my emotions and the relief that I felt.

"I knew it!" I screamed.

Right before we left, I pulled Cooper onto my lap to slip his coat on. In a rare moment of affection, he reached up and touched my ears and smiled. I burst out laughing. That's my Cooper. He knew.

That night Jamie and I sat on our deck, our chairs facing the window to the living room so we could watch Cooper watching TV. I was feeling a mixture of relief, validation, and exhaustion. Part of me was expecting a thank-you from my husband. I had gone to war over our son's hearing, and I had won. Or so I thought.

"I knew he wasn't deaf, Jamie. I could feel it in my gut. Why couldn't you just back me up?"

"I wanted him to be deaf, Kate. I wanted an answer, one that was simple and had a solution. If our kid can't hear, then he wears hearing aids. Simple."

"I want an answer too, Jamie. Can't you see that? I'm killing myself over here to get answers. But I also want it to be the right one. Our kid can hear. He doesn't need hearing aids."

"Then why isn't he talking? Last week I stopped by my client's house to drop off some paperwork, and I had an actual conversation with their son. He was born three days after Cooper. Words, Kate. Back and forth. He brought me my shoes and his bat and ball. Cooper doesn't even know what a ball is."

"It could be a speech delay. Or a developmental delay. Or autism." At the last word he seemed to shut down, lifting up his phone to look at something. I tried to get him to open up, to make a plan of what to do next, but he was done talking.

For months I had been sending him articles about autism and developmental delays, even tagging him in blog posts written by parents of autistic children on Facebook. It's something I now see wives do to their spouses all the time on my own blog. I tried to get him to read books, even to watch *Parenthood*, a popular show at the time that had a character with autism. But he refused to read and to watch and to learn. It frustrated me immensely. I thought knowledge was power. He told me eventually, many years later, that it was just too sad to read about. Too hard. Too soon.

I was on a roller coaster—up and down, trying to figure out the mystery that was Cooper. But that wasn't the hardest part. Instead, it was the notion that I was on the ride alone with very little support. I desperately needed my husband to get on the ride with me. But it felt like the more I tried to convince him, the more he pulled away. Whether it was perception or reality, I was alone.

There is a viral image that went around the special-needs moms' groups and Facebook pages a few years ago. It was titled, "Nevertheless, We Persisted." It shows a mother holding her child looking up at a wall. The wall is covered in sentences, fifty or more, each one circled in a thought bubble. It's meant to show you the thoughts and worries that run through a special-needs parent's head on a constant reel. It's meant to show the weight of what we carry at all times.

*Did I do something wrong?*

*You're overreacting.*

*She just needs discipline.*

*You are stronger than I would be.*

*What's wrong with him?*

Never have I related to a meme more than that one. When I saw it, I immediately felt seen, heard, and validated. I printed it out, put it on our refrigerator, and waited for my husband to comment. He did, immediately, that night as we cooked dinner together. In a strange moment of clarity, I said to him, "The beginning would have been so different, Jamie, if you would have given me more emotion. It was so lonely to go through alone."

He nodded and said, "I'm sorry. I gave you everything I had at that time."

And I believed him.

# FOUR

Sawyer Jamie, my little buddy, was born on January 20, 2013. He had red hair and a ruddy complexion that I swear must have come from a love of strawberries during my pregnancy because no one else had red hair in our family.

On our drive home with our new son, heading home to meet Cooper, Jamie and I spoke very little. He was navigating icy roads and I was studying Sawyer and worrying how all of this was going to work. Two babies, both in diapers, both needing me. I know mothers do it all the time, and with way more kids, but Cooper was challenging to say the least. His meltdowns were increasing, and tiny things seemed to set him off. He was aggressive toward himself when he was angry, and his biggest trigger seemed to be loud noises, like a baby crying. He was very impulsive with quite a few unsafe behaviors too. He would frequently throw things, as if throwing were a form of communication for him. The living room walls of our new home already had multiple dents, and we were preparing for a broken window or two. Jamie and I learned to think fast and dodge, but we knew a baby would not stand a chance. We also didn't have family close by, the nearest being three hours away.

A few months earlier, we'd had a breakthrough with Cooper. He fell in love with toy trains. While we were thrilled that we could now check the box "plays with toys" on his milestone checklists, something felt off. Cooper had rules when he played, and while he could not verbally communicate them, he made them known, his rigidity coming on strong. The track had to be set up the same way every single time. The trains had to be in a certain order. The trains could not stop and pick up imaginary passengers. The trains had to go a certain speed at all times. Once it was all set up and in perfect order, Cooper would crouch down on the side of the track, put his cheek to the carpet, his nose practically touching the track, and watch the trains go round and round. It would be fun until it wasn't. The train would slow down or slip off the track and before we could even step in to fix it, he would grab the track and throw it against the wall. Within seconds his toys and room would be a mess. Then he would scream for us to rebuild.

It was stressful to say the least. But in my mind, he was playing. And that was a step in the right direction. I had recently stumbled upon an online test called the M-chat, used in the diagnosis of autism. I took it often, typically late at night, every time getting a different answer. Cooper made eye contact, pointed, waved, and acknowledged people. And now he played. His chances of having autism were getting lower. I found comfort in that.

When we arrived home from the hospital, I set Sawyer's car seat down in the living room and held my breath, and Jamie did too, as we called Cooper to come meet his baby brother. Our nurse had asked, just like countless other people, if Cooper was excited to become a big brother. I said yes, to avoid the heartache of the conversation. He didn't understand or notice my belly getting bigger or the baby gear that now filled the house.

But I told myself he had only just turned two, and he was a busy boy who didn't care about new baby brothers.

It ended up being fine, surprisingly. Cooper never once acknowledged his brother, barely giving a second glance at the car seat. When Sawyer's cry filled the room for the first time, I held my breath. Cooper glanced at us, then turned back to the television.

Before my parents left, I tried to get a photo of our family of four and one of my two boys together. I had dreamed about taking a photo of Cooper holding his baby brother, even kissing his forehead, just like all the photos my friends shared of their kids. It didn't happen. Not even close. Cooper adamantly refused to touch Sawyer. He would scream if we tried, and we didn't want to force it. And he wouldn't come near me if I was holding him.

My favorite memory of Sawyer's newborn days, and one I tell him often, is of his first night home from the hospital. I wrapped him in a fuzzy blue blanket and tucked him in his bassinet by my side of the bed at 10:00 p.m. For the next eight hours, Jamie and I played musical beds with Cooper. I went to his bed. He wandered back to ours. I followed. Jamie took him to the couch. He was awake the entire night. By 6:00 a.m., Jamie and I were standing over Sawyer's bassinet, wondering if he was breathing because we couldn't figure out what he was doing. We contemplated poking him and laughed. The answer was that our son was sleeping. It was an entirely foreign concept to us.

Shortly after Sawyer was born, Cooper started Early Intervention, speech therapy, and occupational therapy. He was finally two and could most definitely hear, so his doctor agreed it was time to start services. It was not necessarily how I planned to spend my maternity leave, but I was thankful that I did not have to juggle work while managing four appointments a week. The way I looked at it, I had sixteen weeks to get him help. Sawyer would go on to be nursed and raised in countless waiting rooms around Duluth.

As we sat in the waiting room for Cooper's first speech therapy appointment, I felt rather confident. I was in no way an expert on speech delays but was fairly certain the words would come quickly now that we were finally getting Cooper the help he needed. Speech therapy was the medication to fix this. When the nice young speech therapist called Cooper's name, my confidence rose to cocky when he walked back willingly. I followed behind with Sawyer strapped to my chest, thinking, *Is this actually going to be easy?*

The therapy room was small but a child's dream. A bookshelf held interactive toys and activities; a train track was set up squarely in the middle of the room on a brightly colored A to Z rug. But instead of grabbing a toy or moving a train along the track like most children would, Cooper first cased the room, touching all four walls and the observation window before trying to leave. I dropped to the ground to sit, my back pressed firmly against the door, a move I had perfected in countless doctor's appointments. Once he realized we were here to stay, he started pawing at my purse for my phone.

The therapist sat down next to the train in the center of the room and called Cooper over to her. He seemed mildly intrigued as she pushed the train up the hill, stopping it when it got to the top. Before she would push it down, she used her hand to make a circular motion around her mouth while saying, "GO," and pointed to Cooper to say the same. He dropped to his knees and reached his hand up to push the train down the hill. She stopped him, repeating, "GO!" And that was when it went south. Two minutes in, the train track was in pieces around the room. At one point she ducked and took cover. Balls, books, even tiny chairs bounced off the walls as she tried to engage him in play. She was trying to build rapport. It didn't happen. Not in that session and not in the ones that followed either.

I often called Jamie on our drive home from therapy. He was at work and I'm sure busy, but he always answered. Sometimes I would cry. Sometimes I would yell. And every time I said, "This is serious, Jamie. Something feels really wrong with him." I said those words so many times they started to lose their meaning.

I was thankful when Early Intervention with the school district finally started. It was different from other therapies we had tried. The teacher would come to our house to play with Cooper, saving me from having to bundle two children up, drive to therapy while Cooper screamed, and then take seven flights of stairs with Sawyer in a carrier because Cooper was afraid of elevators.

I assumed play therapy was supposed to be fun and enjoyable for both parties. This was not the case. It was more like a workout. I spent the whole session chasing Cooper, trying to encourage him to engage with the teacher, but because we were home, he knew he could just run away.

The therapist would sit on the floor of our living room, pulling brightly colored toys out of her Mary-Poppins-sized bag, hoping to find something that would interest him. Puzzles, blocks, balls, you name it, her bag of tricks had it. But he didn't care. The television was behind her, off of course. He would scream for it. Sometimes hitting her, sometimes hitting the TV, sometimes hitting himself. I never knew what to do during those sessions. I always felt like the teacher looked at me to stop him, to make him cooperate, but that made no sense. I was looking to her for help and to tell me what to do. She was the expert. Or so I thought.

Each week she would try the same things. It felt like the movie *Groundhog Day*. She used a bubble wand to blow bubbles in front of Cooper's face, moving his hand to pop each one, while encouraging him to say, "POP!" He would run away screaming as if the bubbles burned his skin. I would bring him back and try again.

Each week, it was like the first time all over again. I started to dread the sessions. As parents we are supposed to be amazed by all the things our children learn and know, but with Cooper, it felt like I was continuously being shown all the things my son could not do. I would often ask his teacher questions, wanting to understand what she was seeing in my son, but she was tight-lipped. I learned later that the teachers who come into your home are not supposed to mention words like *autism* or *ADHD* even if they see it. Instead the data gathered has to go back to a supervisor. But I didn't know that, and I think that gave me a false sense of security.

I also felt sad after the sessions. Each week the things my son could not do seemed to stack up. I hated seeing how hard everything was for him and the resulting behaviors. It just didn't make sense to me, why he had to struggle so much just to do things that almost all children take for granted.

After a few months, I received a phone call from the director of the Early Intervention program. She felt it would be best if Cooper had a full evaluation because his needs appeared to be greater than in-home therapy could accommodate. Their goal was to determine if Cooper qualified for preschool through the district, which was offered to children who needed extra help. What she didn't tell me is that in order to qualify, he would have to be educationally diagnosed with either autism or a developmental delay of some sort, which is in fact different from a medical diagnosis. There are many differences between a medical diagnosis and an educational diagnosis of autism, with the big one being the impact on a student's learning, and neither diagnosis has to acknowledge the other. So a child can have one and not the other.

Over the next two weeks, Cooper had eight different evaluations. Some were in our home; some were at school. Some were hopeful. Some felt pointless. They would give him objects, like a brush or a phone or a baby doll, waiting to see if he engaged with the objects appropriately. He did not. Next, they would demonstrate what to do with the brush, phone, and baby doll and expect Cooper to mimic their action. He did not.

They asked me endless questions too. "Does he know what money is?" "Does he know where he lives?" "Can he use scissors or open a pill bottle?" I found myself being defensive sometimes. Even annoyed. Often, I didn't know what the right answer was. Why would I want my two-year-old to open a pill bottle or use scissors? Sometimes I could not tell if we were failing or succeeding.

It was scary to me that Cooper didn't seem to know what they were asking him to do. Or what the objects even were. I would try to justify it, saying we didn't play with dolls in our house or he had never seen me brush my hair or that as a busy mom of two I didn't have time to talk on the phone. And money? Why would a two-year-old know anything about money?

The evaluations at the school were even more disheartening. It felt like I had the only challenging kid, and no one understood him. I would lace up my tennis shoes, strap newborn Sawyer to my chest, and run through the halls of the school, chasing after Cooper, trying to corral him in the room. Sweat would drip down my face as I crawled around on the floor, encouraging him to do whatever task they wanted him to do, feeling like my parenting was on display and I was failing epically.

After the last evaluation, something amazing happened. As we were walking out, Cooper happened to pass by the gym. When he saw children running laps in a circle, he made a bee-line at full speed. He ran right to the center of the large room and started flapping his arms with excitement as the kids circled around him. The children all waved and smiled at him. Watching his joy as he took in their sounds was incredible. For once, I walked out of there with happy tears, telling myself this was all going to be fine.

In the end, it all came down to a vote. I had always assumed a diagnosis of developmental delay or autism was scientific, black and white. But it wasn't in our case. It was Jamie and me and a team of people sitting around a table being asked to raise their hands if they thought Cooper had autism spectrum disorder.

I listened to the director read the report that she and her team had compiled over the last few weeks. She held a stack of papers a mile high.

I felt vulnerable as I listened to this woman, who had never met my son before today, speak about him and our family. To her, we were little more than characters in a play. As she read our demographic information aloud, I let myself slip away for a second.

Many people thought I was overreacting about Cooper's delays. Sometimes it felt as though I was screaming into a void. But one person did not think I was overreacting. Lately Cooper's in-home day care reports had begun to get less shiny. "Cooper refuses to follow the schedule," she would say. Or, "Every other child painted a Mother's Day craft today, but Cooper did not. He refused to hold the paintbrush." She added, cruelly: "I didn't bother making you one because I assume you don't want to see my work." I sensed that he was going to get kicked out, a very real fear for parents like me. Most day cares, in-home and even some centers, are unable to accommodate kids with special needs, leaving parents without care.

I cried that night to my mother on the phone, telling her of the sting I felt in my heart watching Cooper's day care buddies toddle up to their moms with decorated gift bags for Mother's Day, while Cooper had nothing to give me. Her decision to not make one for me stung and felt deliberate.

Each day my anxiety started to rise as pickup neared. Because I knew. I could tell something was building. I knew my son was different from the other children. I felt it in my bones. There was nothing I was more certain of. But I was doing everything I could to figure it out and coming up empty-handed. I assumed that was obvious.

On this Thursday, it was different though. As I turned to leave, his day care provider followed me to my car.

"There is something wrong with Cooper, Kate. And it seems like you aren't doing anything about it," she said flatly.

My mouth dropped open and I stepped back, bumping into

my car. I felt like I had been slapped by her words. I could tell by the tone in her voice that she was serious and that she'd obviously had to build up the courage to tell me this. Before I could speak, and defend myself and Cooper, she went on to say...

"I know kids like Cooper. My father is a speech therapist and I had him meet with Cooper. He agrees with me. Something is wrong and it is *not* just a speech delay. Cooper needs help. It seems like you are living in denial."

The silence hung between us. Was she kidding me? I was practically killing myself to figure out what was happening. All the therapy, the early intervention, the endless research and seeking out answers.

Cooper was on the waiting list for a clinic that treats children with language disorders. I was doing everything I could to get him help.

And then she said the most painful thing that had ever been said to me.

"Kate, something is wrong with Cooper. You need to prepare yourself that he will never ride a bike, make a friend, or learn to talk."

My face burned hot. This woman had just confirmed my greatest fears. The rest was a blur. I'm not sure if I said much. I'm not sure if I defended Cooper or myself. I think I just got in my car and left.

I spent much of the night staring off into space, imagining the future she predicted. Never before had another person's words impacted me so much. I felt worthless as a mom as I studied Cooper, tears falling from my eyes, wondering if she could possibly be right. Was it possible he might never talk? Or make a friend? Or even ride a bike? I kept telling myself she was wrong. It wasn't possible. How could she know what the future held? I sure didn't.

That night after Cooper fell asleep, I crawled into bed with him, something I would do for years to come. It was rare that he was ever still, and on that night, I needed to feel him, breathe him in, and will all my love into him. I wrapped my arms around him and held him as tightly as I could. And I prayed. I prayed to God to fix him, to make him better, to bring him back to me. Some nights I would cry as I held him. Some nights I would feel peace holding him.

Some nights Jamie would lie with him too. Even beat me to it. I asked him once why he did it, wondering if he prayed like me. His answer was simple. "I need him to know I am here." While Jamie and I clearly were not on the same page with where our son was developmentally, he felt the loneliness too. In a way, that made it more real for me.

My son was disappearing before my eyes. Evaporating. I could see him. He was right there. But parts of him were turning off, disappearing even. Or maybe not turning on. I didn't know the difference. I just knew that I was losing him. I was doing everything I could to hold on to him. An arm. A leg. Whatever I could grab. Because I knew in my heart, once he was totally gone, in his own world, I'd never get him back.

"Cooper is a two-year-old boy who lives with his mother, father, and younger brother. Mother has concerns about a speech delay and lack of imaginative play. Mother had a vaginal birth with no complications..." And then I was back in the small room, talking about our son's education.

That was not the first time my vaginal birth was read in a report. In fact, it would be read hundreds of times in the years to come.

As the director spoke about my son, our day care provider's sentence kept running through my head.

*"He will never ride a bike, make a friend, or learn to talk."*

It took her nearly twelve minutes to read the report from start to finish, paraphrasing our son's entire life. As she spoke, I realized they must have recorded every word I had said and written about Cooper.

"Mother says that Cooper does not sleep through the night

and has no spoken language. He makes eye contact, points, and waves but only eats five foods. Mother says he seems anxious and noted his obsession with watching his shows on television. Mother says he is never content and seems not to know what to do in most situations."

It felt weird, talking about Cooper like he wasn't in the room. Almost as if we were discussing someone other than our own son. I pushed myself away from the table subtly and peered underneath. He sat there, perched in between my legs, his face illuminated by my phone.

"Cooper was unable to stack three blocks, did not know what to do with the baby doll and bottle, refused to blow bubbles or walk in a straight line… Cooper failed to complete most of the evaluations due to behaviors with self-injuring and elopement." Before Cooper, I thought eloping was a happy couple running off to get married. After I lived it, I learned it can also be when a child wanders or runs away, typically with no regard to safety.

They noted that Cooper sat in the W position, which is when a child sits on their bottom with their knees bent and feet positioned outside of their hips. If you're standing above your child, you will see their legs and body make the shape of a W. They also noted that he walked on his tiptoes, both common red flags for autism and a developmental delay. He also flapped his arms when excited. Another red flag.

I looked at Jamie. He was stoic, listening to what the woman was saying about our son. Was he surprised? I couldn't tell. The farther we got along in this process, inching toward a diagnosis, it seemed like he was pulling away. It wasn't just my son. I was losing them both to autism.

The woman then transitioned to communication, saying Cooper's language was that of a six-month-old. I had the overwhelming desire to run. Hearing it out loud. Six months old. It was like a jab to my gut. I squeezed Jamie's leg, hoping that our years of marriage had perfected our telepathic communication. *Let's run, Jamie. Let's go. Let's get out of here.*

He squeezed my leg back.

"Kate and Jamie, after careful evaluation, it appears that Cooper exhibits signs of autism spectrum disorder."

There it was. The label that had been haunting me for years now, but this was the first time someone had said it out loud in relation to our son.

"But the team gathered around the table has mixed opinions." My head perked up immediately. I kicked Jamie under the table. Thomas the Train sang from the corner of the room.

She went on to explain that a child can have an educational diagnosis of autism but not necessarily a medical diagnosis. One does not impact the other. She and one of her colleagues thought Cooper had autism. Two others did not.

She asked us how we felt about the diagnosis of autism. I told her that the term had crossed my mind a few times but the medical professionals in our life quickly shut me down when I brought it up. They all thought Cooper was fine. That he was just a boy and a late bloomer. Lazy even. Speech delay, yes. Autism, no.

She then went on to do something that struck me as bizarre. She brought it to a vote.

"Since we are not all in agreement on Cooper's diagnosis, raise your hand if you think Cooper is autistic. Keep your hand down if you think he is not."

While I had been mostly avoiding eye contact up until this point, staring at the paper in front of me, my head snapped up and I looked directly at her. A vote? I felt like we were playing some weird twisted game about my son's future. She could not be serious. If it was that simple, autism or not, I obviously would vote no.

Neither Jamie nor I spoke. For once we were both speechless. Music continued to sing out from under the table as the first person raised her hand. Then the director did. The other two did not raise their hands.

The director, with her hand raised, asked each person to explain their vote. Two explained why they thought Cooper had autism. The other two explained why they thought he was merely delayed. It felt as if they were talking about someone else's child.

Then the director said, "Kate and Jamie, you two need to vote. With everything you have seen and heard during the evaluation process and at home, do you think your son has autism?"

I gasped and then giggled awkwardly. So did Jamie. I thought to myself, *What in the actual hell?* We were the deciding votes.

The silence hung in the air. The director went on to say that an autism diagnosis in the school setting would help Cooper considerably. It would get him more services. It was like she was trying to talk us into autism. Every part of me wanted to get up and leave, but I was frozen.

How could they expect me to label my own son? A label for people to judge him, treat him differently. I assumed a person was either autistic or not autistic. And they wanted *us* to decide? Weren't they experts?

Jamie just sat there, listening. I wondered what he was thinking. Was he as stunned as I was? How would he vote?

"This will help Cooper and get him the services he needs?" he asked, and the director nodded.

"Then I say yes."

I felt sickened. The way he nonchalantly agreed to something I had been running from and fighting for simultaneously made me feel betrayed. This whole time, I had been screaming that something was wrong with Cooper, desperately wanting Jamie to see it. I couldn't speak, so I just nodded my agreement.

We left with an educational diagnosis of autism and a plan to start services in the fall. I asked at the end of the meeting if we should pursue a medical diagnosis. I didn't quite understand the difference between the two. Did we need both? Was my son *actually* autistic?

"We can't give you that advice. Not legally."

As we gathered up our things to leave, I sensed an awkwardness in the air as I mentally tried to figure out who was on whose team. I honestly couldn't tell.

The next morning, I went in to work early. I closed my office door and pulled a crumpled piece of paper out of my purse. I dialed the number I had found the night before after a late-night Google search. It was for an autism diagnosis center nearly three hours away. It was time to get to the truth, once and for all. I couldn't live in this in-between place anymore.

While I waited on hold, I pulled up the website for the clinic. Happy faces filled my screen. Kids of all ages, boys and girls, sitting with therapists, and smiling. And then there was a man on the other end of the phone. He asked questions about the child to be evaluated. My Cooper.

I went on to tell him about Cooper, about the ordeal we had gone through, trying to read his reaction through the phone. We scheduled an appointment for six months from then, the first available appointment. It seemed so far away, but maybe this would all work itself out by then. Maybe we wouldn't need the appointment after all.

That weekend I took Cooper to an indoor playground, just the two of us. I wanted some special time with him alone. Back then, and even today, whenever we went places, I would always do my research to find out the quieter days and times. Cooper struggled so much with sounds, crowds, and waiting in line. I knew we'd have our best chance at success if I chose wisely.

On this day, there were just a few other families at the park. I had hit the jackpot. Cooper was free to roam, touching and feeling, at his own pace. As I followed behind, encouraging him to try the slide or maybe a swing, instead of just touching the walls and carpet, I saw a woman with a girl I assumed was her teenage daughter. The girl stuck out because she was much older than the other children running around. Yet she behaved far younger than she appeared. I watched her flap her arms, much like my own son did. It was as if fate had placed this girl in my life at this exact time.

I was drawn to the mother. After an hour or so, we found ourselves standing side by side, watching our kids dance and chase color from a projector. Just two moms. Our children at least ten years apart. I introduced myself and made small talk about where we lived and the weather. I asked how old her daughter was. And she told me about autism. She wasn't afraid to talk about it, the diagnosis rolling smoothly off her tongue. Something I wasn't able to do yet.

While we were chatting, her daughter, who I now knew was fifteen, ran up to her mother and began jumping excitedly in front of her. She wanted something, but I couldn't tell what. When her mother didn't immediately respond, the girl started yanking at her mother's shirt, pulling the top down with both hands, exposing her bra. The woman tried her best to stop her but couldn't really do much. Soon the girl was screaming, and aggressively pulling at her mother's breasts.

Cooper, the boy who didn't like sound or affection, ran up to me, alarmed. He climbed in my arms, burying his head in my shoulder. I held him close, not sure how to help the woman. She dropped to the ground with the girl who was nearly as tall as her, pulled a package of fruit snacks from her pocket, and fed them to her daughter one by one. Once the screams stopped, the woman looked up at me, her eyes filled with tears.

"When she gets nervous or anxious, she tries to touch my breasts. It provides her comfort. At home it is fine, but in public, well, it's humiliating."

I didn't know what to do or say to her. Was this my future with Cooper? Part of me wanted to run away. But I also didn't want to leave her alone. She seemed so vulnerable. I dropped to the ground with her and we sat there for a few minutes, neither of us really saying much. Most of the room was staring at her daughter. Did she notice? I couldn't tell.

As she got up to leave, she said four words to me that I'll never forget.

"This has broken me."

I sat for a while longer, holding Cooper, breathing him in. It was so rare that he let me hold him, and I didn't want to rush it. I was shaken. The woman's words ran like a ticker through my head. *This has broken me.* But our life would never be like theirs. Cooper would be different. That wasn't our fate.

I thought about my love for him, how strong and powerful it was. But I was terrified. Yes, of autism, of being different, and of standing out. But of being broken too. Was that my future?

I am a confident woman. I know my role as a wife, a daughter, a friend, and an employee. But as a mother, I have found myself in a place of uncertainty, where I can't figure out who I am, or what my role is. I know many if not all mothers feel this way at some point, the pressure sometimes suffocating. We are our own biggest critics. I don't feel confident in how to help my son, yet I am expected to. The decisions to help him felt monumental, while I felt like I was playing a game with ever-changing rules. And on top of that, I am in between two entirely different worlds and I don't feel whole in either of them anymore. I long for them to overlap, but as the boys age, they rarely do.

When I am with Sawyer, who is developing as he should, hitting all the appropriate milestones, we blend in. I am not consumed with worry or uncertain for the future. We do all the things other mothers and sons do. The things I imagined we would. We go to playdates and parks and hit baseballs off tees. I sit and drink coffee with other mothers while our children play, in that club that I had so desperately wanted to be a part of. But I miss Cooper. And as he ages, he needs me more. I am feeling the invisible tension, pulling me into his world. A world with no rules and no guidebooks to tell me what to do. A world of isolation. His needs pull me in and away from people, away from friends, away from the life that I once felt so comfortable in. Together, Cooper and I wander the perimeters of parks while Sawyer plays, sit in the basements of churches during events, and hide upstairs during holidays. While with him, I can hear my other son. I can see my husband. I am missing their lives.

I am a mother split in two, straddling two worlds. I hold my hands outstretched, a little boy on either side, pulling me, each needing me more. Will I forever wonder where I belong?

While we waited the six months for Cooper's diagnostic appointment, financial worries loomed over us. Jamie quit his job to start his own insurance business, a decision we agonized over. I felt it wasn't a good time, with all the stress I was feeling with Cooper, but he wasn't happy working long hours in banking, and it showed. In the end we decided to take the leap, but the financial strain of a family of four living on my measly part-time salary brought our stress level up even higher than it already was.

What we didn't know before we had a child with developmental delays—and why would we have?—is that without a diagnosis, help isn't typically covered by insurance. And getting help is expensive, money that we did not have. So, the therapies that Cooper needed were being put on a credit card weekly. And adding up. Jamie and I had many late-night debates about how we were going to pay our mortgage for the month. But the choice was awful. Our son never learning to speak, or debt?

We of course chose debt. And we cut corners. We could not really travel or go anywhere because of Cooper's challenges away from home anyway, so we stopped trying. We ate a lot of cheap food and paid the minimums on our credit cards. Life was not easy by any means. But at our core, we were a happy family.

Sawyer celebrated his first birthday and was not only developing typically, but I would even say early. When he said his first word, *mama*, at ten months old, I immediately started crying. I picked him up and twirled him around the room celebrating. No one had ever called me Mom before, and while I knew it was true, hearing it out loud was everything. But at the same time, I felt a longing in my heart for Cooper to speak. He had recently turned three and still had no words. He didn't babble or make speech-like sounds either. He was no closer to speaking than he had been at six months old.

My parents tried to assure me that Cooper would begin speaking. The possibility of Cooper being nonverbal forever never once crossed my mind. It was as foreign a concept to me as one could be. Autistic, maybe. Nonverbal, no. During every conversation with my mother, she said the same sentences in response to my concerns: "Everybody talks, Katie. Do you know anyone who doesn't talk?" My dad similarly started every phone conversation with, "Is he talking yet?" until one day I told him he had to stop asking. I couldn't take it anymore.

Right before he was diagnosed, I had a dream about Cooper. Which was a little strange because I rarely dream about my family. I typically dream about people I haven't seen since elementary school and the cashier at Target. And the occasional nightmare where I can't remember my locker combination in high school. And if I am being perfectly honest, I rarely dream at all because that would require sleeping. Something I've hardly done for nearly nine years now.

In my dream, we were walking along, Cooper and I, hand in hand, on a high bridge. It was made of rope and wood, very junglelike. I seemed to have my wits about me because I said to myself in the dream, *Why on earth would Cooper and I be in the jungle? This is dangerous but I'll go with it.*

We walked along for a while, very calmly, each pointing out the colors in the landscape. Vivid greens and blues and reds. It was incredibly beautiful. I could feel the wind in my face and even sense that it was somewhat dangerous. But we were fine. I felt a calm that I had never experienced before.

Suddenly, I heard a voice. Then it dawned on me. My son was talking. I couldn't believe what I was hearing. He grabbed my face with both hands and pulled me down to his level. He looked right into my eyes and said, "Mama," a word I have never heard before out of his mouth. He went on to tell me a story. I can't remember what it was about. I was too busy studying his mouth and watching his lips move. The sounds coming from his mouth were beautiful. I never wanted them to stop.

*Keep talking, keep talking*, I silently prayed. *Don't stop.*

The most intense joy suddenly washed over me.

I had a million questions for him, and I could sense that my time was limited. We stood there, laughing, and talking, like mother and son should. I didn't have to hold him with two hands. He wasn't running away or dropping to the ground screaming. He wasn't hurting me or himself. His body was calm and at peace, something I had yet to see in real life. His mind was too.

"Cooper, I love you. Do you know that?" I said to him.

Before he could answer, I woke up. My pillow felt cold, wet from my tears. Suddenly, I felt angry. I didn't want to wake up. I willed myself to go back to sleep. I squeezed my eyes shut, trying to get back into the dream. I wanted to hear his answer. I wanted to hear him talk more. I was frantic. "Take me back. Take me back." But the dream was gone.

I quickly analyzed every aspect of what I had seen and heard. The bright colors. The overwhelming sense of calm. And my son, he was at peace. He was able to stand still and walk along with me. He was talking. He was understanding. He told me a story. It was all unbelievable, really.

Suddenly, it hit me where we were. We were in heaven. And I had died before ever hearing my son speak.

I felt an immense sadness, no longer able to hear the sound of his sweet voice. That was the first time, but not the last, that it occurred to me my son might never speak. And of all the parts of autism I knew were probably coming, that thought devastated me the most.

While we waited for our diagnostic appointment, Cooper was

discharged from three therapy centers for behavioral problems. I found the last place in Duluth that would take him. A clinic for children with language disorders. As I described Cooper on the phone to the receptionist, explaining that we more or less had been kicked out of the other places, she laughed kindly.

"He will do great here," she exclaimed.

The first few sessions were exhausting. Cooper running. The therapist chasing. It had become obvious to me over the prior months that people didn't know how to work with Cooper. He was definitely a unique little boy. Nothing seemed to motivate him, which can make teaching challenging. Not food. Not play. Not toys. Getting him to try anything was impossible. I understood because I had the same problem when I worked with him at home. But what scared me terribly was how different Cooper seemed from the other kids at the center. I would observe them sitting with their therapists, engaging and even playing.

After our third week, his therapist said, "My boss wants me to diagnose Cooper with autism. I'm not going to though. Once you give a child that label, it sticks with them forever. And I truly believe he does not have it." I didn't know if I should thank her or not for saying that. Was she doing us a favor? I didn't know, honestly.

One of the goals of the therapy center was to bring families together and help foster relationships while educating us about our children. When I heard about the once-a-month evening class, I immediately signed our family up. The thought of meeting other families like ours excited me. Jamie and I sat at a table with twenty or so other parents, books on various speech disorders and neurological disorders placed in front of us. I looked around, taking it all in. These were our peers now. While my friends' kids were starting preschool and dance and T-ball, we were starting more therapies. Pizza was served and eaten, and then it was time for the kids to leave and go play. Only Cooper refused. As the therapist reached for him, he went limp and dropped to the ground, rolling, taking a folding chair down with a crash.

Jamie jumped up to take him back, but he refused again. He scooted his body, wedging it in between the wall and the backs of people's chairs. I watched their backs and necks lurch forward as his feet kicked ferociously.

"He can stay here with us," the therapist said. I was thankful for her accommodation. As the speaker went on about the importance of early intervention, Cooper picked himself up and made his way around the room, dragging his right arm along the wall. When he reached the stove, he stopped abruptly. The knobs had huge plastic covers on them as a form of babyproofing.

He spent the next forty minutes with his nose pressed to the cool stove, spinning the plastic covers. Faster and faster, the hum filling the room, forcing the speaker to talk louder. I desperately wanted to jump in, redirect him, or grab him and go. I wanted people to stop staring at him. When I looked up, ashamed, I made eye contact with a woman across the table. And that's when I knew. I couldn't pretend anymore.

That night I sat at the kitchen table, staring into space, and I heard Jamie say to our boys, "Mommy's broken." He was mostly joking, but his word choice stuck out to me. I had flashbacks to the woman at the indoor park. *This has broken me.* I told myself I was ready for the diagnosis of autism because then maybe someone would tell me what to do and how to help my child, and ultimately how to put us back together again.

We were technically twenty minutes late for Cooper's appointment. The one we had waited so long for. Jamie had one job, to get us there on time. He had the clinic name, but what he didn't know was there were multiple locations. We were going north when we should have been going south. I knew it was a harmless mistake, but to me it felt like he didn't care. I needed more effort from him. I was livid, frantically dialing the phone to the intake line, begging the woman on the phone not to give our appointment away. She said they would wait fifteen minutes, but after that, the appointment would be canceled.

I had done all the prep work for the appointment, pages and pages of paperwork. Question after question asking if Cooper could drink from a cup, smile at a stranger, or pretend to feed a doll. I had to sign release forms and have records transferred. I made endless phone calls to our insurance company and to every place that had seen Cooper since birth. Other people in our family had to complete evaluations as well. It was all-consuming. Jamie didn't understand how easy he had it and what I had been through to get us to this point.

Once we arrived, late, the three of us were placed in a room with a small table and a play structure. It was hot and the lights were dim. I felt agitated and uncomfortable, not wanting to be there in the first place. I swear that every hard situation in my life happens in a hot room. I looked at Jamie and wondered if he felt crowded too.

Cooper was given toys to play with, but he mostly just climbed the rocking canoe placed in the center of the room. Every so often the psychologist would ask us a question, and one of us would answer her. Since Cooper wouldn't respond to them, they asked me to prompt Cooper to perform different tasks.

"Point to the apple."

"Give the baby her bottle."

"Stack the blocks."

I started to feel like I was on display, like I was the one being evaluated. I sat with Cooper in between my legs, holding his hands in mine, willing him to be successful.

"Come on, buddy, just like we practiced."

The psychologist asked if he lined up objects or had an obsession with wheels. The answer to both questions was still no. Cooper continued to wander around the room, engaging when he felt interested, which seemed to be more than the usual.

After several hours, I had a sinking feeling. This was going well. Too well. *They aren't seeing the real Cooper. We came all this way and it's going to end up like every other medical appointment, wait and see.* I couldn't imagine leaving without an answer.

And then, with the thought still running through my mind, Cooper picked up my purse and brought it to me. He was tired, ready to go. When I didn't jump up, he moved his way to the light switch, flipping it on and off repeatedly. When neither Jamie nor I reacted, he took the lady's clipboard, the one the woman was using to determine if he was autistic, and threw it against the wall. I watched it shatter, the metal separating from the plastic.

Cooper looked at me, with fight or flight in his eyes. He swung the door open and took off down the hallway. I could hear him drop to the ground in screaming protest as Jamie caught up with him.

I smiled awkwardly. "That's the Cooper I know."

Finally, our three hours were up. Four of us, Jamie, me, and two psychologists, sat on little chairs at a tiny table, while Cooper sat in the brightly colored canoe, watching my phone. The older woman slid a folder across the table, almost discreetly. Like it contained secrets. I stretched out my hand and slid it toward me. I felt like we were spies or something.

I flipped it open, ready for our fate. Pamphlets and resources stared back at me. I flipped through it. Speech delay, developmental delay, autism, etc. Nothing specific to Cooper.

*This is it?* I thought.

In Minnesota, there is this awkward goodbye that most residents have perfected. Chatter turns to small talk, usually about fishing or the weather, neither party wanting to be rude and end the conversation. As Jamie spoke about his favorite lake, I had had enough.

"Is he autistic or not? I'm not leaving here without an answer."

"Well, typically we send you something in the mail and then follow up with a phone call. It will be two weeks. We don't tell you today."

"But obviously you know. I can't leave here without you saying it. I need to know." You could hear the desperation in my voice as it shook.

Jamie was standing to leave, uncomfortable by my forward question. Cooper was pulling on my arm, but I held my ground.

"Yes, Mr. and Mrs. Swenson, Cooper has autism spectrum disorder."

And then everything faded away. I looked down at Cooper, pulling not so gently on my arm, whining to leave, and all I could think was, *I made it. We made it, buddy.*

I had my answer. The last four years of fighting and begging and trying to figure out the mystery of Cooper were done. *He has autism.* And for the briefest of seconds, before all the other emotions hit me, I felt relief. I might have even smiled. And I told myself the hard part was over. Now we would get help and move on.

I heard her say "special needs" as she continued to speak to Jamie. That term that felt so heavy. She said something about the possibility of him never talking or using the toilet. I heard "planning for the future" and "lifelong care." But I was done.

I bent down and scooped up Cooper in the biggest hug and turned him away, shielding him from her words and future predictions, and I basked in my feeling of relief for as long I could.

# FIVE

On my desk, in my office, I have a picture of Cooper and me. The now weathered brown frame has moved with me over the years, from bedside to living room to office, never getting replaced by a more recent photo of us. It's my favorite. Cooper is eighteen months old and wearing a hand-sewn blue sailor suit, something I thought for sure he would be mortified about when he got older. When we took the photo, I even imagined bringing it out years later at his graduation or to show his future partner, much like Jamie's mother had done to him the first time he brought me to meet her. Only in his case it was a red cowboy hat and boots.

In my photo, Cooper's white-blond hair is long, maybe longer than a boy's hair should be, but I didn't care. I loved the way it curled around his face, making him look like an angel. My mother-in-law has always said about Cooper, "All kids are cute, but Cooper, he is beautiful." And she's not wrong. There's just something about him. Almost magical. He makes you want more of him.

In the photo, the sun is setting behind us in the trees, so the lighting is perfect. I am holding him tightly in my arms and smiling at him like we are the only two people on this earth. He is staring directly at me, both of his hands cupping my cheeks, pulling me close, as if he is telling me some amazing secret.

I often find myself staring at that photo when I should be working. I study the parts I can see. My blue dress. How young I look. Cooper. How young he looks. The baby fat on his feet and hands. The way he is staring at me so intently. I study the parts that can't be seen too. The worry inside of me. The fear that I was feeling. The diagnosis that was coming. The answers to my question just out of reach. The love I have for my son.

Sometimes I want to go back to the beginning. To the moment that photo captured. Before the official diagnosis created a stark line of before and after. Parts of me long to go back to that version of me, having no idea what was ahead. Back before the weight of autism was placed firmly on my shoulders, motivating me, and crushing me at the same time. Back to holding that complicated, confusing, beautiful little boy in my arms and believing it would all be okay, eventually. I just had to get to the finish line.

But I remind myself too, autism was always there. It wasn't given to him by a doctor who said the word out loud. It was inside of him, woven through him like the sunlight shining between our faces. I just couldn't see it yet. But I could feel it.

The day Cooper was officially diagnosed with autism, absolutely nothing changed and yet, in the most subtle way, everything about him and me and us felt different. Kind of like how overnight your baby turns into a kid. There is no way to explain it really, but as a mom, you look at them and just know they are no longer a baby. Or how every September I can pinpoint the day summer turns to fall. My mom always says the sky looks yellow when fall arrives. That's how she knows. Some years I see that yellow tinge in the sky as the days shorten and some days I don't, but I know the season has changed because I can feel it inside of me.

That's what getting a diagnosis was like for me. Nothing changed really. Not on the outside. The little boy I brought into the appointment was the same boy who came out. He still loved trains and Goldfish crackers and running at full speed. He was no different once the word was said out loud, but I could feel it inside of me. With the word *autism*, those strangers, those psychologists, had taken the road map of the life I had imagined for him and altered its course. Ever so slightly.

And isn't it just that? A word on a piece of paper. It doesn't have power. It's not something to be feared. It's not a death sentence. And it most certainly doesn't transform a child when said out loud.

Yet when we walked out of that room, Jamie, Cooper, and I, everything felt different. Like I was walking through a fog and trying to find my way out. I even felt like we looked different. As if the word *autism* was tattooed on our foreheads. A brand of sorts. It didn't feel fair, to put something so permanent on such a little boy. As we walked through the waiting room, I felt stares from onlookers. Did they know? Was I being paranoid? Did they pity us?

The sense of relief I had felt from finally having an answer was slowly fading, but I couldn't pinpoint the emotion that was replacing it. I felt lost when I should have felt found.

Once Cooper was buckled in his car seat, I waited for the tears to come, thankful that it was all done. I finally had my answer. There was no more wondering. But the tears didn't come. Instead I felt numb. That finish line moved farther away.

I peeked back at Cooper as I clicked my own seat belt. He was already watching Jamie's iPhone. I knew exactly what he was watching by the sound that was coming from it. He looked so content as he sat there in his seat, munching on a snack from his cup holder and smiling at his friends on the screen. Cooper had no idea that something huge had just happened. He was just happy to be going home with his mom and dad. He wasn't different at all.

I looked at my husband as he entered our destination into the GPS. I looked for signs of sadness on his face. A reaction. Anything, I guess. He had been silent since we left the observation room.

"How do you feel?" I said, trying to pull something out.

His response was nonchalant, his focus on the road.

"Sad, I guess. At least it's over now. But it's probably not as serious as they make it out to be."

His sentence trailed off as we drove. I didn't even bother responding. I felt alone as we navigated our way through the city. *Who is this man?* I thought. He felt like a stranger to me. We had just gone through this huge, exhausting, life-changing thing together. I felt as if I had been to war, yet he looked unfazed.

His lack of emotion toward everything—autism, me, life— was a big problem for me. Tears pooled in the corners of my eyes as I stared forward. How could he have nothing more to say about what we'd just experienced? This was his firstborn son. The one he bought the baseball glove for when I was pregnant. The same glove he brought to Cooper's newborn photos. He'd beamed with pride as the photographer placed a curled-up Cooper inside. How did he not feel anything more?

I wanted him to pull the car over. I wanted him to say he was sad and scared. I wanted him to hug me and for both of us to cry, if only for a few minutes, before taking our first step into our new roles as autism parents. I wanted him to say that everything would be okay, and we would get through this together. Take charge, even. But he didn't. I don't know why I even expected it at this point.

Then something dawned on me. Yes, Cooper had autism, but no one knew yet. Just us and those doctors.

"Let's run away, Jamie. You've always wanted to move to

Alaska. We can live in a cabin with the boys. You can fish. I can work remotely. And Cooper can just be Cooper. Who cares if he doesn't talk? Autism can only follow us there if we bring it with us." We began fantasizing a whole new life.

"That would be nice. We can live off the land!"

We both had a good chuckle knowing what terrible gardeners we both were. For a brief second, I actually considered this. I was having a fight-or-flight response. This was my flight. For the rest of the three-hour drive, I busied myself, like I always do when I'm avoiding feeling. I didn't want to break down until I got home. I didn't want Cooper to see me cry. I went online and ordered books on autism and a few more on speech delays. I joined a Facebook group for autism moms. I made a list of what needed to be done over the next few days. Phone calls that needed to be made and emails that needed to be sent now that we had a diagnosis.

I called my mom and told her the news. I knew she was waiting by the phone to hear. Like almost everyone in our life, she thought for sure it wasn't autism. She worked her career in the office of a school and often told me, reassuringly, that Cooper was nothing like the autistic children she had seen. When the words, "Yeah, it's autism," left my lips, I heard her burst into tears. My mom is a crier, and sometimes I have felt pressure over the years to sugarcoat hard things for her, but not this time. This one couldn't be sugarcoated.

I told her the truth and the words the psychologist had said. *Disabled. Special needs. Severe. Nonverbal. Lifelong care.* Each one feeling heavier than the last. When the call ended, I felt terrible. Saying the words out loud for the first time made me feel dirty. Maybe even a little bit like a traitor. I had pushed for this. I saw the signs and I blew the whistle. And I was right. It's a bizarre feeling being right when all you want is to be wrong.

Next, I called my dad, and even though he knew we were going to the appointment, he seemed confused when I gave him the news. I explained what I knew about autism and how this would affect his grandson socially, cognitively, even emotionally. He didn't understand and asked me if he would grow out of it. My heart broke even more when I had to say no to him. He gave me his old standby response. "Trust in the Lord, Katie. I will pray for Cooper. I just know he's going to talk." I felt angry as I hung up. I hated statements like that. While meant to be kind, it felt devoid of any real help or feeling.

Once we were finally home, hours later, and the boys were both tucked into their beds, I let myself plummet. It was finally time to feel. I closed the door to our bedroom and crawled into bed and screamed into my pillow until my voice was gone. I knew Jamie wouldn't come to bed that night. I was too sad for him, my emotions too big, and it seemed like he pulled away in my moments of grief, thankful to be able to avoid the huge swings of emotion. When I left him on the couch, he had just poured a drink, and I knew that was the last time I would see him until morning. In my head, while I hugged my pillow, I repeated one word. *Why?* I wanted to know why. Why my son? Why not some other kid? Why me? Why our family?

The word seemed like a black hole. None of this felt fair. I had done everything right in my life. I didn't break the law or do awful things. During my pregnancy, I took my prenatal vitamins, and I ate healthy. I even exercised. I thought about mothers who are careless during their pregnancies, doing drugs or drinking, and yet have perfect babies. Why Cooper?

I tried to bargain with God too. We weren't on the best terms, but I still tried to make a deal with him. *Take my voice, or my arm, or my leg, or punish me. Just let my kid be okay, please…*

My emotions roared through me, and I did nothing to quiet them. I let myself slowly unravel. Piece by piece. I felt anger. Then sadness. Then worry and fear. Jealousy was mixed in too as I thought about all the kids in my life who were the same age as my son. And who were fine. I felt slighted and robbed of all the experiences I had missed up to this point. And now what did the future hold? No one could tell me or dare predict.

For a few moments, I let myself doubt the diagnosis. I convinced myself it was wrong. Maybe instead of autism it was something else. Something simple. Maybe he just needed a supplement or maybe he was allergic to something. Maybe it was some mysterious lock that we just had to find the key for and then voilà, he would be fine.

Or if it was autism, maybe his wasn't severe. *Severe* felt so much scarier than *high-functioning*, a term used to describe the spectrum of autism. The psychologist had put him at the left, but maybe she was wrong. He was so young. Maybe he would move to the right-hand side of that spectrum and live a somewhat normal life. Maybe.

I convinced myself that he would talk. I had to in that moment, because the thought of him never talking to me was scarier than all the rest put together. All the emotions seemed to be spiraling around inside of me. I felt manic and out of control. A feeling that I was not used to.

Later, much later, I would learn what I was feeling was grief. But not the typical kind. I wasn't grieving a death, but the life that I had envisioned for my beautiful boy. A life that I had expected.

I pulled out my phone and searched *severe nonverbal autism*, a term that I hadn't let myself search before. For the next few minutes, I watched videos on YouTube of children screaming, rocking, and flapping their arms. I read articles about some children never really growing up. Never being potty trained. Some were aggressive. Some were dangerous. I felt ill. I felt scared. These kids weren't my sweet boy. That couldn't possibly be our future.

As the sobs shook my body, I thought about my son's teenage years. All the rites of passage we experience as we go through those complicated years. Driving a car, first date, first kiss, sneaking a beer even. I went farther into the rabbit hole of grief. I thought about proms, first jobs, graduation, and so on. The dreams I had taken for granted were endless. But now, I didn't know.

My son wasn't even four. Why was I torturing myself like this by thinking about every lost hope and dream? And then I faced my fears. Just for a second. I dipped my toe in… I thought about Cooper never talking to me. Not ever. And what that would look like when he was twenty and thirty years old. I thought about shaving his face for him when he became a man. Eventually it was too much to think about. I had to stop. I had gone too far into my own grief too soon. I had to pull back.

The last thing I thought about before falling asleep was my son being the one in a million. I knew autism wasn't going away. I knew there wasn't a cure. But I also knew, because I'd read stories online, that some kids get better. There are breakthroughs. They start talking. They start to understand this world and want to be a part of it. As I drifted off, I told myself that this would be Cooper, and this would all be fine.

The next morning, at 5:00 a.m. on the dot, I heard the pitter-patter of little feet come into my bedroom. I reached my arm out for Jamie, but he wasn't there. He'd never come to bed. I kept my eyes closed as the feet shuffled to my bedside, like they did every morning. And I smiled as the hand touched my cheek. As I opened my puffy eyes, Cooper grabbed my hand and attempted to pull me out of bed. Together, hand in hand, we made our way to the living room. He brought me right to the DVD player, holding my hand to it, nonverbally telling me what he needed. Before I got Thomas going, I scooped him up in the biggest hug and apologized for every worry I had the night before. Guilt washed over me as I replayed my thoughts. I vowed to tuck every one of those dark thoughts down inside of me. My moment of weakness had passed.

As I sat in the living room drinking coffee, watching Cooper dancing in circles, I felt reborn in a way. As if my lowest night had reset me. I felt motivated. I had hit what I thought was my bottom, and now it was time to pick myself up and help my son. I was a strong, smart, devoted, capable person and I could make this better. I had the power to make this better. And now that we had a diagnosis, it should be easy. Someone, I wasn't sure who exactly, would tell me what to do. Like a prescription of sorts. Cooper wasn't the first autistic kid diagnosed, nor would he be the last. I would just help him. Simple as that. By my calculations, he could be fine by kindergarten. That was the goal I set for myself. *By kindergarten he will be fine.*

The next few weeks were odd, to say the least. You know that old saying, "Hurry up and wait"? That's what I was feeling. I was all ready for the marathon of autism. I had my shoes on, I had trained, I was at the starting line waiting for the gun to go off. But there was nowhere to go. Cooper was already receiving all the help our area had to offer. He was getting speech therapy and would start preschool in the fall. But to me, that wasn't enough. I could tell that he needed more but I didn't know what. I felt like a failure.

But then a miracle happened. I received a phone call from the clinic that had diagnosed him two weeks before. The woman on the phone said that they could significantly change Cooper's life.

She told me about their program, *day treatment,* she called it, where Cooper could learn daily living skills such as how to sit and play and be with peers just like him. He would get his other therapies there too, occupational, speech, and feeding therapy. The only caveat was that they needed us to be there October 1, which was only one month away.

No one had ever given me hope like this before. Not the countless speech therapists, not the school district. I felt like she was dangling a carrot in front of me. After all, we lived three hours away from this clinic.

I know I sounded hesitant on the phone. Jamie and I both

had jobs and friends, and we owned a home. Moving wasn't a simple thing. Plus, Jamie truly loved it here.

"The earlier we can help these kids the better. Early intervention services are vital," the woman explained. I knew she was right. I had done enough research to know that the sooner a child gets help, the better their future looks. Some professionals even refer to it as a *window of time*. A window that closes.

Recently, the window was brought to my attention. A friend had reached out to me after hearing about Cooper's diagnosis, and connected me with a friend of a friend, who was a top neurologist at some big university. I emailed her all about Cooper and asked for advice. I did not hold back my desperation. I told her that he was just a few months away from turning four and had no words or communication. I told her about his limited diet and how he rarely slept and never sat down and how potty training felt impossible. And I told her how smart he was and bright but that I felt like he was slipping away from me. My hopes ran high as I poured out my fears and concerns to a stranger.

Her response came back almost instantly.

"The brain closes by age four. You've missed the window to help your son. Sorry, there really is no hope."

I was livid. What a sick thing to say to a mother about her child. I would learn, though, that this wouldn't be the first time someone would limit Cooper's future because of his diagnosis and age. Soon after this, a speech therapist would tell me that if a child doesn't have words by age four, then game over. Another would tell me to prepare for a life without words. Another would tell me that children like Cooper all end up in institutions. To parents, these statements are crushing.

But in time I learned not to let these people limit my child's future. Professionals are here to help us, and often they do. But they don't have a crystal ball, or the ability to predict a child's future. Regardless of whether they end up being right or wrong, the one thing we can't let them do is destroy our hope.

I told the lady on the phone from the clinic that yes, we'd be there. I couldn't control much with my son's autism, but I could control this. I could give him a chance. I could try one more thing to help him. If I could give one piece of advice to parents of children with additional needs, always try one more thing. My joke is that our autism manual got lost in the mail, or maybe sent to the wrong address since we moved so often. And if I ever happen to write one, it will say, "Try one more thing. Always one more thing."

With that, I walked downstairs to Jamie's office and told him the news. I told him about the clinic's offer and the treatment. "We're moving," I said, "and you can't fight me on this. Please don't fight me. I have to help Cooper."

In my marriage, when it came to decisions, Jamie and I were typically a team. We would talk big decisions through, weighing the pros and cons. But in this one, I refused to take no for an answer. My only focus was Cooper. We talked through the logistics and how we could make it work. We would have to live with his parents since we most likely couldn't afford to buy a house on my salary alone. We would need day care for Sawyer. I would need to be able to transfer my job. Our home would need to sell. The list of concerns was endless. I didn't care though. I would make it all work.

Jamie didn't fight me for once, but I know he didn't want to move. And I knew there was resentment building toward me. I could feel it.

After a frantic call to my boss, a real estate agent, and Jamie's parents, it was official. I could transfer down to the Twin Cities, keeping my same job with the same company, and Jamie, who was a self-employed insurance agent, could work from anywhere. And our forever home—we had been updating it along the way, bringing it into the modern era. It sold after the first showing. It all felt meant to be. Almost easy.

Less than a month later, we moved, practically overnight,

complete with two U-Haul trucks filled to the brim, eventually landing at Jamie's parents' house, two dogs and two boys in tow. The next day, October 1, Cooper started at his new program. The pieces were falling into place.

The next few months were chaotic to say the least, and Jamie and I felt the pressure build between us as we worked to start our lives over in a new place. Jamie took the lead on finding us a house, while continuing to grow his new business, and I kept managing Cooper's services, while working. It felt like a full-time job. I had assumed when we moved, the hard part would be over. I didn't know the fight had only just begun. Daily, a large amount of my workday was spent making phone calls and completing paperwork. We had found out from Cooper's new therapy center that help was available to families of autistic children, but you had to jump through their hoops first. And it felt like there were hundreds of hoops. For four years I fought for the diagnosis, and now I felt like I spent my time proving it was actually real. The amount of paperwork that went into it was astronomical. There was always another release that needed to be signed or an evaluation that needed to be completed. I wrote and said Cooper's birthday so many times that when asked my own, I often said his.

The whole time I felt like I was working toward a moving target. But soon we had another win. We found out that along with attending day treatment weekly, Cooper could also attend a preschool program for three-year-olds with autism at the local school district. And they provided transportation. With Jamie and me both working full-time, and day care not an option for a child with such significant needs, this was a huge win. Cooper would attend preschool in the morning, then attend day treatment, and we could both work a full day. Plus, we found a house. A beautiful home with a decent-sized yard and a swing set. It was near a park and close to Jamie's parents' house too. The way life was working out should have provided Jamie and me so much happiness, but it didn't. I think in our hearts, neither of us wanted to be there. We missed our old simpler life in the country. I felt alone a lot of the time, even when I was in the same room as Jamie. I hoped that moving out of his parents' house and into our own place would help get us back on track.

"I think the parents who have autistic children are the lucky ones."

I just stared at Cooper's new teacher when she said that. At this point in our autism journey, not one person had said anything positive about autism or my son's future with autism. Let that sink in. Everything we heard was dark, and while I am typically a glass-half-full kind of person, the constant negative was wearing me down.

I have often wondered if the beginning would have been easier for me, for our family, if just one person had spoken positively about our son's future. What if, instead of telling us about all the things he would supposedly never do, they said, *"It's going to be hard at first, like most things. You will bend and almost break, but you will survive, and it will be great. Your child will be great."*

That never happened though.

So you can imagine my surprise when this young, sweet teacher called us the lucky ones. I looked around to make sure she was talking to us. Cooper had just thrown a small child's chair across her classroom, barely missing the SMART Board. Jamie was trying to manage the chaos that came from bringing him to a new space while I tried to pay attention to her presentation. I smiled a fake smile at her as another chair bounced off the wall with a thud. We certainly made our presence known.

We were visiting the preschool program that Cooper would start the following day. It was an open house at your typical neighborhood elementary school, full of loud and happy kids. Only it didn't feel that way to me. I think this new teacher probably assumed I was feeling anxious about sending my nonverbal son to school in a new city. Of course, I was nervous. He couldn't communicate his wants or needs. I worried about him being able to ask for a drink or wandering off. I worried about people being nice to him. But it was more than that too.

I felt sad. This wasn't what I had imagined for preschool. Sending my sweet boy to a special education program for half days, then sending him on a van for people with disabilities to an autism day treatment program for the rest of the day. I kept trying to figure out how we got here. This wasn't what I pictured.

My friend's daughter had started preschool the week before and it was nothing like this. I know because I saw a photo of her on Facebook, holding a giant sign that said, "My first day of preschool!" The caption was all about their mother-and-daughter shopping trip for the perfect backpack and her excitement over the yellow school bus.

It wasn't like that for us. Cooper had no idea he was starting school. He didn't care about a backpack, and shopping was out of the question. He hadn't been in a store in almost a year. And while most kids learn their ABC's and 1-2-3's, we were hoping that Cooper would learn to sit and pay attention and talk.

My son was starting his first school, and while I was hopeful that this would help him, my heart was broken at the circumstances.

But we were lucky. Looking back, I know that now. Our son was not yet four and had just made the age cutoff for an autism preschool program through the school district. It was a godsend because he had been kicked out of every day care he had attended. This is all too common for children with significant needs and why typically one parent must quit their job to provide care. But in our case, we both wanted and needed to work.

When we arrived thirty minutes earlier for the open house, we were met by a huge sign that said, "WELCOME PRE-K'ERS" and directed by neon-green arrows down a long hallway lined with little lockers. I was nervous, my stomach in knots. Our experience with the last school district had been less than stellar. We were made to feel almost as if the word *autism* was dirty. I'd have to explain Cooper's diagnosis during every phone call, never really getting anywhere. One step forward and two steps back. So, I wasn't sure what to expect with our new school.

Cooper didn't see the arrows, nor did he understand why we were there. He didn't care about meeting his new teacher or seeing his new classroom. In fact, he was really in a mood. The second he saw the long hallway and wide-open space, he took off running. Jamie took off chasing, around the corner and out of sight. Jamie and I often divided and conquered. He went after Cooper so I could meet the teacher and get ready for tomorrow and hopefully motivate him to come to his classroom eventually.

As I walked along, following the arrows to pre-K, I felt out of place, like an impostor. Moms and dads were all around me with their children, Cooper's age, little bodies marching along with their backpacks on. Some clung to their mothers while others made a game of hopping from arrow to arrow. I wanted Cooper to be here with me.

When I reached the end of the hallway, I peeked inside a classroom. It was filled with parents and children, brimming with an energy that only a dozen three- and four-year-olds can bring. Music was playing, and a few of the kids were dancing on the blue mat in the center of the room. I heard little voices babbling on about desks and lunch. Tears sprang to my eyes as I took it all in. This wasn't Cooper's room. I knew it in my heart. Yet I wanted to go in. I even took a step forward. If I just went in, I thought, maybe we could blend in.

"Ms. Swenson? Are you Cooper's mom? I recognize you from the photos you sent."

I turned my body to the door on the right and nodded to the kind-looking young lady who I assumed was Cooper's new teacher. Her smile was huge and inviting, just what I hoped for in a teacher for my son.

"Welcome! We are so excited to have you here. Where is Cooper?"

I was busted. I stepped away from the bustling class of children and into a much quieter room with her. As she shut the door behind us, I felt a ping of grief as I peeked at the small sign next to the door. "ASD Classroom Pre-K." And with that one step, our label was known. We were different. But we weren't alone. I counted four other families spread out around the room.

Like the room next door, this one was brightly colored. There were little tables and chairs and a rug in the center. There was a big sensory swing hanging from the ceiling in the corner and bean bag chairs scattered about for children who needed breaks. It wasn't sad by any means, just different. There were fewer children, there was no music, and the lights seemed to be dimmer. And it felt like the parents were all whispering as if trying to stay anonymous, which felt far different than the loud, excited room next door.

The teacher told me there would be five children in her class, which was wonderful because each child would get one-on-one attention. She told me they would focus on daily living skills, communication, and peer interactions. She handed me a folder marked ASD, and I sat down to wait for Cooper and Jamie, who were still apparently roaming the halls of the school.

I pulled the folder to my chest and turned to study the other four families. At this point, I didn't know anyone else in my life with autism. You hear the diagnosis rate is one in fifty-nine, but I couldn't figure out where all the kids were. We sure weren't seeing them. It felt like one in a million to us.

I noticed the other four children were boys too. Each was with his parents, scattered in different parts of the room. One was doing a puzzle. Another one was climbing on the giant swing. I was very surprised by how calm these children were. And engaged with their parents. I heard a few of them talking.

Suddenly, I started to get nervous. Was I in the right classroom? This wasn't our autism, at least not what I knew of it.

Cooper's energy level was unlike anything I had ever encountered in my life. He didn't sit. Not ever. He woke at 4:00 a.m. and went to sleep at 9:00 p.m. In between, he ran. Even when he watched television, he paced and bounced. He didn't speak and he most certainly didn't play. I felt scared. I wanted so badly for this to work.

*Maybe it will be fine*, I thought to myself. *Maybe he will come in and want to go on the swing or roll on a bean bag.* And then the door burst open, slamming into the wall, and Cooper and Jamie were here. My little blond-haired boy in his button-down shirt for his big day flashed a huge grin when he saw me. He immediately scanned the room, took in his surroundings, and took off. He was like a tornado as he pulled out the contents of every cubby. He dumped a giant tub of crayons on the carpet. He even swept the papers off the teacher's desk into a pile on the floor.

He ran from spot to spot, making messes, while Jamie and I chased behind. I could feel my anxiety rising and the sweat gathering in the small of my back. All eyes turned to us. Suddenly the room was very noisy.

I let Jamie move with Cooper while I spoke a bit more with the teacher, who did not seem to mind our chaos at all. I felt an instant connection to her and her excitement to teach my son. Something I hadn't felt up until this point. I could tell this woman was different from Cooper's previous day care and therapy providers, who had given me nothing but dread and anxiety.

"Children like Cooper are special. I wouldn't be sad at all if my own children were born with autism. It makes them unique."

There she went again. I was taken aback. I continued to stare at her, mouth open. Was she pulling my leg?

As the open house came to an end, the other four families eventually left. Jamie had taken Cooper out to the car to wait while I filled out the last of the paperwork. I needed to ask the teacher a few more questions. As I sat there waiting, I felt incredibly alone. And I felt lonely for Cooper. For children with autism, it's hard to fit in with other kids. And it's even harder for children with severe autism. Our peer group was already small, and after the open house, I felt like it had gotten even smaller. My son was different than these kids. Far different.

"Those other boys, they have autism like Cooper?" I asked the teacher tentatively.

She nodded yes.

"It sure feels like my son is the most…spirited."

"They all have their struggles and their strengths. We just have to find Cooper's. You are a lucky mama, Kate. He's a great kid and I'm excited to have him in my class."

"But can you help him?"

"I'm going to try."

As I walked to the door, I turned and said, "He won't be able to tell me anything about his day. Like if he's sad or hates his lunch or whatever. I won't know what he did. And he might get upset. You saw him. Please be nice to him. Please love him like your own. He's so fragile and vulnerable."

And with that I broke down right there in front of his teacher. I was given the most precious, vulnerable gift in the form of a child, one that wasn't always easy to understand or to teach. All I could do was trust that the world would treat him well and deliver him back to me in one piece.

I was terrified.

Shortly after we moved into our new house, I received an unexpected email that brought me to tears.

For the last couple of weeks, we here at Kacie K Photography have been asking for nominations of other families affected by autism. I have two children on the autism spectrum myself and know firsthand how difficult it can be to get a family photo or individual photos of my kiddos. There are a million things that go into the struggle...sensory overload, inability to sit still, wandering, poor eye contact...and sometimes the hardest part...finding a photographer that "gets" it. We had 15 families nominated, but the nomination that your dear friend sent me about you was beautiful and moved me. I felt so connected to your story...like it was part of mine. It was an automatic YES when I read it...and I wanted to work with you!

As I read the email, tears flowed from my eyes. I was overwhelmed with gratitude. Grateful to my friend for nominating us and grateful to the woman who picked us. For the first time I felt like someone saw how hard we were struggling. When I connected with the photographer over the phone, I immediately fell in love with her. She was the first person who spoke to me about autism from the mother's point of view. She was candid, open, and full of faith and love for her children. She spoke of the sleepless nights, the exhaustion, the fear and worry in a way that I hadn't felt confident enough to say out loud yet. She spoke her truth, which felt a lot like mine as well. I had found someone who understood. And she spoke about grief, a topic that no one had discussed with me openly until now.

After talking with her for five minutes, I felt like I had known her for years. The questions poured out of me and we talked for a long time, bonding over our shared experiences. Finally, I worked up the courage to ask one last question. I asked her about her journey to acceptance. That word, *acceptance*—it's a buzzword on the tongue of every special-needs parent. To accept the question, *Why my child?* To accept the things they might never get to do. To accept that this isn't going away. Acceptance to me was the finish line, or so I thought.

I asked her when she found acceptance, because Cooper was only four, and I just couldn't believe this was our forever.

We both cried as she told me her answer.

"Five years," she said. "It took me five years to get where I am today."

"Five years from birth?"

"Five years from the diagnosis..."

I gasped. That couldn't possibly be true. Would I be living in this upside down, inside out place for five more years? She had to be wrong.

A week later our family met her at a local farm to take the photos she so graciously gifted us. Cooper wore bright yellow pants and carried an 8-by-10 photo of our family in a frame, a quirky thing he had started doing. Our family photos went everywhere with us, and I mean everywhere. Sawyer wore a yellow tie and had a black eye from a baseball. Jamie and I were in the middle of an argument and not on speaking terms. We were quite the crew.

We stood on top of the bridge for a posed photo. Cooper, suddenly anxious, threw the beloved frame he was holding over the edge and into the river. It landed with a thud. As all four of us turned to watch it float away, the photographer snapped a beautiful photo. It was a symbolic moment now looking back. Almost as if the old us was drifting away.

The photos turned out perfectly, showing a beautiful, happy family of four. As I studied the proofs over a glass of wine, I struggled to choose which ones to put on the walls of our new home. We looked so happy. No one could've known that behind closed doors, my marriage was over.

# SIX

Shortly after Cooper was diagnosed, I found a study online that said the divorce rate in families with special-needs kids was upward of 80 percent. It showed up as an ad on my Facebook feed, some study done by some big university. I normally never click on those things, but this one I did. It was as if my phone knew what was happening to my family behind closed doors.

Not many people know that Jamie and I were married, divorced, and then remarried to each other again. We don't talk about it all that much. In fact, not long ago, I went to a sign painting party at a neighbor's house. A sign painting party is a very Midwestern thing where middle-aged moms drink wine and make pretty things for their walls. The wooden sign I was making said our last name, "Swenson" and "Established in..." I laughed as I tried to decide what date to use.

Was it 2008, the year we were first married, or 2018, the year we were remarried? I went with 2008 when it was all said and done. The buildup, separation, and divorce took about two years of our lives and a whole lot of our money, time, and energy, but we were still together. We were still a family, just an unconventional one. That two years apart did something else too. It provided us with a much-needed pause button and a way to relieve the pressure that had built up between us. It provided clarity and time to examine what we both needed. And ultimately what was most important.

Our children. And giving them their best life.

When we do share our story now with other couples, typically over a few drinks, people are shocked to hear that we were actually divorced. That we "actually" went through with it. And that we "actually" healed enough to get back together years later.

They laugh at Jamie's time spent fishing in a boat and my stories of mowing my lawn while drinking a martini, and pausing every sixty seconds to check on Cooper to make sure he wasn't destroying my home. They love that I bought a house by myself and that we attempted to stay good friends the entire time. Jamie will usually chime in at that part with, "I hated her," which will bring another laugh. He did though. He really hated me. I hated him too. But you wouldn't know that now.

Someone, typically the wife, will always pull me aside after and ask if I dated. Or if Jamie did. They want to know the fun, scandalous parts. Often the husbands will follow up with Jamie later, asking if either of us recommend a marriage time-out, saying it sounds like a free pass.

We both get it. People are intrigued by our nontraditional love story. They look at us now, happy, and assume that because Cooper is doing better, our marriage is better. And they assume autism caused our divorce.

On paper it may look that way. We might have even thought that for a while too. But the answer is no. Autism did not cause our divorce. And he didn't cheat, and I didn't lie. In fact, we still loved each other very much. It just got too hard and over the years we became strangers walking parallel paths that rarely intersected. It was easier to do it apart.

I asked Jamie for a divorce. Yes, it was me, because while he was generous, loving, and kind, he was oblivious to what was really happening with Cooper. When you have a child diagnosed with something, it comes with a weight. A heavy one. And my husband was more than fine with letting me carry it all alone. As Cooper aged, and the weight intensified, I started to turn invisible, completely consumed by all of it. The pressure of helping our little boy was just too much to carry alone. And my husband did nothing to save me. That is why I divorced him. If I had to do it all alone anyway, I might as well truly be alone. It would be easier that way.

Months after we moved into our new house in the Twin Cities, it probably appeared on the outside like our life was going well. The pieces were all falling into place. I was thankful for my project manager job and the flexibility my employer gave me to manage my chaotic life. Jamie was able to work from home and was having success growing his insurance business. Cooper, who was now four, had his supports in place. His days were busy with his therapies, and he spent his evenings with Thomas the Train and Dora the Explorer, a new favorite. And while he still had no time for people in his life, I watched the characters in his shows become vital to him. I watched a documentary once about a man with severe, nonverbal autism who later learned to communicate. He told his parents that the characters in his shows were his friends. When people would shame me for the amount of programming my son watched, I took comfort in this. I knew he wasn't lonely.

Despite all the services he was receiving, he wasn't making much progress in any areas. Sleep was still hard to come by, which made everything more stressful. He also developed quite a few behaviors, the challenging ones I had heard about from parents of older children. He would elope out unlocked doors and run into streets at any given moment. When something set him off, he would yell and rage for hours. His communication was still nonexistent, his recent speech therapist once again comparing it to a six-month-old baby's, a statement that gutted me. I continued to stay positive that progress would come. He just needed more time. And it was my job to give him that.

Sawyer, who was now two, started a new day care and was thriving being closer to his cousins and grandparents. He was such an easy little boy, talking nonstop and staying busy with his toys. He loved going places too and struggled sitting at home, which was the exact opposite of Cooper.

On paper, we were great, all smiles in the photos I shared on Facebook. But on the inside, it was a much different story. My resentment toward Jamie, family, and our situation was building. Like a volcano ready to blow. I felt trapped by my life, which was all work and autism. And the isolation from not being able to leave the house was suffocating.

Our life had come to a standstill after Cooper was diagnosed. The list of places we could go was dwindling rapidly, but yet everyone in our life still expected us to show up for parties and events. So we'd go, try to keep up appearances and do what was expected of us, but it would always end in disaster. Cooper and I once had to leave a wedding early. There was a barbecue where Cooper and I spent half of the event sitting in the truck while he watched a movie.

The pressure this put on Jamie and me was astounding. He wanted to keep attending these gatherings, keep pretending that everything was fine. But I didn't. It made me too angry. Part of me wanted the world to accommodate us better and make it easier for us to be included, but the other part of me knew that wasn't always an option and it was no one's fault.

We fought having autism consume us. We fought having it control where we could go and how we could spend our time. We fought being nothing more than autism parents. For years we searched for hobbies and a life outside of our home. We tried.

People often asked why we didn't get a babysitter, which is comical. One does not easily get a sitter for a nonverbal child with autism. How would I explain to a teenager that our son was a runner? That if the door was unlocked, even for a second, he would escape. That they'd have to lock not just one lock, but three. The dead bolt, chain, and a flip lock up high, and then jiggle them, just to be sure.

How would I explain that our son only watches a fifteen-second segment of a two-hour Thomas video and they would need to sit at the television and rewind it over and over again?

Even if I could provide the elaborate instructions for watching Cooper, the truth is that we couldn't trust anyone. Or at least it felt that way. It was too scary to leave Cooper alone with someone else. He didn't speak. He didn't understand safety or danger. Finding a person I could trust to keep him safe felt impossible. And I know we are not alone in this way of thinking. I hear from parents constantly that getting babysitters for children with autism is simply not an option. But without a break, other parts of your life will inevitably suffer. For us, that was our marriage.

Jamie and I had become strangers. Our conversations were solely about our son's care. I'd talk about new therapies with a renewed excitement and anticipation almost weekly. I'd find a new diet, supplement, or tactic that was going to help our son. I'd read about a child who started talking after his parents removed gluten from his diet, or a nonverbal boy who spoke his first word after his mother gave him fish oil. I'd tell Jamie about these things and while he always had doubts, I remained hopeful. I would be on top of the world. Until the remedies failed. They all failed. And with each failure we would be out money and wasted time. But even more than that, my hope would be crushed. Jamie would always give me an *I told you so*, making me feel silly for even trying. Each time the resentment would grow. He resented my willingness to try new things and I resented his unwillingness to try anything at all.

The other issue that drove a wedge between us was how to juggle Sawyer's needs. He shouldn't have to miss a birthday party or skip a family picnic just because of his brother. So Jamie and I would split up. Typically, Jamie would go with Sawyer, and I would stay home with Cooper. Often, I would cry as photos of my younger son having fun and playing with other kids would pop up on my phone. I was jealous. But Cooper needed me, and it was just easier for me to stay home. Yet the resentment that I had toward Jamie, because he was enjoying himself as though our world was okay—it was thick.

I felt like I was on the roller coaster alone. I'd send Jamie blog posts about autism, links to YouTube videos, even tag him in articles on Facebook. He'd barely give them a glance and I didn't know why. It felt like such a simple thing to me. I was desperate to find other families like ours, stories of hope, even stories of overcoming the struggles. Many of our fights were me trying to understand why he didn't seem upset or worry like I did. But I couldn't force him to feel. I couldn't make him get on the ride with me.

Before we had children, one of my favorite things about my husband was his laid-back personality. No matter how intense our life got, my husband stayed calm. It was the perfect match for my energy. And after Cooper's diagnosis, it was the thing I hated the most about him. It wasn't that Jamie was unhelpful. He went to every appointment. He was next to me when I needed him to be. What he couldn't do, not at that time anyway, was help me carry the *emotional* weight of our son's diagnosis, a weight that was placed firmly on my back and only getting heavier as he aged. It was almost as if he was numb.

I didn't want to do it alone. I wanted my husband to see what was happening, and how serious it truly was. I did everything I could to get him to acknowledge it and understand the scope and severity of it. At a certain point, it became easier to carry the weight alone. I made the decisions. I dealt with the consequences. I know Jamie wondered what had happened to the woman he married, the vivacious, fearless, and adventurous woman. What he didn't know was that I barely recognized myself.

What he needed from me hung in the air. It was always between us. My husband expected me to move on. He expected me to cry my tears, dust myself off, and keep living. He didn't understand that I couldn't do that. My heart was broken. And his wasn't. I had started to accept the fact that our son might never talk or graduate high school or get married and have babies. He had barely even acknowledged it yet. It wasn't like we were reading different chapters of the same book…he wasn't even reading the book. I could feel the perfect life I had pictured slipping away.

Years and years of sleep deprivation, aggressive behaviors, and screaming from a child, or any person in your life for that matter, can wreck a person. We turned on each other. Jamie had become my emotional punching bag. And I was his. He called me a martyr. And probably much worse. I called him lazy and devoid of emotion. Withdrawn. They were all low blows. They were all somewhat true. Eventually I stopped talking altogether. I became silent. I didn't want to fight anymore. Or be sad. Or worried. I thought Jamie would sense that I was struggling and holding it all inside. He didn't though. He seemed to be relieved not having to talk about our problems anymore.

Eventually, the pressure got to be too much. I began searching for something else. I sought out new friends, ones who were a little bit damaged like me and who were looking to escape too. To this day I can't really say what I was searching for. Fun? A release? A life without autism, maybe. A place where I could be more than just a mom. I needed a break from the worry and stress. But I wasn't necessarily going to act on it. Then one day I overheard a conversation that changed the course of our lives.

It was my birthday, and my sister and her fiancé were visiting for a fun night out. My parents had taken the boys for us for the night. As I walked from the bathroom to the living room, I overheard my sister and Jamie speaking in hushed tones in the kitchen. Over the last year I had often confided in my sister about how unhappy I was feeling in my marriage.

"She's unhappy, Jamie. She's been telling me for months."

"Yeah, I know. But I don't know how to fix it."

"She wants a divorce, Jamie. She told me she's even spoken with a lawyer."

He went silent. I felt numb listening to my sister talk to my husband about our failing marriage. For a moment he seemed to be processing the information, and I thought he'd express fear or concern about the idea of me leaving him. Then he said:

"She will never leave me. She can't do this alone."

I gasped. *Never leave him. Can't do it alone?*

That was the moment I decided my marriage was over. I was so angry with him. Livid. After the hell I had gone through alone for the last four years, and he had the audacity to say I couldn't do it alone. I realized then that I wasn't stuck. I wasn't trapped. If I was unhappy, I could just leave. And with that I was done. He could have very easily told my sister that he was trying to make it better. Or that he was willing to work on us. But he didn't. He made me out to be weak and unable to live without him. My marriage was over.

I asked for a divorce days later. Jamie thought I was joking, but he soon realized how serious I was. I contacted our real estate agent to list our house. I told my parents. I asked him to tell his. He refused. From that day forward we slept in separate rooms. I wish I could say it felt different...like a drastic change. But it didn't. We had stopped sharing our lives together long before.

Looking back, I don't think Jamie wanted to end our marriage, but he didn't want to fight for it either. It truly was easier for both of us to be apart.

In the blink of an eye we were divorced. I was surprised how easy it was. I didn't want any money from him, and he didn't want any from me. We'd share the kids. The house sold. I bought a new one. He rented from a friend. We even rode together to the courthouse to make it final. Afterward, we debated grabbing lunch, but he opted to go fishing instead.

I wanted to go to lunch. I wanted to maintain a friendship. After all, our lives were still greatly intertwined. But what could I really do about it? I no longer had any say over his life, nor did he have any over mine. I thought I would feel some big emotion when our divorce was final. But I honestly didn't. I had entered this place of numbness, my emotions dulling. I think that's what gave me strength to go at it alone.

We spent the next year living separately and shuffling the kids and dogs back and forth. They were mostly with me at my house, and Jamie visited daily. During those months we both focused on healing and trying to figure out who we were. Jamie spent his time in a boat, fishing, with friends, and free from the stress of autism. He needed that. To this day he still thanks me for it. I was thankful too. I couldn't share the boys half-time, like most divorced couples do. I wanted them every second. I wanted to tuck them in at night and know they were safe.

Jamie took the space he needed. He continued to meet me at every appointment for Cooper. He was next to me when I needed him. He came to my house and had dinner, he threw baseballs to Sawyer, and he gently and lovingly gave baths to Cooper. Jamie was a doer, and without the pressure of having to show and give me emotion, we actually grew closer.

Me, well, I mothered and survived. I told myself I was broken and flawed and that I wasn't meant for happiness. I was hard on my body. I drank way too much after the kids were in bed. I exercised when I could. I didn't really eat. I still didn't sleep. I dove into my work. I made new friends. I chased a different life.

One day not long after the divorce, I left the kids at home with Jamie to run an errand. When I arrived back to the house, I walked up to my front door, but before going in I peered into the living room window. Inside, I saw my ex-husband sitting with Cooper and Sawyer on the couch, the tops of their three blond heads all looking identical. I could hear Cooper's iPad singing. I could see both boys leaning on their dad. It was a picturesque image. And then I stepped up on my tiptoes to see more, my heart bursting at the loving moment. And when I did, I saw the screen of Jamie's phone. He was on Tinder, a dating app.

I was shocked. I'll admit that I had a dating profile as well, but he always told me that he would never date again. I mean, I would have still been with him if he had given me the time and attention I needed. So why would he give it to someone else? I was crushed.

I wonder if Jamie had ever seen my own profile. It showed happy pictures of a seemingly happy woman, one who appeared available but never really was. We never spoke of it.

Even though we were divorced, we continued to spend holidays together and time with each other's family. Everything that was important we spent together. We said it was for the kids. We even had family photos taken together. I spent hours after receiving the proofs back, studying our faces. Our little not-so-conventional family. I tried to figure out why we couldn't be happy. Why it couldn't work. Were we weak? It was a weird reality. I told myself that some people are just better apart. We focused on our kids and giving them their best life possible. We found a rhythm. I was still hyperfocused on Cooper. I grieved the emotional parts that I felt and the losses alone. I found it easier that way. Being alone with my child's disability. I had no expectations of anyone.

So, as I've explained, I will not say that having a child with special needs caused our divorce, because it truly didn't. Autism wasn't the problem. And it didn't ruin our marriage. What it did do, though, was show how two people who love each other can walk parallel paths of hope, grief, and reality that never intersect.

Parenting a child with a disability is huge and life-changing. What we were going through was traumatic. That's a fact. And through it all we kept our son's care at the center of our lives. We gave him every opportunity. We just sacrificed ourselves in the process.

A few months after our divorce was final, my sister got married in Las Vegas. As I sat by the pool, alone, watching happy couples, I called Jamie and begged him to join me. He needed to be there. He was a member of our family. As complicated as parts of our relationship were, he was undoubtedly a huge part of my life.

It was one of those stories that would make an amazing movie. He dropped the kids at his parents', bought a last-minute ticket, and took the red-eye to Vegas.

When Jamie arrived at the hotel, I was ecstatic. No kids. No autism. I'd truly missed him.

As we dropped his bags in the hotel room, he turned to me. His expression had turned serious. "I have something to say," he said. I could tell he had been drinking, a lot, I assumed. This was his first vacation in years too. He sat on the chair next to the bed, his body hunching forward, as if he was feeling pain.

I didn't know what was happening. At first, I thought he was not able to breathe. But then he started to speak.

"I just spent the last four hours on a plane, thinking about one thing. Cooper. And how we are never going to have a typical relationship. My son is never going to talk to me. You tried to tell me. I *refused* to listen. I just couldn't hear it, Katie. I wasn't ready. Or maybe I haven't allowed myself to slow down and actually think about everything. No baseball. No conversations. Is he going to live with us forever? How can we do this forever? I just don't understand how this happened?"

This was it. This was the moment I had been waiting for. He was finally *feeling*. But instead of relief, I felt frustration. What had taken him so damn long? It was too late for me. The damage had all been done. I had started the process of grief a long time ago, ages before Jamie had, and I didn't want to go back to the beginning again.

We sat there for a while, me on the floor in front of him in the chair. He cried hard, harder than I had ever seen a man cry before. He spoke of his relationship with his own father, how his dad coached his sports teams and never once missed a game, even when he was in college. He spoke of their relationship and how he wanted to be a great dad like the one he grew up with. And he spoke about how it felt as though Cooper had entirely slipped away from him.

I just listened. I understood every word he was saying. I could tell he wanted me to fix the pain for him. But I couldn't. He just had to feel it and walk through it alone.

We never spoke of that moment again, and in the months that followed, sometimes I doubted that it even happened. But I would remind myself that grief is not linear. It's a process, and we all deserve grace as we go through it at our own pace. In my heart I hoped and prayed Jamie would catch up to me. I just had to give him time.

# SEVEN

If you google *autism*, you will find lots of information. You will find signs and symptoms. You will find tools for diagnosis. You will find stories from parents like me. And within those stories, you will find two distinct camps about the spectrum disorder. Some say autism is a gift and that they wouldn't change their child for the world. The other half speaks openly of the challenges and the struggles they face daily. I learned early on that as moms and dads, we typically fall into one camp or the other, a line drawn firmly in between us. The two groups spar on Facebook, neither really listening to the other, both wondering how the other can think so differently. We are all in the same boat. All parents. All raising unique children. Yet different.

I've spent countless hours over the years trying to figure out the differences between the two groups of parents while wondering where I land. Each group loving their children fiercely and doing everything in their power to advocate for autism. Does one side have it easier? Do they not deal with the aggression and self-inuring that the other side knows all too well? Is one group just glass-half-full while the other is glass-half-empty? Did one group accept the diagnosis with open arms, celebrating, while the other group cried when the word *autism* was said aloud?

I honestly don't know. I've never figured it out. But I have learned you can't tell someone how to feel. You can't make them react a certain way either. You also can't predict how someone will react when their life is turned upside down in an instant. Do I think autism is a gift? It's hard for me to answer that because I know the struggles that my son has faced in his short life and will continue to face for the rest of it. His life will be challenging, and we may never have easy days. But what I do know is that my son is a gift, and I am blessed to have him to love. As long as I keep focused on my love for him, and give him his best life, then my decisions and feelings are not wrong, no matter what the other camp tells me. But it sure can feel scary at times trying to figure it all out.

I want you to imagine your life. You have friends and family, possibly a work life too. You have hobbies you enjoy, things you like doing. When you need food, you go to a grocery store or a restaurant. When you need gas, you pull into a station and fill up with ease. Your life is your own, no one and nothing dictating your choices. That was Jamie and me before becoming parents. We knew after our first son was born that much would change temporarily, but we assumed that after we all settled in, our life would resume as normal. We assumed this because that was how it was for our friends who had children. But our life, it never went back to our version of normal. The world wasn't accepting of Cooper, nor was it made for him. We didn't place blame; if anything, we blamed ourselves.

When Cooper was one and two, we could fake it. That's the only way I could describe it looking back. We would go to an event—a wedding, a birthday party, a family Christmas—and Jamie and I would alternate making it work. One of us would follow after Cooper so the other could socialize. If we were in someone's home, we would spend our time keeping Cooper out of people's beds and from screaming at the door to leave. If we were at an outdoor event, one of us would follow behind as he wandered the imaginary perimeter, eventually taking refuge in our vehicle so he could watch Elmo on his DVD player. I remember countless times sitting in my car with my son, watching the world happen outside the window, like a stranger looking in. We were called amazing parents, selfless. We were told we weren't giving our son enough discipline. We were told he would grow out of it. Jamie and I were excellent actors, doing what we had to do to keep living the life we imagined we'd have.

When three and four rolled around, the grace that we were given when he was younger started to fade away. A toddler having a tantrum is far more accepted than a big four-year-old tearing apart a friend's home because he can't open their Amazon packages or monopolize their television. We slowly started saying no to every invite that came. We had no other choice. But it wasn't one that we took lightly either. We wanted to keep going. We wanted to keep trying, but each visit would end with Jamie and me fighting in the car ride home. There was animosity building between us, as I was typically the one who would be with Cooper alone, wondering if anyone even cared where we were. The invites eventually stopped coming, which in a way was a relief but brought a unique sting when pictures would show up on Facebook of the events we missed.

When Cooper was five, we stopped going places entirely besides grandma's house. Our final outing was a visit to a local park designed for special children, a place I often chose for us to go. I assumed we would be safe there, among our people. Except the park seemed to be inhabited by two groups of children, those who could run and jump and yell, and those who couldn't. Per the usual, I was following Cooper like a hawk as he wandered through the park, seemingly in his own world, unaware of other children. I glanced away for one second and when I turned back to him, I saw that Cooper had scrambled to the top platform of a jungle gym, the only exit being a slide. I held my breath as I watched the kids crowd around him, boxing him in. He dropped to his back, an action he often took when feeling overwhelmed. He spread his body out, making his own space, when his feet bumped a little girl sitting at the entrance of the slide. Down she went, definitely before she was ready.

She wasn't hurt as far as I could tell, not a tear was shed, but her father took one look at Cooper, oblivious to his disability, and pounced. The father screamed at him, and Cooper, who was unaware, giggled and ran off. I learned in that moment that autism is an invisible disability. He looks like every other child his age, only he's not. He is different but yet held to the same standards. And as a crowd gathered, I let every ounce of my built-up pain and hurt out on that man. I gave him the same grace he gave my son. Our outings dwindled to nothing shortly after that. We were homebound yet appearing as if nothing was wrong to the outside world. Our disability invisible.

Eventually we had no good days. We had okay days and hard days. We had days where we survived and days when I didn't fail. Like many kids with autism, his development bounced between being frozen in time or going backward instead of forward. I was forced to lock my house down with us on the inside, only leaving to go to work and therapy. Car rides weren't safe, walks weren't safe, being in crowds wasn't safe. It was as if we disappeared from our life.

We weren't forgotten, not entirely. Friends and family still called, I still texted and shared pictures of backyard picnics and epic forts on Facebook, but eventually people stopped asking about Cooper. It was subtle at first until it wasn't. I asked a friend once, many years later, why she stopped asking about him and her answer was, "I didn't know what to say anymore.

You were just so sad, and I didn't know how to help. It was easier to not ask."

As time went on, and our world got more isolated and restricted, I started questioning my own strength and resilience to finish this race alone. On a particularly low Saturday, one that started at 3:00 a.m. with screaming and hitting, and didn't end until midnight that night when Cooper's body finally gave in to sleep and was still, I read a quote on Pinterest:

*"Special kids are only given to special people..."*

As I sat alone in my house, in the world I was forced to create for myself and my two boys, exhausted and feeling a little beat up, I let those words wash over me. *Special kids are only given to special people.* And they filled me with rage.

I understood that the words were well-intentioned, but it was toxic positivity. It brushed over the realities of disability. It made parents like me feel shame for having anything but positive thoughts about our difficult situations. And it was a disservice.

I wasn't special. Cooper's diagnosis wasn't a rite of passage. *"Congratulations, Kate, you are now special as well. Here is extra strength, patience, and resilience and the ability to always find the joy."*

It doesn't work like that. I was just a person, a mom, with very real emotions and feelings.

It's not that I was resistant to the grief that came with the diagnosis. Or the pain that came with the possibility of never hearing my son speak. I'm his mother, and a mother's love can meet any challenge. But the pressure was crushing.

There's no manual for how to raise a child with special needs. The decisions I had to make about his care, future, and well-being felt monumental and sometimes had no right answers. No one could make them for me, or even tell me what to do. It was all up to me. And I was scared a lot of the time.

The aggressive side of autism can break even the strongest of mothers, and I was not spared. I endured snickers from people who judged Cooper and me as his parent. I just did it. I just held my head up and puffed out my chest, and then I would break down later when no one was watching.

I wasn't given extra hours in the day to research, advocate, and fight. I had the same amount of time as everyone else. I wasn't given a dose of extra energy or the gift of not needing sleep. I didn't have superhuman strength to take the abuse he gave my body. I just did it.

I wasn't given an off switch either. There is no turning off the worry and fear that consumes a parent of a child with autism, not ever. Not when I get an hour out for a coffee or a precious weekend away with friends. Autism is always on my mind and will be until the day I die.

And I most definitely wasn't handed the precious gift of acceptance. Instead, it took years of walking through the darkness to get there. A walk that no one could take for me.

I am not special. I am no saint. God didn't give me Cooper because I had all the qualities that I would need as his mother. I was just an ordinary person who fell in love with her son. But what God did do, and I believe this deep down in my core, is make children like Cooper so special, so beautiful, and so magical, that parents like me gain the skills we need at lightning speed. Because we are smitten. We are goners. We may not jump headfirst into the secret world of autism, we may need a gentle push, but when we get there, we demand a life that is worth living for our children. Because they deserve it.

Special kids are not given to special people. Special kids make special people. And for that, I am thankful to be chosen.

The first night I spent in the house I bought after leaving Jamie was wonderful and exactly what I imagined single life could be like. Jamie had the boys for a few nights so I could do all the things that go into purchasing a home and moving a household. A girlfriend came and helped me unpack. We arranged furniture and hung pictures on the walls, exactly the way

I wanted, and no one fought me. We blared '90s music, drank margaritas, ate junk food, and stayed up way too late watching a romantic comedy. She told me she was jealous of my freedom and proud of me for choosing happiness. I told her the freedom was what excited me the most and the happiness part, I did not know if that was meant for me. When she left the next day to go back to her husband and kids, my hangover felt stronger than it probably was. It was the first day of the rest of my life, and I was scared.

I was alone. The house felt way too quiet without the boys, who were with their dad. As I stood there in my living room, I told myself that it could only go up from here. I had relieved the pressure of my marriage and I could make my own decisions and do whatever I liked. I had wanted a different life and I had gotten it. But it didn't feel that great. It felt lonely.

I spent the day getting the boys' rooms ready for their return. I filled Cooper's room with Thomas the Train books and photos of things he loved. I filled Sawyer's room with Nerf guns and Legos and *PAW Patrol* bedding. I made it a home like only a mother can do. That night I lay in bed, listening to the silence, and wondered if I was doing enough to help Cooper. And were they the right things? We were a year past the window of no return, the wrong side of age four, as that neurologist had referenced, Cooper's brain allegedly closed. Hope was dwindling. My son was five years old, almost ready to start kindergarten, something that terrified me. He had no words yet, not even a speech-like sound. He seemed to be worsening or staying the same. It was hard for me to pinpoint which one. All I knew was that it felt as though we were being left behind.

Many of the other autistic children in Cooper's programs seemed to be thriving. Their words had come. Their parents and teachers had found the right key to unlock their development. And they transitioned on. Not us. Our peer group continued to shrink, and it felt terribly small. The autism diagnosis was a blow, but severe, nonverbal autism was a hurricane. And on top of all that, Cooper had developed quite a few health complications that were causing him pain—one ear infection after another, chronic bursting of his eardrums, severe stomach issues.

We became regulars at Children's Hospital. I desperately wanted to help him, but it felt impossible. Cooper couldn't tell us when something hurt. Instead he showed us in other ways. He stopped sleeping. His aggressions toward others increased, and his self-injuring behavior doubled. I felt like I was playing a guessing game where I didn't know the rules or even how to win. I struggled to get doctors to take me seriously. I started receiving daily phone calls from his school and his autism center with bad reports.

I felt I was screaming into a black hole. I knew my son didn't feel well, but I also didn't know how to help him. One afternoon, Cooper brought me his speech device, an assistive technology tool that allowed him to speak by simply touching pictures. He had been whining and crying all day and I was exhausted and worn down. He crawled up onto my lap and in a rare moment of communication, he pressed two buttons on the screen, one a picture of a head and the other a picture of "pain," an image of an arm with a wound.

The robotic voice said, "Head pain." He looked up at me with these huge angelic eyes and without flinching, pressed the button a dozen more times. "Head pain, head pain, head pain," the voice said. It was eerie. There is nothing quite like the sickness a parent feels when they know their child is in pain but cannot help them.

Days later his fifth set of ear tubes was placed, but the doctors couldn't seem to get a handle on what was going on with his ears or why he was in so much pain. I couldn't understand why in the days of modern medicine, my son couldn't be helped.

I soon heard a phrase that would haunt me for years to come. "Oh, that's just autism." It became a phrase doctors and other professionals would use when they didn't know how to help my son. To me, it became a replacement for good care and an excuse to give lesser care to people with disabilities. Instead of trying to figure out why something was happening, they presented me with options that seemed to only make him comfortable. It was a very confusing time for me. I would look at my son, my beautiful son, and not know how to help him.

I learned quickly after reaching out to advocacy organizations in my area, and other parents, that disabled adults who were on Medicaid were not given the same health care as nondisabled adults. For example, when a disabled adult needs dental work, the answer will always be to pull teeth. It's cheaper and quicker. That sickened me. I looked at my son and refused to let that be him. He deserved the same care as everyone else.

A fire was lit inside of me. The fire motivated me to start researching, advocating, and speaking out on behalf of children, teens, and adults with disabilities. And I made a promise to myself and a vow to Cooper. I would never listen to a professional whose answer to pain was, "Oh, that's just autism." Never again. I didn't care how many dead ends I encountered; I would never stop fighting for my son.

Just a few months later I found us at what I thought was our lowest point. When I had researched autism years before, I saw a few glimpses into our future. It felt like a fate that we couldn't run from. The research told me that nearly all kids with autism eventually turn aggressive. Whether that be kicking or hitting, it was inevitable. Up until recently I'd thought we had been somewhat spared. Cooper did have aggressions, but they weren't every day. If he got mad, he would yell and throw but never once had he hurt anyone with his hits and kicks besides me.

But then something changed.

With all of his health complications, nonstop ear infections, constipation, not sleeping, and being unable to communicate, his aggression had started to appear. I knew that the aggression was just his way of communicating. Imagine living in a world that doesn't understand you. You can't say your sock feels funny or your head hurts, or you are thirsty. So you lash out.

The aggression started small at first. A kick here and there. But it was growing, like him. I was also hearing reports of aggression from school, and public schools don't tolerate this sort of behavior. But I didn't know how to fix it. It brought a unique sort of shame and frustration to my life. I began to dread the phone ringing. One afternoon I got a call that Cooper had torn apart his classroom, throwing chairs, hitting, and kicking. I needed to pick him up immediately. I learned later, when I read his communication log from his teacher, that they had misplaced his lunchbox for nearly thirty minutes. To Cooper, that must have felt like an eternity. I'm sure he was looking for his lunchbox, but no one understood.

Around this time, a friend informed me that our county offered emergency interventions. Initially I was terrified. I didn't want anyone to know that my son could be mean and violent. I wanted to protect him from the judgment. But I had reached my tipping point. Bruises now covered my thighs from Cooper kicking me every morning as the bus pulled up. It was time to get help.

So I called for intervention. Days later, an emergency social worker visited our home. As he stood in our living room, explaining the process, our oblivious blond-haired little boy lined up kitchen chairs throughout our living room. It was a new behavior Cooper had started when he turned five. I learned later that it was his way of gaining control in a world where he mostly had none. He would spend hours dragging chairs throughout the house, lining them up, and screaming if anyone went near them. He found them wherever they were hidden, in closets, the basement, the garage. At this very moment, I counted seven chairs so far, four from the kitchen table and three carried in from the patio. Each chair was placed meticulously in a row, the logic clearly making sense to him, but not to anyone else.

The room was visually split in two. The man stood on one side, and Jamie and I stood on the other. Cooper was in the middle, standing in front of the seven chairs, moving his hands in a conductor-like motion, as if he was directing an orchestra. It felt as if a line had been drawn. Only it shouldn't have. We were all on the same team. Our focus was to help Cooper.

The social worker spoke with Jamie and me at length while he observed our home. He looked at our son's bare bedroom and mattress on the floor. I worried he would judge the missing box spring and quickly explained that Cooper tore our beds apart, down to the ground, daily. He noted the locks on the doors and alarms on the windows. He laughed when I said our home felt like a secure prison at times. "If I had a quarter for every time I've heard that!"

I told him about the hoarding, another new behavior, and how it was consuming me. "Thousands of pieces of paper, blankets, family photos, even the decor from my walls are brought from room to room and placed in a nest around him and then eventually under and in or behind furniture." As I explained, I lifted up my couch to show him the evidence. I watched his eyes get wide.

I felt ashamed as I shared our life out loud. It's such a weird process…asking for help. I felt weak. I felt embarrassed. I think it's safe to say I was a little defensive. Asking for help meant admitting that there was something really wrong and that I was unequipped to manage it.

He asked about our other son, Sawyer, who was two years younger than Cooper, and if he was safe. I told him yes, thankfully, Cooper didn't acknowledge Sawyer in any way, which, while heartbreaking, also meant that he didn't get the brunt of his brother's aggressions. While Cooper's care demanded so much of us, we had made the decision the day after Cooper's diagnosis that his little brother would have a normal life. He wouldn't resent him…or us.

The man asked a lot about Cooper's self-care and if he was potty trained. "As a child ages, the toll on a parent increases drastically…"

I told him no. He had no self-care and he had no desire to potty train, which was getting harder to manage as he aged.

He asked us how Cooper communicated. "Mostly nonverbally, with sounds and pointing or bringing us things. Yesterday morning I tripped over a gallon of milk at 3:00 a.m. He was telling us he was thirsty."

"Can you leave the house? Go into the community? Ride safely in your car?"

"No," I said. And to me that was the hardest part. The isolation. A whole world was happening, and we were locked inside our home, each door with three locks and alarms on the windows. I've spoken to many other parents over the years, and they cite isolation as being the hardest part for them too. Being cut off from your world…it's the silent killer of special-needs parents. Add in sleep deprivation and you've got a real party.

Cooper hadn't gone anywhere besides school and grandma's house in ages. During our last trip to Target, many months prior, while I moved items from the cart to the conveyer belt for checkout, Cooper was attempting to stand in the cart. Already probably too big for it anyway, he was doing a good job rocking it from side to side. With one hand I held on to his arm, and with the other I threw items toward the cashier. Out of nowhere Cooper's open hand connected with my cheek, and the sound echoed in my ear. It didn't hurt as much as it shocked me. I had never been hit in the face before. My eyes immediately started watering. I am sure it looked like I was crying. The cashier, an older woman, who had seen the whole thing, scolded Cooper. I was humiliated as I looked around to see people staring at us. Cooper wasn't slowing down either. He wanted out of that cart. I had no choice but to apologize to the cashier and leave our stuff behind. That was the last store Cooper had been in. Now if I needed something, it had to be delivered or we had to go to a drive-through.

The man asked us if Cooper slept, although I suspect he already knew the answer. I told him how every morning started at 3:00 a.m., Cooper bursting into my bedroom with an almost indescribable amount of energy. He would pace my room, touching the walls, making happy sounds, until I got up and started his movie. I told him that the sleep deprivation was really starting to affect me. So much so that even on my night off from the boys, I still couldn't sleep. My body was now programmed to wake up at 3:00 a.m.

He asked Jamie and me how we made our relationship work, obviously referencing our divorce. He asked about our mental health. He asked if we had a good support system. I felt drained by the questions and the negativity coming from deep inside of me.

"We have no good days anymore. Just okay and hard. He's… um…started kicking me." I said it quietly, almost like a whisper. I showed him the permanent bruises on my thighs and arms from the repeated kicking that happened every morning when the bus pulled up. I hadn't shown anyone the bruises up to this point and I felt guilty doing it now. I didn't want anyone to ever think differently about my son, or think he was a monster. It was my job to protect him, but it was just getting so hard to do alone.

Every five minutes or so, Cooper would run up to me, screaming, either leading me away or shoving something in my hand. If I didn't immediately respond, he would climb up my body like a jungle gym, reaching for my face, turning it to his face. This is how we communicated. I felt like we were tethered to each other, an invisible umbilical cord, the two of us always together. I am Cooper's person. He demands a lot from me, twenty-four hours a day. I explained to the man that it's a lot of pressure. "Sometimes I just wish I could have a break from the emotional weight of it all."

I watched the man study Cooper as he climbed on me, taking him all in. His blond hair, his pale skin and ruddy cheeks. He was in a diaper and a blue oversize sleeveless T-shirt. I wondered if he thought we were lying. Or terrible parents? Like most other special-needs parents, we had heard it all at this point. *That kid just needs discipline* topped the list of advice we got. People just didn't understand. The typical rules of parenting didn't work for Cooper. I wish I could say at this point that I didn't care what people thought. But that would be a lie. I very much cared.

With each answer Jamie and I gave, he nodded and made a "hmm" sound while he scribbled notes on a clipboard. I noted his poker face. I imagined him checking little boxes, *good, bad, really bad.*

I told him about the shattered mirror from the night before and how Cooper had zero understanding of the danger of the shards of glass covering my bedroom floor. Nor did he even attempt to show me what had happened. I went on to tell him about eating dinner in the dark with headlamps because Cooper hated the light. I explained in detail how Cooper put everything we owned in the bathtub and how I spent nights awake worried that he was going to get hit by a car or drown. I made jokes and told stories about our hard times, making sure to keep it light and as upbeat as I possibly could. That was me. Kate. The woman sitting in the burning building, drinking a coffee and saying, "This is fine."

Only, it wasn't fine anymore. I had failed at trying to help my son. I had turned myself inside out and upside down and put everything else on the back burner as I worked to help Cooper. But he seemed to keep regressing. In fact, most parts were getting worse. His health, his meltdowns, insomnia, aggressions, self-injurious behavior, property destruction, eloping. All of it. My marriage had crumbled. I drank too much wine, lost too much weight, let the wrong people into my life, and didn't know how to sleep anymore or even talk about something that wasn't related to Cooper.

I hated that we needed a social worker. I hated that we were forced to air our dirty laundry. It felt like we were begging for help. It made me feel weak.

My father-in-law once said to me, on a particularly hard day, "You and Jamie are the most positive people I know. Your life is hell most of the time and you choose to stay upbeat." After he said that, I spent hours wondering if I was lying to myself. Had my positive attitude toward life been a mask?

After an hour discussing our day-to-day ups and downs, the social worker turned to me and said, "Your son has one of the most severe cases of autism I have ever seen. There is no way you can do this forever."

The words hung in the air between us like a cartoon.

*MOST SEVERE?* That wasn't possible. This man had no idea what he was talking about. Suddenly I felt like the walls were closing in around me. *Most severe* meant my son was one of those kids I had seen on the YouTube videos that rocked in a corner and screamed and hurt. That wasn't my son. And *FOREVER?* That wasn't possible either. My son was going to improve. That's why I was doing all of this. If I put in the work now, he would be better eventually. It had never crossed my mind that it could be this hard forever.

"You need to understand," he continued, "that your son is getting bigger. I am not seeing the communication and understanding of safety that I should be seeing at this age. At some point, I'm not saying right now, you need to decide if this is the life that you want for yourself and your other son."

I knew what he was saying without saying it. He was predicting that Cooper would eventually need to live in a group home or residential care. He was saying that Cooper would soon be so big and so aggressive that I wouldn't be able to care for him. He was saying Cooper wasn't going to improve.

I felt the urge to scream, "GET OUT OF MY HOUSE." But instead, I finished up the evaluation like I was supposed to. I smiled and nodded. I took his pamphlets and agreed to weekly crisis intervention sessions and walked him to the door. I calmly shut it behind him, turned the three locks on the door, and took a deep breath before turning to see Cooper standing in front of his chairs, moving his hands in some motion that I didn't understand. I felt every emotion flood me as I studied my misunderstood boy. Anger that someone who didn't know my son had predicted such a dark future. Sadness that he could be right. Devastation that I couldn't fix it. Desperation that I might not be able to keep him with me forever, the one thing that provided me comfort when I thought of lifelong care. I let the heaviness of yet another weight sink onto my shoulders and wondered if I was strong enough to continue to carry this alone.

When I share this part of the story with the world, people assume that his words didn't affect me at all. They know the me now, the me who continuously tells parents of younger children like Cooper to never give up hope, and they assume that I let the man's words go in one ear and out the other. Maybe that I even laughed them off, my hope so unwavering that I knew deep down anything was possible for my son. But it wasn't one of those moments. I won't lie. That man's words crushed me, my already paper-thin hope taking yet another hit. I was like a Ping-Pong ball, bouncing back and forth between hope and giving up, sometimes daily. I didn't know how I could keep fighting for my son to get better when even the experts thought he was a lost cause. My determination and resilience were fading.

This was such an important time in my life. It was one of the lowest I'd ever felt. From the outside looking in, I seemed to be doing it all and taking it in stride. I was happy and bubbly on the outside, but I was dying on the inside. The intensity of my life was breaking me.

Usually, I could take on any challenge. I loved a fight, and I loved the payoff after hard work. But this fight, it was simultaneously a sprint and a marathon with no end in sight. As humans, there's only so much we can do. For days, months, years the challenges had been piling on daily. And on top of all that, there was so much heartbreak. My biggest critics think I hate autism, or worse, that I hate my son. But that is the farthest thing from the truth. I loved my little boy fiercely, and his autism is part of him. I didn't hate autism, never once. But the hard parts that wore me down to a nub, those I hated.

On my one night off a week from my boys, I would drink. A lot. Instead of resting and sleeping and processing, I would get dressed up, stay out all night long, and live an entirely different life, free from the restraints that I lived the other six days. My family didn't know. Nor did my ex-husband. Until one day, just days after that man told me my son had the most severe case of autism he had ever seen, I hit my low.

I woke up somewhere I didn't recognize after a long night of drinking. I didn't know how I got there, or who I was with. I wasn't in Minnesota and I wasn't alone.

I've learned since then that feeling the need to be busy all the time is a trauma response and fear-based distraction from what you'd be forced to acknowledge and feel if you slowed down.

I hadn't slowed down since Cooper was born. And I hadn't truly accepted anything since he had been diagnosed. The chaos that his diagnosis brought to my world was a double-edged sword. It kept me busy and in this perpetual state of limp that kept me from feeling a lot of the sad feelings, because there was simply no time, but it also kept me from processing and eventually healing. My healing was frozen.

As I showered the embarrassment off that morning, I didn't rush to not feel. Instead, I sat down and let the water wash over me, black mascara dripping down my face into my lap. I let the social worker's words, *"Your son has the most severe case of autism I have ever seen,"* pool around me. I acknowledged the possibility that they might be true and what that meant for our future. No more running.

I was ready to leave the land of perpetual grief and do whatever it took to get to a place of acceptance.

I wish I could say I crossed right over. That the next morning I woke up different. Healed, even. But the process was gradual for me, teaching me that once again, grief is not a linear process. Instead, it's up and down, forward and backward. But I was finally ready for the journey.

A year ago, my stepmom lost her battle with pancreatic cancer. The night before we lost her, I was driving my dad back to his house, from the nursing home where she would spend her last days. It was nearing midnight. He was exhausted, close to eighty himself. He needed to rest for a few hours. It was foggy and cold, and I found myself weaving through the backwoods of northern Wisconsin, driving his truck.

I was white-knuckling it, focusing the best I could through fuzzy eyes and trying to listen to his sporadic words of grief and say the right things. I felt scared, not knowing how to help him. We both knew she had mere days left.

Watching him sit next to her, holding her frail, pale hand, was almost more than I could take. When she would cry, the morphine not enough to dull the pain, he would hunch over her body, whispering, "Go to Jesus," in her ear.

As we wound around the dark road, I wondered how anyone could watch their partner die this way. The pain she was experiencing was unbelievable. She was not spared. Neither was he. I prayed for it to end for both of them. But I didn't know if I was praying for the right thing.

He said, "She's still here, Katie. She's not gone yet. Even

though she can't talk, or communicate, she is still here. I can touch her and hold her hand. I can sit near her and I can talk to her. I'm not ready to be without her. I need her. She doesn't have to speak; I can do the talking."

At that moment in my life, my son was still nearly entirely nonverbal. He wasn't really trying to communicate either. Maybe a request on a speech device for a cookie or a sign for more but that was about it.

Of course, I talked enough for the both of us. And his dad and brother never seem to stop making noise either. Our house is filled with love and chatter. But when it's just the two of us, Cooper and I, the silence overwhelmed me. It was deafening and would eat me alive. To help my heart and mind, I would blare the television all day or have the radio going in the background or even talk to myself.

I was sad that my son and I had never had a conversation. And possibly would never. But that car ride with my dad, without even knowing it, in his hardest moment, he taught me an important lesson. I don't need words; I just need Cooper. I just need him to hold and to love for the rest of my life. I can do the talking. Just as long as he's with me.

He is a gift. My gift. And I will spend my life opening him up to this world.

# EIGHT

When the professionals first told me about autism, they described it to me as a spectrum. I immediately thought of a spectrum of light, like a rainbow through a prism. But it wasn't that kind of spectrum. Or at least the experts didn't explain it that way. They described it as a long line, with one end being the most severely affected and the other end being less affected. They threw terms at me like *high-functioning, low-functioning, severe, moderate,* and *mild,* even *levels one, two, and three.*

When Cooper was diagnosed, I told myself he was on the right side of that spectrum, that he was high-functioning, and that we had won the autism lottery. I convinced myself that when his diagnosis was handed out, we got the good kind. I held on to that term, that safety blanket, so tightly, as if it could protect us. After I learned to say the words, "My son has autism" out loud—and that took me time to be able to do—I started saying, "My son has autism, but he's very high-functioning." Our hearts eat lies when we are hungry. And I was ravenous.

I soon learned, like most parents do, that Cooper's autism

was being ranked on that spectrum. And before I knew it, instead of being Cooper, the little boy with blond hair who loved trains and smelled like the wind, he was a number. A listing of ASD on a file folder. He was data and checkboxes and eventually a graph that would put him on the most severe end of that spectrum until my sunshine boy became a black-and-white list of diagnoses in my desk drawer, void of his light.

When I pictured that spectrum, the one they described to me, I imagined a long line drawn with a thick black Sharpie across a white wall, down an endless bright hallway. It was straight as an arrow, no bumps or hills, no crevices. It felt clinical. I felt like I was standing alone in that hallway, with the white walls and white floor, watching Cooper toe the line, moving from right to left and farther away from me and everyone else. It almost felt like we were doing autism wrong, moving in the wrong direction, bucking the traditional path and dripping bits of color everywhere.

In the early years, I would look at veteran moms with older children like my Cooper is now, and I would wonder when I would get to acceptance, like them. I had felt so close at different times, but something would always set me back. A child the same age telling me a story. My niece singing me her kindergarten graduation song. My younger son having his first playdate. Acceptance felt like a moving target, something just outside my grasp. Something I so desperately wanted to obtain.

And while I chased that white unicorn, I packed my bags and I walked that line with Cooper, sometimes crawling, sometimes trying to push him in the direction I thought he should go. But no matter what I did, we did not move toward high-functioning. And as we reached the end of the line, my version of the spectrum started to change. Probably out of necessity, because my heart had to see this differently or I wasn't going to make it.

I hated the black-and-white and the dark, sad, clinical parts of autism. I hated straight lines too. So I started to think of my son and his autism as a spectrum of color, like I did in the beginning, before the fear and worry consumed me. A huge circle full of bright colors. Think of the happy reds and oranges on the trees in the fall, and the sometimes ominous teals and the blues of the ocean, and the yellows in a field of flowers. Cooper had dashes of all of them. Some harder. Some scarier. Some easier and happier. And they were all mixed together on his palette that he paints the world with. His spectrum is his color. And his autism is where the light shines through.

As I started to embrace my son's often too bright color, I learned that the colorful kids, the sometimes challenging kids, the not easy to teach kids, they can sort of fade away. Their light sometimes becomes dulled as the world spins away from them. As Cooper started kindergarten, my real fight began. We were entering another phase of the black-and-white world, one where differences aren't always welcomed with grace. A place he wasn't made for.

That label of autism, while it can be helpful and get them the services and support they need to succeed, it can also inhibit so many things. With autism comes preconceived notions. It's like the world had already counted my son out before he even got a chance to live. Yes, I could give up. I could accept that my son has an extremely severe case of autism, and that he will never amount to anything...but what then? If I give up, who will fight for him?

As parents, we need to believe in our kids beyond measure. And then believe in them even more. When you have a child who is developing differently, your hope over the years will waver. But you can't stop believing in them. Because no one will fight harder for your child than you will.

Most mothers dream about their children starting kindergarten. The big yellow school bus pulling up while your child holds the "First Day of Kindergarten" sign. Their giant backpack full to the brim with supplies, new clothes and shoes, and an "I love you, Mom" called from the doorway of the bus. It's a monumental milestone.

I had those dreams too, initially. But as kindergarten neared, and the services that Cooper was receiving were ending, I felt scared. In my gut, I knew mainstream kindergarten wasn't right for Cooper, but I also knew of no other options. I agonized all summer over what to do with him. I couldn't quit my job and teach him for financial reasons. I also didn't have the skills to teach him what he needed to learn to succeed. I felt trapped and I didn't know what to do. Many parents I talk to have felt this same way. Trapped. And because of it, many parents are forced to quit their jobs so they can be with their children because no other options are available. But I was a single parent. I had no choice but to work.

I knew my son was smart. I had taught him his letters, numbers, shapes, and colors, and he could point to the corresponding one when I asked him to. But for anyone else, he wouldn't do it. All questions were met with his version of no. He refused to sit or play. And even harder yet, he couldn't be motivated. There seemed to be nothing that he wanted to work for. Not treats or toys or iPad time. I also worried about bullying and people not being nice to him. While Cooper had this challenging exterior, he was delicate like a flower and so vulnerable. Who would protect him and make sure he was clean, safe, dry, and loved? I couldn't figure out how this was going to work.

The day we received the letter in the mail welcoming Cooper to kindergarten, I knew it was sent to us by mistake. The letter was printed on colorful paper with teddy bears around the edges. It introduced his assigned teacher and invited us to a class meet-and-greet at a local park.

The letter said nothing of the self-contained classroom that Cooper would be in. Cooper would not be in the general education kindergarten class. Instead, he would be in a classroom with a teacher and a paraprofessional, a person who will be assigned to work with him throughout the day. It said nothing of autism. It said nothing of special education. The school supply list that accompanied the letter had crayons, scissors, and other items that Cooper had never used before. I immediately called the school and asked if we were sent the letter by mistake. The nice woman on the phone said that every special education student is placed in a general education classroom, even if they don't attend. They need a "real" class in the system. I felt a sting as I thought about special ed classes not being real classes. So many times on this journey, I had been made to feel like I wasn't a "real" mother, or my son wasn't a "real" boy because he had autism. As if because we were different, we were fakes. It angered me.

The woman on the phone went on to tell me that we should attend the event at the park anyway because the goal was to get Cooper in the general education classroom as much as possible. "If he improves, that will be his teacher and class." With school starting in just a few weeks, I wondered where our letter was from his actual teacher.

I felt sick to my stomach as Jamie, Cooper, and I drove to the park that weekend. I did my best to avoid public situations like the one I was walking into. My heart couldn't take it. The differences screamed too loudly at me when I was surrounded by other children Cooper's age. This was my worst nightmare. And I wasn't spared during this event.

I stood and watched twenty kids climb a jungle gym. I watched twenty kids play in the sand. And I watched their parents stand around and talk about T-ball and dance classes. Jamie thankfully offered to follow Cooper around as he wandered the perimeter. I think he could sense that I wasn't feeling all that strong. I felt saddened as we changed Cooper's diaper in the back of our truck and even considered leaving. My heart told me to stay and keep trying.

When we returned to the event, a line had formed to greet the teacher, complete some paperwork, and drop off our school supplies. As we tried to casually blend in, Cooper refused to stand still, screaming, crying, and eventually dropping to the ground and rolling under the picnic table. We were learning as he aged that doing simple things like standing patiently in line wasn't possible. We knew this, but we also live in a world with social norms.

In this moment, we tried to make Cooper's life easier. We stood in the line while he distanced himself under the table. In my mind, if he felt safe, then it would be perfectly fine. But his behavior under there was perplexing. He yelled at us, not with words, just sounds. Loud enough to disrupt conversations. He used his foot to repeatedly tap the metal of the bench, the loud tinging seeming to aggravate the people around us.

We felt the stares. We felt different. I've learned over the years that most people want to be kind and don't want to stare. I've also learned that most of my feelings of being judged come from my own insecurities. But standing in a group of people, your peers, and feeling so blatantly different is devastating.

Finally, I couldn't take it anymore, so I grabbed the teacher's attention and asked if Cooper could quickly say hello. "It's hard for him to wait," I explained. It didn't seem like a big deal or an unreasonable request, and she had to see that we were really struggling. All I was looking for was a wave to the little boy I was now holding upright in my arms, his head thrusting back at my chin so he could practice the wave to his teacher that we had practiced for days.

"He will have to wait his turn like all the other children," she responded as she turned away, back to the child she was chatting with.

My mouth dropped open. I just stared at her as Cooper withered out of my arms, screaming. I let him run off. My fight was gone. It's true that she might not have realized Cooper had special needs, or that all we wanted was a quick wave. But in that moment, it felt like such an easy accommodation to give us. We left the event without Cooper saying hello. The teacher never even acknowledged him.

The next week, days before school started, another letter came in the mail. This one was printed on white paper, no teddy bears, no bright colors. It listed Cooper's special education teacher's name and the classroom he would be in. It listed the services he would receive and his therapist's name. It invited us to an open house the day before school started. And it listed the supplies he would need. Clorox wipes, Kleenex, a change of clothes, noise-canceling headphones, comfort items, his speech device, diapers, and wipes. The list was clinical, far different from the list for a typical kindergarten class.

I realized in that moment it takes a strong person to have a child in special education. There are no bells and no whistles. No pomp and circumstance. When I look back now, I wonder if I was being oversensitive. And the answer is, maybe I was. But I didn't think I should have to forfeit the special, joyful parts of school just because my son was autistic. This was his first year of kindergarten and I wanted to celebrate it, but it felt like the public education system was telling me it wasn't going to be special. It was going to be sad and dark.

The letter also informed us that we would need to bring Cooper for a visit so he could meet his teacher and see the school. It was scheduled on a weekday, and I had to take off work to bring him. I'd also have to go without Jamie, something that made me very nervous. The park visit for the main kindergarten class was on a Saturday, convenient to most families. So was the open house for the entire school. But the special education families, our stuff is always during the workday. Every meeting for an Individualized Education Program or IEP, every conference, they are always during the week at a time that is difficult for any working parent.

I felt dread as I pulled into the parking lot of his school. This school was in a different city and unfamiliar to Cooper and me. We had two schools within a mile of our house, but they didn't have a program for children with severe autism. Instead, Cooper was placed at the school that could accommodate him. This is common for kids with special needs. They go where the program is. And in this case, the school was in the same district but a neighboring city. With stops, it would require an hour's bus ride, which felt incredibly long for a kindergartener. Especially when we had a school in our backyard. I was frustrated by the system, feeling like they viewed Cooper as a number rather than a student.

As we sat in the parking lot, I tried to collect my composure, telling myself it would be fine. We would go in, see his classroom, drop off his supplies, meet his teacher, and leave. Absolutely no pressure. This wasn't going to be a crowded open house for the whole school. It was a private visit just for us. I felt relieved knowing that we could take our time. But Cooper felt otherwise and started screaming and thrashing in his seat. He didn't want to go in, but we had no choice. I carried him the best I could, the sweat already dripping down the sides of my face. I was thankful I wore tennis shoes. Once inside the door, the quiet school was filled with Cooper's anxious wails. He took off running and I chased after him.

We eventually found what I thought was Cooper's classroom but felt a sting of resentment when I realized it was the general education room with the teacher who had rejected him at the meet-and-greet. Cooper ran like a hurricane into the perfectly arranged classroom. I tried to talk with the teacher, but Cooper was running so quickly around the room, ripping papers off the walls and clearing off tables, that I couldn't really speak to her. I tried to pick him up, thinking that would calm him, but he thrashed in my arms. I set him down and used my body to block the door, thinking he would eventually find something to interact with. And he did. He found a waist-high cabinet on wheels housing what had to be thousands of crayons and markers. He looked right at me, suddenly intrigued, and with one flick of his arm, dumped it over. I have never, in my life, seen so many crayons. They rolled everywhere, suddenly filling the floor with color. I was mortified and immediately dropped to the ground, grasping Cooper with one hand and using the other to sweep crayons toward me in a pile. The teacher squatted down as well and as she reached toward the crayons, Cooper's leg, angry at me for corralling it, lashed out and connected with her stomach, dropping her from her knees to her butt.

Minutes later we were in the car. I sat there and sobbed. Loud and hard. I didn't even bother driving away. I knew people could see me and I didn't care. I spent the rest of the night waiting for a phone call from the school telling us not to return, but it never came. I thanked God that we weren't being kicked out before the year even started.

On the first day of kindergarten, Cooper woke me up at 3:45 a.m. As I sat drinking coffee, waiting for the sun to rise, I felt a mixture of emotions. This was technically my son's third year of school. It would be the third year I'd put him on a little yellow bus and watch him ride away without a wave or a word. The third year I would feel sadness, resentment, anger, and frustration when I should have been feeling joy. It was supposed to be exciting. Cooper should have been over the moon about his first day of kindergarten. We should have been celebrating. But it wasn't like that.

The night before, I lay in bed and scrolled through Facebook and looked at all of the adorable kids starting school. Gosh, I hate Facebook sometimes. All the smiling children. New clothes. Videos of kids willingly walking to the bus. Videos of kids talking about their new shoes or new backpack. Proud parents. So much excitement. I could tell I was developing a resentment toward other parents, and I didn't like that. I loved my friends' kids. I loved my nieces and nephews and I wanted to know their successes. But as my son's differences became more apparent, the grief seemed to consume me and made it harder to keep things in perspective.

I told myself as I tossed and turned that I wasn't going to make a big deal over his first day. I wasn't going to draw a "First Day of Kindergarten" sign. And I for sure wasn't going to put it on Facebook. I let myself stew in the anger and jealousy that I was so embarrassed to admit I had. But when the morning of school came, I felt different. I told myself that someday Cooper will care. He will want to see photos of his first day of kindergarten. So I dressed him in his new clothes and shoes, gelled his hair in a spike, and handed him the sign. I snapped a hundred pictures as fast as I could and prayed for one good one.

When the bus pulled up, the door opened and the driver, a kind, older woman with a warm smile, shouted out, "Is there a Cooper here that needs a ride to school?" In that moment I fell in love with that bus driver.

Cooper of course took one look and turned and ran the other way, laughing and giggling. So, in true Swenson fashion, I brought him flailing and kicking to the bus. I hugged him goodbye and whispered in his ear, "Be brave, sweet boy. You got this." And he laughed and laughed and gave me a good squeeze.

I gave the aide a handful of Starbursts for the ride and wished her luck. Minutes later, I posted pictures of my sweet boy to Facebook, the caption reading, "Cooper's first day of kinder-garten."

I worked from home that first week. I knew I would be emotional, and I also wanted to be close by if Cooper needed me during the day. I also had volunteered to go to his school and work the lunch line on his third day. An email had been sent to the kindergarten parents asking for volunteers to help direct traffic during the first two weeks as kids got acclimated. I immediately volunteered.

The night before I was supposed to go, another mom I knew, who had a child in kindergarten as well, posted on Facebook about her trip to school to volunteer in the lunch line. She spoke about how cute the kids were as they stood in line for lunch, said their names out loud to the cashier, and sat and ate. I knew that Cooper wasn't able to do any of those things. They had tried the first day, and when he ran through the lunchroom, they opted for him to eat lunch in his classroom with his aide until he got comfortable.

Never up until this point had I let my grief impact what I did for Cooper. But I could not go into that school and work the lunch line. I could not see all the kids walk through, say their names, and eat at the lunch tables, knowing that my son was eating alone in a classroom. I couldn't do it. I asked Jamie to go in my place, and he thankfully did. I cried the entire day, ashamed at myself for not going. When we spoke later about it, I asked if he saw Cooper. He said no, and he didn't want to disrupt him either, so he just snuck in and out. I asked him if it was sad. He said, "Yes, I didn't know five-year-old kids could be like that, so talkative, so easy."

I want to say it got better. I want to say that Cooper settled into kindergarten and thrived there. But he did not. And I learned two valuable lessons that no one had taught me before. First, public education does not work for every child, and it's okay to say that. It is not a dig on teachers. Far from it. Teachers are amazing, but Cooper needed more. And second, stepping off the path that every other child follows is crushing, and one of the hardest steps you will ever take as a special-needs parent.

As the months went on, I got the impression that the school was unable to manage Cooper's needs and didn't know quite how to teach him. The teacher would send me emails that broke my heart, telling me Cooper was "freaking out" again. The reports got so frequent that every ding of a text or ringing of my phone brought a feeling of dread to my stomach.

His teacher once informed me she was withholding recess for bad behavior, and Jamie had to hold me back from storming the school. I can't imagine withholding physical fun time for a child like Cooper. When she did agree to let him go outside during his day, I found out that he went outside alone, and not with his peers. Every day was like that. Something new. Something sad. Never good. I felt like I was always in a battle.

As Christmastime neared, I was ready to try my hand at volunteering again. The kindergarten classes were having a holiday party with treats, card decorating, games, singing, and more. The email came asking for volunteers, and I signed up for the card decorating station. When I walked into the school armed with courage and my bright red silly Christmas sweater, I was led to a room with three other parents. Each of us would man a table and help the kids decorate a card for their parents.

As the kids arrived, I asked multiple times where Cooper was. The teachers in our room didn't know who he was, which surprised me a little bit. This was a tiny school, housing just the kindergarten classes. After an hour or so, I asked again. "Where is Cooper?" I excused myself, made my way to the front desk, and asked where Cooper was. I was informed that there wasn't an aide to take him around, so he was in his classroom, unable to attend the party.

I could feel the heat rising to my face as I turned and marched to his classroom. When I got to the shut door, I peeked in. Cooper stood on a blue mat, watching something on a screen. The lights were dim. There was paper over the windows. This wasn't the happy holiday party I had just left. I opened the door and walked inside. I had so many emotions. I was sad. I was livid. I went to him, sat on the mat, and scooped him up in the biggest hug. I had told him that morning that Mommy was coming to his school. Did he know? I couldn't be sure, but in my heart,

I told myself he was waiting for me. The woman sitting at the desk wasn't his teacher, just someone sent in to watch my son while everyone else enjoyed the festivities.

I took Cooper out in the hallway, and we made our way from room to room. He refused to decorate a card. He did eat a cookie. We lasted ten minutes before I packed him up and took him home. As we walked out, the chatter of five-year-old voices leveled me. I cried the whole drive home again. It wasn't supposed to be like this. This was supposed to be such a fun day.

I called for an IEP meeting the next day with his teacher, who invited Cooper's team, which included therapists, other teachers, and school leadership. I held back the tears as I spoke about inclusion and participation and valuing a child. Why couldn't they see that he was just a little boy and deserved better?

They promised that they would do better, but it didn't feel genuine. One thing stood out from that meeting, one thing that Jamie and I would discuss for years to come. During my speech about how much my son mattered, as I talked about a little boy who spent his days in the dark classroom at the end of the hall, the principal dozed with his eyes closed at the end of the table. He literally fell *asleep*.

When I left the meeting, I didn't feel confident about Cooper's future at the school. I began desperately searching for another autism program, anything but the one the public school system offered. There seemed to be no options available for my son, and no one would tell me what to do. He wasn't learning. He wasn't getting better.

Over the years I've often talked about the linear nature of childhood development. Babies, infants, and toddlers typically learn skills and hit milestones on a prescribed timeline. It's so predictable that you can buy books or subscribe to emails that will tell you what your child should be doing at any given time, give or take a few months. Most parents just have to follow the plan that the system lays out for them. But for Cooper and kids like him, there is no clear development plan.

As spring neared, I knew it was time once again to step away from public education. Schools are set up for the majority. The masses. But not for kids like mine. Public education isn't for every child, but we are made to think that it is. And when it doesn't work out, you feel like one in a million with nowhere to turn. That's how I felt. But the fear of leaving public education behind was almost more than I could handle. I knew this would mean there would be no school plays or band, no sports or dances. I wanted to stay with everyone else. But I also knew what would be best for Cooper.

All along I had been researching for other options in our state. Anything but public education. I found a few places, but the waiting lists were endless. The paperwork was astronomical. I felt paralyzed.

During that time, the stress of it all was getting to Cooper. When the bus pulled up in the mornings, he would drop to the ground, kicking me relentlessly and screaming. I would be unable to calm him and have to carry him over my shoulder to the bus. I will admit I cried during the drive to work every morning for months. Once there, I would sit at my desk and feel ill, mostly just staring at my phone, waiting for it to ding. Waiting for a message that would tell me Cooper escaped from the school or hurt another child. Or that someone else hurt him.

Every night I would study him and ask questions, looking for any type of response. Was he unhappy? Were they nice to him? Was he being hurt? But he was unable to respond. I'd inspect his body for bruises. And I'd wonder what could be so bad that my sweet, misunderstood boy would attack me every morning before school.

But even more, I wondered why no one cared but his father and me. Thankfully, a sign came. And it came in the form of a spring concert.

★ ★ ★

The subject line of the email from Cooper's school said, "Kindergarten Music Performance." The body of the email was short. We are so excited for you to join us on Thursday, March 30th! Our performance will be in the music room during your student's regularly scheduled music class.

Below the text was a chart with seven kindergarten teachers listed, telling parents what time to arrive for their child's performance time. Cooper's teacher was not listed.

In my gut I knew. I knew my son wasn't going to be allowed to participate. Over the course of the school year he had been excluded countless times. The most recent was a field trip to a local apple orchard. I only knew it was even happening because of the mass emails that went out to kindergarten parents. When I asked his teacher if he was allowed to attend, she told me no, that it would be too challenging, and that they would try for the next one. As a mom who was very aware of her son's challenges, I understood. But as a mom who just wanted her little boy to be included with his peers, I was hurt. It didn't feel fair that he would have to stay back while the entire kindergarten visited the orchard. When I offered to go with them, to help combat some of challenges, I was told no, that the volunteers were already chosen. I could have pushed harder, but I felt like I was already fighting so many battles that I didn't have much fight left. When you have a child with special needs, you have to pick and choose what's worth fighting for and focus your energies on that. Because if you try to fight everything, you will get burned out.

This blatant exclusion felt bigger than a field trip though. This was an event that Jamie and I, and Cooper's brother and grandparents, should be attending. We would take pictures and smile at how cute our little boy was. This was a rite of passage for parents, one I had dreamed about for years. I had looked forward to seeing my child all dressed up, standing on risers and singing with his classmates. I knew from nieces and nephews that this was a big deal.

I waited a few hours for an email from Cooper's teacher. I dictated what I hoped it would say in my head. I thought about the special-needs kids having their own music performance in the privacy of their own classroom. That would work, I thought. I could invite the grandparents to that. Or I thought about him attending the big performance for just one song. He could ring a bell. He could feel joy from the other kids singing. I told myself repeatedly that he wouldn't be excluded. There was no way that my son could be excluded from the kindergarten concert.

As bedtime neared, my anger intensified until I finally sent an email to his teacher. The email had one sentence. Is Cooper included in this? Her response came back quickly. We are going as audience members.

I don't even know if I was shocked at that point. Sadly, I think I expected it. My son had been excluded from every single aspect of kindergarten from day one. He was a square peg in a round hole. The way Cooper was being treated was wrong. Yes, he had autism. But he was a little boy who deserved a seat at the table of life. He deserved to go to that concert like every other kid. He was being purposefully excluded, I assumed, because he was autistic and loud and couldn't stand still. I could think of at least a dozen modifications they could have made to give him and his family the same kindergarten experience. My eyes were opened.

Shortly thereafter, we were officially done with public education. I am often asked by exhausted and overwhelmed parents if it is okay to quit something that isn't working. With countless therapy and medical appointments a week, wondering if any of it is working, families feel stretched thin and are afraid to make hard changes. That was us. Every morning Cooper fought me when that bus pulled up, kicking and fighting as if he was being injured. My gut told me it wasn't working, but quitting was terrifying. When we finally did it, the first day he spent at home with Jamie was like a breath of fresh air. There was no screaming. No aggression or self-injuring. He seemed content. I knew we had made the right decision. You have to trust your gut.

For the next two weeks, Jamie and I alternated working from home, which both me and my employer hoped was temporary, and teaching Cooper the best we could. I knew my time was running out to find a program for him when a miracle happened. A year before I had put him on a waiting list for an autism center in our community but was told the waiting list was years long. When I called, they said he was still many names down for in-center services, but we could start in-home immediately. This would mean staff would come to our home daily and do therapy with Cooper. I didn't know how we would make it work with both Jamie and me employed outside of the home. I spoke with my boss that night about a modified schedule, and Jamie, who had more flexibility being self-employed, agreed to be at my house with Cooper when needed. We vowed to make this a success.

Days later Cooper was evaluated by their psychologist for services. He had to be diagnosed with severe, level three autism to be able to receive services. Once again, Jamie and I found ourselves seated at a table, waiting to hear the results of the evaluation.

"Your son has autism, Mr. and Mrs. Swenson." Jamie and I both smiled, as if she was telling us something we didn't already know. "He qualifies to receive services from us."

And with that, I could breathe again. On the drive home, Jamie and I laughed at the irony of life. For three years I wanted it not to be autism. Anything but autism. And today, I prayed for it so our son could have the help he needed. Life is funny like that.

# NINE

Many years ago, I had a conversation with an acquaintance about his brother who had a disability. Cooper had been diagnosed with autism a few years before, and I had reached the point where I had questions about his future. More specifically, his relationship with Sawyer.

As he described his own brother, I pieced together a picture in my head. He told me that his brother was two years older than him, which would put him in his forties, I guessed. He never learned to speak and was unable to go to school. He was aggressive at times and unable to care for himself. He was never diagnosed, no name given to his disability. But if he had been diagnosed today, it most likely would have been severe, nonverbal autism.

His brother was my Cooper, just years ahead. He made me think of my own two boys, two years apart. One with autism, one without.

"What was your relationship like growing up? What is it like now?"

His eyes looked sad when he said that they had no relationship because they didn't grow up together. His brother was placed in an institution thirty miles away from their house at the recommendation of his pediatrician. He called it a state hospital. He said they visited him as often as they could, but it was still only biweekly. And as he aged and started a family of his own, he rarely saw his brother.

An institution? I didn't even know those really existed. Scenes from a scary movie I'd seen years back flashed into my mind. Images of stark white concrete walls, bright lights, and children and adults in long gowns. That couldn't be it...could it? I thought about Cooper and how much he loved soft blankets and when I tickled the skin under his arms. Why would a boy like him be placed in an institution? He wasn't dangerous. He just couldn't talk. He just learned differently.

I could tell the man felt guilty.

"My parents weren't bad people. Please don't think that. It was a different time. When my mother had him, he wasn't breathing. He almost died. It was her first baby. When he was just a few days old, the doctor told my mother, 'Go home, and have another baby. Forget about this one. He most likely won't live, and if he does, he will need to be placed in an institution.' My mother tried, Kate. She tried to keep him home, but he was more than she could handle. She had six other kids including me, and Johnny needed more than she could give. He left when he was four and I was two. I don't even really remember him ever living with us."

I tried to take in his words without reacting. I couldn't imagine a doctor saying something like that to me... *"Put him in an institution and go home and have another baby."* I have learned since then that this was an all-too-common occurrence years ago, parents being told to give up their disabled children and go home and forget they were ever born.

Tears sprang to my eyes. He was four years old. I thought of

Cooper at four, unable to communicate but still able to show love. He would stand by the window and wait for me to come home if I left to run an errand. He would wake me up in the morning, far too early, by touching my cheek. He wouldn't survive if I disappeared. He wouldn't be able to understand.

The man then said his brother died a few years ago, after his parents passed as well. His state institution had closed years before, and he had moved to a residential group home.

I felt an unbelievable sadness that night. A sadness for all the mothers who were forced to give up babies and the babies who grew up without mothers. I reached out to my brother and his wife, who have an adult son with special needs, although significantly different from Cooper, and asked about their experience. They confirmed what my friend's family had experienced. Their son was born in Germany, and days after delivery, they too were told to institutionalize him and go home and have another baby. This was not a hundred years ago. It was thirty years ago.

I stayed up way too late researching the history of disabilities, and I learned of a world I knew nothing about. My son's world. My world now. I remember my dad once saying, "When I grew up, there was no autism." I realized that there probably *was* autism when my dad grew up; it just wasn't diagnosed. As I looked at the black-and-white photos on my computer screen, of the forgotten children, the same age as my son, I was overwhelmed with emotion. My son could have been one of those children.

I just couldn't believe it. The institutions are all closed now, and from what I hear and see, there is still not a lot of help for parents like me. In my research, I read about parents needing immediate help from a hospital for their children and being told there were no beds. I read stories about aggression so scary that I almost couldn't keep reading. The parents were helpless.

I thought about having to do this forever, raising a vulnerable little boy who will become a man and still not understand the world. And then I thought about what will happen after I am gone. Will Cooper's care fall to Sawyer or will Sawyer have no relationship with him? They are too young right now to even think about that. I just pray that I am creating a world where individuals like Cooper are treasured instead of feared and seen as a burden. And that I am raising my other son to see the gifts his brother brings to this world.

When my boys were six and four, I visited a therapist for myself. I felt selfish about it because I was so busy with kids and work that fitting in time for my own mental health seemed impossible. But after some gentle urging from a friend, I managed to find sixty minutes to block off for *self-care*. It's a buzzword that makes most special-needs parents cringe. We don't have time for extras in our world. Once I counted Cooper had on average seven additional appointments a week on top of school and being a kid. Think a combination of speech therapy, occupational therapy, play therapy, feeding therapy, medical appointments, and appointments with his social worker. I also had another son to care for, and a house to manage, and a job to work. Self-care was not a priority.

I found myself in a busy parking lot of a medical office building. As I sat there in my parked car, waiting to go in, I thought about what I wanted to speak with the therapist about. The options were endless. On the outside I was fine. I had a fantastic job in public media, one that I was incredibly proud of. I paid my own bills, owned my own home, and managed to keep all the different plates not only up in the air, but spinning too. But on the inside, I felt much different. I felt like a failure. I had spent the last six years trying to find my son's voice, and I had lost mine in the process. Instead of thriving, we were surviving. But with my independent, tough exterior, most people had no idea that I felt that way. And opening up and being honest about our day-to-day struggles and my heartache didn't come easily to me.

So I had pulled away from most people. I had fifty unanswered text messages on my phone and a dozen unopened voice mails. My friendships were suffering. I sugarcoated the challenges with family. I wanted to believe that if I just kept going, and kept doing more for Cooper, that one day, he would get better. But it wasn't happening. Autism had woven its way into every aspect of my life and had consumed me. I had become my son's disability, and there was no Kate left. Should I ask a therapist how to find myself again?

I could tell her about my divorce and how I was in love with my ex-husband but deep down I knew it would never work. Because I felt broken and destined to carry the burdens of autism alone. When I pictured my future, it was Cooper and me, rocking on a porch, frozen in time, the rest of the world having moved on. And I was coming to terms with that.

I supposed I could talk about the stages of grief. I had cycled through them all but the last one. Denial, anger, bargaining, and finally depression were no strangers to me. But the gift of acceptance was still elusive. Instead it felt like a moving target, remaining just out of reach as Cooper aged. Some days, even weeks, I would walk around thinking I had made it, and then something would happen. Cooper's niece, just four months younger, would sing me a song, and I would be leveled, blindsided by the grief that seemed to lie dormant and then resurface when I least expected it. In a way, part of me secretly wondered if acceptance meant giving up. Was it going numb? And what was I really accepting? That my son would never learn to talk. Or make a friend. Or ride a bike. I wasn't sure if I was really ready yet. I was in the in-between place.

But lately, those weren't the parts that were troubling me the most. Instead, I was thinking about Sawyer and how the night before he had stood on a chair in my kitchen, stirring chocolate cupcake batter, and I almost didn't recognize him. He had grown up. His hair was spiky and long and he was wearing a red Power Rangers costume. He spent almost all of his time dressed in costumes lately, something I wholeheartedly encouraged him to do. As he stirred the big wooden spoon, he talked a mile a minute, telling me a long story about a dinosaur bone hunt they had at school that day, and how he had found bones but his teacher wouldn't let him keep them.

I stood there in my kitchen, trying to remember when Sawyer had grown up. I felt like I had missed it entirely. But that's how life goes. It just happens.

Since his dad and I separated, I had grown incredibly close with each of my boys. Sawyer, he was my little buddy. We cooked together. He would follow me from room to room while I cleaned, shooting me with Nerf guns, and demanding we play every game in the house. I appreciated him so much in those days, when the isolation felt the most suffocating. And while he watched his programs, or played games in his forts, I stole snuggles from Cooper, forcing my way into his world any way I could. People would often ask me how I communicated with my son, since he had no words and very little communication. Well, it was easy. Cooper and I developed our own language. I knew every sound, every squeal, every look and gesture. I even compared us to a little old couple, sitting in silence together. Our bond became undeniable. That doesn't mean I didn't long for words, or for Cooper to join us for a game of Candyland. I absolutely did, but I didn't long for those things quite so often anymore. It was as if the pain, while still present at times, had dulled a bit. We were settling into our normal.

There is a silence that comes with nonverbal children that is hard to explain. It can be deafening, sitting at a table, across from your child, wanting nothing more than to hear about their day and what they are thinking. But there is nothing. For years it was like that. Until one day, Sawyer started talking. And he filled the silent rooms and car rides with noise. Suddenly it wasn't so quiet anymore.

Sawyer fell in love with his older brother at six months old. He would sit in the living room, watching Cooper jump and squeal with joy in front of the television. As Sawyer neared a year, and Cooper three, I wondered what their relationship would be like. Many people in my life told me that having a sibling would be the best thing for Cooper. They told me that Cooper would want to be like Sawyer, do what Sawyer was doing, talk like Sawyer, play like Sawyer, and so on. That wasn't true though. Cooper barely seemed to notice his younger brother was even there.

I have a photo of the two of them set as the wallpaper on my computer. It shows their personalities perfectly. Sawyer is sitting on the floor outside Cooper's room, his back pressed to the wall. He is playing with a Nerf gun, dressed in a ninja costume. Cooper is sitting just inside of his bedroom door, spread out on his fuzzy train blanket. The blanket had to be perfect at all times; no one could touch it or walk on it. If we did, or a dog dared to, Cooper would break into hysterics. He is surrounded by a dozen DVD cases and watching his iPad. Same house. Two very separate worlds.

When Sawyer was around three, he asked if Cooper hated him. It was the only reason he could think of to explain why Cooper didn't play with him. I did my best to explain autism. And from that day on, Sawyer referred to it as his "brother's 'tism." Without a brother to play with, Sawyer turned to me to play. A role I gladly filled. I made sure to invite Cooper to join us in our play. I knew in my heart that he wouldn't, but that didn't matter. I wanted him to know he was invited, and we would be ready if and when he wanted to join us. I also wanted Sawyer to understand inclusion and the importance of including kiddos who may be different.

In those early years, Sawyer slept in my bed nightly. At first, I fought it, walking him back into his room and tucking him in a dozen times. I needed my alone time too. But once he said to me, "Mama, I just need time with you to snuggle," I was a goner. I felt like he got the leftover shreds of me. And that wasn't fair to him. Nightly, we would lie in bed and chat about dinosaurs and whatever was on his mind. I felt so much joy from those moments with Sawyer, but deep down, buried inside, I felt sadness for never having them with my oldest son. I once said this on the blog and received some scolding from those who felt that I shouldn't compare, that I should be thankful I have a "normal" child. I think it's important to know that I could have a dozen kids and still long for Cooper to tell me his favorite color and why he loves trains. One child doesn't make up for another. They are both my sons, uniquely made.

I spent the next sixty minutes talking to my new therapist about sibling guilt, a very common and confusing occurrence for parents of children with special needs. I told her about how I created a good life for Sawyer. I put him in the best preschool, one that cost more than I could afford. I signed him up for sports, and playdates, and field trips. I kept him busy. I sent him to stay with friends and family. I watched him experience life through photos and videos sent to my phone. I spoiled him rotten with gifts because I couldn't always give him time or experiences. And I told her how days before, he had told me he didn't need me to cut his food anymore and that I should focus on Cooper, because Cooper needed me more. He was just barely four. That gutted me.

Sawyer associated me with Cooper. With home. With autism. His dad was the fun parent, the one who coached sports and brought him outside of our home to experience the world. I knew I had to make a change. I had to figure out a balance before the guilt consumed me. But I didn't know how. Cooper's needs were so intense, and I was the only one who could calm him. But I had another little boy too, one who needed me as well.

The therapist's prescription was simple. Write a letter to Sawyer, one that he could read when he was older. One that could help him understand why our life was the way it was. She said it would be therapeutic to get it all out.

That weekend, I climbed into my bed and started writing. I didn't sugarcoat my words. I wrote from the heart:

My little Sawyer,

I want to tell you a few things. At four years old I know you won't understand them, so I am writing them down for you to read when you are older. Someday, when Mom is old and gray, I want you to read this letter. I want you to understand. It's a thank-you, and an apology and a dose of reality.

First, I want to thank you for simply being. Thank you for being with me. Thank you for being my son and a brother to Cooper. That probably sounds silly, but the world is such a better place with you in it. And on your hardest days, kid, please know that. You have so many gifts to give this world.

I want to thank you for growing up too. Again, probably silly. But you are so unbelievably lucky because you get the gift of aging and becoming a man. And you and I both know that not everyone does. You are lucky, Sawyer. You hit the genetic lottery. You get to learn independence and success and failure too. You get to sneak a beer and feel the thunder in your chest at your first concert. You get to drive a car, kiss a girl, walk across the stage at graduation, and vote. These are gifts, son.

Thank you for giving me so many precious moments. Your first word was *mama*. I cried. I can still see you catching your first fish. You were wearing a fleece camo jacket. You were so proud of catching a fish just like your dad. You learned to ride a bike at three. That's amazing. You potty trained yourself by watching me work with your brother. You have always been fiercely independent. You were never sick. You learned everything so effortlessly and simply. You gave me a part of motherhood that was free from worry. Thank you.

I have a feeling that you won't always be easy. You're going to be just like your dad and give me lots of trouble. Your Grandma Swenson tells me stories about your dad that give me heart palpitations. Go easy on me. You know I am a big baby. And please don't ever ride a motorcycle.

I want to say I am sorry too. I don't ever want you to think I missed out on your life because your brother needed me more. I was faced with choices, Sawyer. So many more than most parents. It wasn't fair. Having to choose. And I like to believe I made the right ones. You may think different. I don't know yet. I worry that you may resent Cooper. I hope not.

I want you to know that I was always watching, Sawyer. You may have been throwing a pitch at a baseball game or scoring a goal in hockey and looked to the stands and just saw Dad. Or Grandpa and Grandma. I was watching, kid. I am always watching. Even if you can't see me, I see you. I may be watching from the car with your brother or wandering behind him in the bleachers or seeing it on a video. I will never miss a second of your life. I promise you that.

I learned early on that if I wanted to give you a normal life, I would have to share you. So I found people I trusted who would bring you along. I will never be able to thank them enough for including you. There were so many days that I missed you too and I would feel tears spring to my eyes as I watched you run off to go to the park with the neighbors or visit the zoo with family. I was jealous. They got you.

For years, I watched you grow up through photos and videos sent to me by other people. They will never know the gift they gave me for taking you and showing you the world when I had to be at a therapy center, or a hospital, or keep your brother safe from himself.

And last, I want to tell you something that may surprise you. But maybe not. I don't know what your relationship is going to look like with Cooper. I have hope though. So much hope. That someday, you see the gifts and beauty that he brings to our lives. And not the aggressions, the struggles, or the missed events.

You are lucky that you have autism in your life. Because you get to see a side of the world that most adults never get to. You get to see hope, resilience, differences. And you get to see the fight, the evil, the sad parts too. When you were younger, I felt bad. I no longer do. You get the gift of knowing Cooper. And you have a choice, kid. You can change the world for him and help me give him his best life. And that is a blessing.

Let having a brother with a disability change you for the better. See differences. See the underdog. See the discriminated and the forgotten. And give them a voice, kid. Speak so loudly that your voice shakes, even when you are scared. I love you, buddy.

When I finished writing the letter, I immediately put it in Sawyer's mostly empty baby book. It joined his tiny hospital bracelet, mine as well, the blue hat that was placed on his head after birth, and a piece of paper with his footprints. There are a few other dates and notes written in as well, but noticeably less than in Cooper's book. But I did manage to write down the first time he smiled, rolled over, sat up, crawled, and walked. The last entry I wrote in his book was his first word, *mama*.

Many years before, when Cooper was diagnosed, I met a woman in the waiting room of one of the many therapy centers we visited. I can't even remember which one. Her son was ten years older than Cooper and nonverbal. We had a very short but very profound conversation. She said, "When you enter the world of special needs, your happiest days will also become your saddest." I didn't fully understand that sentence until the day Sawyer surpassed his brother in development. The joy I felt filled me up. But the sadness for my other little boy felt bigger. For the rest of my life, in moments like these, the joy will battle with the sadness. My conversation with this woman left an indelible mark and changed me. But at the time, I just didn't know how much.

I hardly remember anything from my pregnancy with Sawyer and I don't remember a lot of his first few years, but I do remember that we almost died during his birth. I don't share this with a lot of people. Probably because it feels so far-fetched. But it happened and it was very scary.

On the day of my induction, forty weeks exactly, I was leaning, hunched over the side of the hospital bed, feet dangling near the ground, with my face crushed into Jamie's chest, waiting to get the relief that only an epidural can bring.

This was my second epidural in my birthing career, so I was not scared. I knew sitting still was the hardest part. I knew that the pain would all be over in a minute and I would finally be able to take a deep breath and relax for a minute.

While Cooper's birth was long and drawn out, Sawyer's was going to be fast and ferocious. I could tell from the second I felt that first contraction. In hindsight it's funny. Each child's birth matched their personalities perfectly.

The anesthesiologist was talking me through the process. "You will feel pressure. You should not feel any pain." I felt the tape. And the cold of the swab used to clean my back. I felt the pressure.

Once done, the nurse told me to sit up straight and swing my legs around, but to do it all slowly. I could be woozy, she said. I followed her instructions and lifted my head from my husband's chest. With the help of a nurse, I turned to lift my numbing legs up to the bed. I looked her in the eye and very calmly said, "I'm going down."

That is the last thing I remember. When Jamie tells the story, he laughs about how calm I was, like I was just lying down for a quick nap. Before I tell you what was actually happening in my delivery room, I will tell you what I was feeling.

I was feeling amazing. I was floating. I had this black swirling around my head and a voice telling me to go to sleep. Finally, I could rest. If only these people would all leave me alone. I vividly remember feeling the best I had felt in ages.

The second I lay down for my much-needed nap, the room filled with sound. Buzzers and alarms started ringing. My blood pressure had dropped to zero. And my heart stopped beating, which practically never happens in childbirth. I was essentially dying.

Jamie said the nurse climbed on top of me, trying to wake me. She was shaking my shoulders. "Katie. Katie. Can you hear me?" When she could not wake me, she reached over me behind the bed and slapped a button on the wall and screamed, "I'm calling the code!"

Jamie said within seconds, microseconds even, the room was full of people. When he tells the story, he says dozens. He says he was pushed back in the corner and there were so many people gathered around me that he could not see my face.

I was sleeping and then I was awake. I opened my eyes, but I could not move my body, so I looked up. I knew there were people around me because I could hear their voices. But I couldn't move my head. It felt like I was in cement, my limbs heavy. The talking heads were all gathered around me. I felt trapped in the bed, and I had this desperate feeling that I should run away.

I was darting my eyes around, trying to avoid the bright lights, looking for my husband. I just needed to see his face. I was scared. Really scared. Something was wrong, but I didn't know what, and Jamie, well, he is my calm. He always has been.

I often joke that our house could be on fire and Jamie would be sitting in the recliner telling me, "Relax, we have time. Let's make a list of what we should save, but first let me finish what I am doing." His calm sometimes drives me crazy, but in that moment, I needed it more than ever.

When I realized he was crying, my fear started to build. I had never seen my husband cry. I tried to reach for him, to say I was alright, but I couldn't speak. The nurse kept repeating my name, trying to get me to focus. After what felt like an eternity, I was able to focus.

"Katie, you're back. You gave us quite a scare there. How are you feeling?" asked my nurse. I just looked at her. All of these people were standing around staring at me. I felt confused about what had just happened.

Then I heard someone shout that the baby had no heartbeat. I will never forget that sentence.

"The baby has no heartbeat."

At first it caught me off guard, like an out-of-body experience. *Whose baby has no heartbeat? Not mine*, I thought.

Frantically someone lifted my gown, no modesty for me, and moved the heartbeat monitor around my tummy. Multiple hands were pushing on my stomach, trying to move and reposition all at once. Nothing. No baby.

I distinctly remember thinking, *I can't lose this baby. He is mine. I want him now.* I looked at Jamie, willing him to do something.

In those moments, they were all focused on me. I was the priority, getting my heart going. They had to save me. But now I needed them to save my baby.

I heard the word "C-section." I heard "Prep for surgery." I heard beeping. I heard the blare of a flatline. I made eye contact with a doctor. Gosh, he was young. He was not my doctor. I don't even remember his name. My doctor, the same man who delivered me and my sister and Cooper, was probably in his seventies. He was always calm and reassuring. I had no fear with him. None. But he hadn't made it to my room yet.

The other doctor, the younger one, did not seem like he knew what to do. He was wiggling my stomach, moving the whole entire thing as if to shake Sawyer awake. He was visibly scared. I saw his face. He looked panicked. I could have very well misread that look, but it scared me deeply.

Someone screamed, "Get the doctor here! Now!" This is the dramatic part, the part that always makes Sawyer smile when I tell the story before bed. Suddenly my doctor was there, beside me. He walked in looking unnerved. Machines were beeping. People were running around. It was like a scene from a movie where the hero walks in through the fog, unrattled.

He looked at me and squeezed my arm and said, "Hang on, kid." I don't know if he meant me or the baby. Then my doctor's arm was up inside me, and he gave Sawyer the biggest shake. I felt all of it and it didn't feel good.

Beep. Beep. Beep. The fetal heart rate monitor let out the familiar sound it was supposed to. The room let out a collective sigh. We were both okay.

My doctor, gray-haired, a larger-than-life man, had saved him. Sawyer loves that story. He thinks he was saved by a superhero. He loves how he gave us all a huge scare before he was even born.

I'd like to tell you the rest of his birth was Zen and peaceful. Nope. The rest was just as chaotic. That's my boy. My loud, wild, exhausting boy. I should have immediately known that he was going to put me through the wringer.

Thankfully, he gave me a few hours to relax and recover from the trauma. I sucked on ice chips, and Jamie and I played on our phones and joked how this felt like a vacation. You know, besides the whole almost dying part.

One second, I was saying to Jamie that I wanted to stay an

extra night and have these wonderful nurses take care of me, and the next I was screaming bloody murder for Jamie to get a nurse.

"Jamie, press the call button," I demanded. "The baby is coming."

"The nurse was just in here, Kate. It can't happen that fast."

"Press the DAMN BUTTON!" I screamed.

Jamie responded, "I did, Katie. I pressed the (insert sarcasm) DAMN button."

"PRESS IT AGAIN!"

Nothing.

"Run and get the nurse right now. I can feel his head, Jamie. Do you want to deliver your son?"

Now, this is one of the moments when Jamie's ever-calm demeanor was not helpful.

He sighed, pushed himself out of the chair, and slowly, like a sloth, made his way to the door. His shoes. They were clomping. Flip-flops. Who the hell wears flip-flops to the birth of their child? He was taking his time. I made a mental note to finish him off when this was all over.

I know I swore. I know I was screaming. Can this man never have any dang urgency in his life? I heard him and the nurse joking on their walk back.

I heard her say, "I just checked her, but it can happen quickly. Especially with a second baby." She sat down, took one peek, and told Jamie to hit the button again. It was time to have a baby. Then she told me to stop pushing. She could see Sawyer's head and we needed to wait for the doctor.

Finally, after what felt like eternity, the doctor arrived. A nurse gowned and gloved him as he turned the corner. I watched him take one peek, and then Sawyer came out like a rocket. The doctor caught him like a football.

It was incredibly dramatic. And then Sawyer was in my arms. The baby who almost wasn't. He was perfect. All eight and a half pounds of him. Like with Cooper, I fell in love with him immediately.

★ ★ ★

My family tree is complicated, never easy to explain in a sentence. I have a half sister, five years older than me, who grew up with her father. I have two much older half brothers, who grew up with their mother. I didn't have a relationship with them until well into my twenties. I essentially grew up as an only child in rural Wisconsin with my mother and stepfather. My sister stayed with us sometimes, but again, it was complicated. As she aged, her visits lessened. My parents worked, so I was alone a lot. I spent my summers talking to my dog, building forts in the woods, and watching soap operas and Bob Barker on daytime television. I had an amazing imagination and a love for independent activities. But oh, how I longed for siblings. Someone I could ride the Tilt-A-Whirl with at the fair. A built-in friend.

Long before Jamie and I got married, I knew I wanted at least three kids. I loved the chaos of loud, messy families, full of kids. As far back as when I was pregnant with Cooper, I remember envisioning future Christmases full of kids and grandkids.

Even though I didn't spend much time with my sister growing up, I do have precious memories of her visits. Growing up in the '90s I loved her huge bangs. I was secretly jealous that Mom made me have a short boy haircut and she had long, beautiful hair. I was in awe of how she rolled her jeans, the tighter the better. And I will never forget that when she came to stay, I was sometimes able to sleep in the same bed as her, which I thought was amazing. She would read V.C. Andrews books, and I would pretend to be annoyed that the light was on. In those moments I had a sister, and it was everything I wanted for my boys.

Cooper and Sawyer often share a room by choice, something that warms my heart and gives me hope for the future. When I tuck them in at night, I give hugs and kisses, whispering *I love you* into each of their heads. One little boy says it back and to the other, I say it twice, just to be sure he knows. Every night I pause outside their door, the silence once again consuming me.

Some nights, I hear Sawyer chattering to himself, and I wonder what Cooper is thinking.

I don't know what the future holds for Cooper and Sawyer. I don't know if they will ever have a typical relationship. But I have hope. So much hope that it carries me through.

I am watching Sawyer turn into an amazingly kind, patient boy who seeks out kids who are different. I've watched Sawyer instinctively grab his older brother's hand in a parking lot, guiding him to safety. I've watched him buckle Cooper's seat belt, even feed him a bite of food.

I've witnessed Cooper run to Sawyer for a hug at the most random moments. Or show him something special on his iPad. I've had multiple teachers tell me at his conferences throughout the years that Sawyer is compassionate. That means more to me than any math or reading test score.

I've also watched them wrestle and argue like all siblings do. No, it's not the relationship I imagined for them. But it's blossoming. There is something there. And Jamie and I will continue to nurture it as they grow older. We will do this by continuing to talk about autism in our home and the community, modeling to Sawyer what advocacy means. I know people who whisper the word *autism* as if it's a dirty word. Not to us.

We will continue to introduce Sawyer to kids and adults who have different abilities, so he knows there is no one-size-fits-all in this world. I firmly believe that people stare at us not with disdain but because they don't understand. And also, they fear. I want Sawyer to seek out people who may look or act different, not hide from them. And that starts with us as parents.

For Jamie and me, it has never been our autistic son and our normal son. They are both our boys, and we love them equally and fiercely. Of course, times will arise when Cooper may need accommodations, and we will face that head-on, with honesty and grace, so Sawyer understands. These boys are so lucky to have each other. I know that. And one day they will too.

★ ★ ★

"Did you know that I'm going to live in an apartment some-day, Mom?"

"You are?"

"Yep. When I'm eighteen. I'm going move out to live with my friend Derek. Will you be sad, Mom? Who will help me get dressed? Who will drive me to school? We are going to have a hot tub in the living room!"

"Well, bud, of course I'll be sad. I don't want you to leave."

"But you'll have Cooper forever, Mom. I heard you and Dad talking about it."

"Well, yes. That's a possibility. He might, er, um, well, yes, probably live with us forever."

"That's good. I really don't want you to be sad when I leave. Because I have to grow up. You know that, right?"

Pause.

"What about after forever, Mom? After you are gone? Who will take care of my brother then? Do I have to take care of him?"

"Well, Sawyer, we don't worry about that right now."

Pause.

"I guess maybe he could live in my apartment. But maybe not. Do I get to choose, Mom? Do I get to choose where he lives? You'll be in heaven. Right, Mom?"

"You, Sawyer, can choose whatever feels right for you, honey. And that may change many, many times. And the good thing is, we have a long time until we have to think about it. Forever is a long time away, Sawyer. Mom and Dad will take care of Cooper as long as he needs us to."

"Maybe Cooper can live with me. Maybe we can all take care of each other."

As I watched Sawyer climb inside the fort made of blankets and chairs, I let myself think about the future. It's hard for me to acknowledge it. I'm not ready yet. But I dipped my toe in just for a second.

Cooper will probably need lifelong care. And someday, I will be gone. Will Sawyer take care of his older brother? Will he shave him and bathe him? Or will he go to a group home? I will never put that pressure on my younger son. It's not fair to put that on a sibling. But these thoughts are starting to plague me more. I can't always run from them. My boys are growing up.

I want Sawyer to go to college, get married, and have babies. I want him to live his life to the fullest and not have to worry in any way about Cooper. But, and it's a huge *but*, he does have a brother with special needs. And when it's my time to leave this earth, I pray that he will love his brother as much as I do. And whether that means in his own home, or managing his care, I just pray that he will.

# TEN

It was early. Before 7:00 a.m., although it felt like midday. I had been awake all night, mostly due to insomnia, but then officially up at 3:00 a.m. with Cooper. I felt like I had been hit by a freight train when he pressed the remote into my hand. But I survived and got him on the bus at 6:30 and raced out the door.

I was sitting in the parking lot outside of my work, the ten-minute walk into the building ahead of me. I didn't want to go in. I had been crying most of the night, and my face did not hide it. How was I going to walk in and act normal? Like nothing had happened.

I pulled out my phone. I had recently started a Facebook page called *Finding Cooper's Voice*, so I could talk about my life with Cooper. I was tired of keeping the fear locked inside. It was paralyzing to pretend that my son's autism wasn't severe. It was suffocating not being able to talk about how we couldn't leave the house or feel welcome anywhere. It was devastating not being able to say the fears out loud.

My audience was small but mighty. It was mostly other mothers like me, moms of relatively newly diagnosed kids. I knew they would understand what I was feeling.

Talking about autism, but even more, talking about the journey of being a parent going through an autism diagnosis and beyond, was freeing. Even if no one said anything back. It saved me. And I was quickly learning that my openness and honesty were helping other parents too.

The videos I posted were nothing special. Just me, typically in my car, talking about the hard, sad, good, and worry. I never made a script or did any editing. I just spoke into the camera. This morning was no different. I spoke from my heart.

*"I want to talk about something that I think all my autism parents will understand. I want to talk about the last time. Which is a funny phrase. You hear it a lot. Like the last time you'll pick your child up, or the last time you'll nurse your child, or the last time they'll hold your hand.*

*"There is a last time in the world of special-needs parenting that I don't think anyone else would get. There is the last time you think that this is going to be okay. What does that mean?*

*"Yesterday was a really rough day in our little autism world, and I couldn't sleep, at all. Cooper lives in his own little world, in our home, and he is safe, and he is happy, and he is healthy, and he is a complete joy.*

*"But there are times when we have to leave that world. And we have to go and do things. And when we do, I plummet after."*

That was where I was at. I had plummeted. We were nearly three years into our autism diagnosis, and I had always sort of assumed that every year would get easier. I thought you get the diagnosis, you get help, you move on.

And maybe it is like that for some families. Not us though. We were stuck, almost frozen in time. But not just frozen in Cooper's development, services, and resources. I was frozen too. I was unable to see the future, to see reality.

The day before, I had received a special invite through work to visit the Mall of America, the biggest mall in the United States, which happens to practically be in our backyard, to meet Elmo. I had agonized over whether we should go. Cooper loved Elmo with a passion, but we had also not had a successful trip outside of our home in years. The list of places we could go had dwindled to nearly nowhere.

Jamie and I weighed pros and cons and ultimately landed on one simple factor. Our son loves Elmo. We are bringing him.

I meticulously planned out our trip, right down to where we would park, even the walk in. I pulled up maps and made phone calls to the group hosting the meet and greet. In our world, nothing is left up to chance. To have success, we need a plan.

We arrived early, with hopes that Cooper would get his wiggles out by running around the somewhat deserted mall. I was thankful that our time to see Elmo was before the mall officially opened and that there would be no crowds. Cooper ran from store to store, peeking in windows and never once slowing down. Seniors walked past us, getting their steps in, as Jamie and I followed our son. To anyone else he probably looked like a typical little boy enjoying his freedom.

At one point I caught him, scooped him up, and held him tightly for a photo. Taking pictures has always been my thing and I often try to get many during events like this one. Just like every other photo of ours over the last few years, I squeezed him tight as he arched his back and pulled away screaming. I plastered a fake smile on my face as the sweat dripped down my neck.

Jamie tried to get Cooper's attention but had no luck. "Just take the photo," I snapped at him. I heard the click of my camera right before Cooper brought his fist to his own head, hitting himself repeatedly and screaming. I set him down, sighing, as he took off. The walkers spread apart as he wove through. Jamie and I took off running after him.

We made our way to the center of the mall, preparing Cooper up as much as we could about the crowd, noise, Elmo himself, and even waiting in line. I couldn't tell if he was excited or if he even really understood. As we neared, I ran ahead to chat with the person running the show. I was looking for the woman I had emailed the day before. I had explained to her that my son had autism and waiting in lines was nearly impossible for him. I'd asked if we could skip that part and just see Elmo first and be done.

I received the sweetest response back from her. "Of course. When you arrive, just sneak under the rope and ask for me. When Elmo and Abby Cadabby come out on stage, your son can go up first. No problem."

I found the lady with the headset immediately, and she waved our family in. We ducked under the rope, skipping the check-in line. I looked around, sizing up our surroundings. I knew my son better than anyone and the danger he could find in an instant. He could cause damage too. I was the classic autism mom, sweeping the room like an FBI agent.

I saw sets from *Sesame Street* set up for photo shoots. I wondered if they were flimsy. I saw train tables and coloring tables that could easily be flipped over. Tiny chairs. Dammit. Tiny chairs could be thrown. I saw a big table stacked high with Elmo dolls that could easily be ransacked. Cooper could clear a table in seconds with one sweep.

I saw my coworkers and their families, lined up inside a roped area, waiting. I took notice right away that my son was by far the oldest child. Most of the kids were toddlers. Some even infants. They were all dressed cute, waiting patiently in line. I felt the familiar sting in my stomach reminding me that we were different and then quickly shoved it way down deep inside. I was excited at the chance for Cooper to meet a character he loved. I didn't care if he was five or twenty. And deep down, I think I already knew that we would be watching Elmo forever.

Once inside the roped-off area, Jamie and I did our best to contain Cooper as we waited for Elmo, who obviously didn't know there was a little boy waiting for him. Cooper dropped to the ground as I reached for his hand. He rolled. He screamed. He flailed and reached for anything he could grab to throw. I felt the stares. My cheeks turned hot instantly as I tried to reach my hands in and pick him up. I know people wonder why he is behaving this way. The answer is I don't know. Since birth, Cooper struggled with being still. No matter where we were, or what we were doing, he was running away. It was like he just couldn't be present.

We attempted to distract him with trains and crayons, but none of it worked. The lady with the headset was trying to talk to me, trying to tell me Elmo would be right out, and that we could make our way to the stage. Jamie attempted to pick Cooper up, and he slithered like Jell-O out of his hands. He whispered to me, "Do we just go?" I knew that desperate tone well. "I don't know!" I whispered back. I felt trapped. I felt like crying. I could hear the frustration in Jamie's voice. I knew we would turn on each other soon. This always happened. Cooper's intensity had a way of bringing our stress levels to a ten every single time.

I looked at Jamie, and he was beet red too. I saw sweat on his forehead. It was like we were running a dang marathon. Finally, music, clapping, and cheering erupted from the stage. Elmo and Abby sauntered out, waving to the kids and dancing. From the ground, Cooper sat up, took one look, covered his ears, and ran the other way screaming. Under the far rope he went, and he was gone. I stood there with my mouth open as Jamie chased him.

"Do you want us to wait for him?" the lady asked. I stammered awkwardly. I told her to skip us.

I watched as a mother and father were waved on stage, their toddler taking big clumsy steps toward Elmo. He walked right into a hug, and the whole room said, "Aww." I felt the tears spring to my eyes. They looked so happy, their actions so effortless. They went on to pose for a family photo. "Say 'Elmo,'" the photographer said. "EMO!" the little boy shouted.

And then Cooper was back, next to me in his dad's arms. Jamie whispered, "Let's just go, Kate. This was a bust." But Cooper gestured toward Elmo. I looked at him, my sweet, little, misunderstood boy… "Can't we just try? Please, Jamie?"

As we looked at each other, having an all-too-common silent conversation with our eyes, the heat rose to my cheeks again. I wanted to try. Jamie wanted to leave. It was a standoff. This is how it always went. And when it failed, I would be at fault. Me, the one who pushed.

"Fine." Jamie set Cooper down, and again he was gone. On the stage he went, waving at Elmo while screaming, happy or sad I do not know, cutting a family off on their way up the steps.

I ran up after him, tripping on the third step, apologizing to the family as I pulled myself to standing again. I knelt down next to my little boy, and for a microsecond I could breathe. We had made it. Cooper smiled and reached his hand out to touch Elmo's giant red arm. I felt relief. Was he smiling? Yes! He was! But then he was done. Just like that.

Cooper dropped to the ground, hitting his head against the floor over and over again. I felt frozen for a second before I scooped him up, shielding him from the stares burning into us. I turned him in to me, his long body, almost half my size. I whispered in his ear, "All done, buddy?"

"Would you like a photo?"

I looked out at the crowd. I saw the woman in the headset, the photographer, and Jamie. "Sure," I said through gritted teeth. I plastered that fake smile on my face while Cooper rocked back and forth, his forehead eventually striking my chin and mouth. Tears immediately sprang to my eyes. I could taste the blood, but I kept smiling.

I realized the room had grown very quiet. Everyone was staring at us. I made eye contact with a mother as she hugged her infant daughter tight. I scanned the room and I saw their faces. Some held pity. Some looked shocked. I'm sure some were happy when we left.

I suspect some were wondering why we were even there. The answer is, because our son loves Elmo. And like every other child, he should get to go and enjoy himself. But for some reason, the things that bring him the most joy also bring him unbelievable anxiety. As his mom, I felt trapped, not knowing when to encourage or pull back.

When we don't go, we are judged and feel guilty because our child is missing out. When we do go, we fail. We feel judged and feel guilty. And of course, there is always hope. Hope that it will work out for once.

We left immediately after the photo, Jamie coming to the edge of the stage to scoop Cooper out of my arms. He turned without a word and left. He just walked right out. I followed, grabbing our things that had been dropped during the commotion. His jacket, my purse, a water bottle. The woman with the headset smiled sadly and handed me an Elmo doll.

"Maybe this will cheer him up."

I spent the rest of that day in a fog, unable to clear it from my brain. Everything felt muddled, all squished together like I was upside down and inside out. Words flew through my mind. *Autism. Severe. Nonverbal. Forever.* And then finally the sentence, *He will be autistic forever.*

As the day drew on, and the scenarios of forever played through my head, I turned to wine to take the edge off. I thought about autism. His autism. No one told me it would all be so challenging, that every day would feel like climbing a mountain. They also didn't tell me it would be so emotional. That seeing other children his age speaking and playing would almost drop me to my knees. It felt as if the world had long passed us by and forgotten about my beautiful boy.

I let myself wonder what life would be like if Cooper didn't have autism. What would be different about him and what would remain? He would be speaking by now, saying *mommy* and *daddy* and *brother*. He would be learning to play games and hit a baseball and ride a tricycle. We would go on family vacations to Disney World and camping. I choked out a sob as I envisioned each scenario, torturing myself.

That night as I bathed him, I listened to him hum and watched as he rocked back and forth. I reached my hands down to scrub his legs and his feet, overwhelmed by how much I loved him and wanted to make his life easier. He was right in front of me, the little boy that I had prayed for. I could touch him and even hold him if I wanted to, but there were parts of his mind that were closed off to me. I suddenly missed him. And felt an urgency to be closer to him.

As I held his foot, scrubbing each toe with a washcloth, I sang "This Little Piggy" to him. He giggled as the fifth and final piggy went "wee wee all the way home." I felt tears pool in my eyes. I studied the little foot in my hand. This was not a baby foot. Not anymore. As I scrubbed, I looked up at my son's face, and for the first time in Cooper's life, I saw him as a man. And me as an old woman, with wrinkles and gray hair, scrubbing his feet.

And it hit me. Really hit me. Like a freight train. Autism, his autism, was forever. And it wasn't going away. I had felt this before, numerous times, but never like this. In the past it was like I was acknowledging it was forever, while secretly thinking maybe it wasn't. There I was living in that in-between place, the emotions too big for me. My son may never speak. He may never live on his own. And it is out of my control. *Who will care for him? Who will love him after I am gone?*

I was suddenly angry at the unfairness of it all. I thought, *Why him?* I wanted my baby to know all the wonderful parts of life that everyone deserves. I wanted him to hit a home run, feel the butterflies before leaning in for a first kiss, know the stress of a job interview, even the anguish of getting a D on a paper.

I wanted him to graduate, get a job, get married, and give me grandbabies. I wanted to dance with my son at his wedding. But suddenly I knew those things were never going to happen. I had been at the edge of the acceptance cliff for months now and with one trip to see Elmo, I jumped over feetfirst.

That night, after both of my boys were tucked in bed, I could barely get off the couch. I let myself crash to my lowest point. I thought about forever.

Will Cooper understand when I die? Or will he still be a little boy?

Will Cooper be able to go to my funeral? His own mother's funeral? Or will he be kept home because he can't sit or stop stimming, which is a self-stimulating behavior or behaviors, usually involving repetitive movements or sounds. Will he understand that I am gone? Or, instead, will I just disappear one day? Will he wait at the front door for me, like he does every single day of his life? I am his person. I am his world. Will he say "I want Mom" repeatedly with his speech device?

Hopefully, I will be in my eighties and Cooper will be in his fifties. And even then, will this delayed, vulnerable, innocent boy know his mother is gone? The tears started streaming down my face. I could feel it coming on before it started. The thoughts. The fears. The worries that no one outside of this world will ever understand.

Who will steal a kiss every single time he runs by? Who will wipe his face, nose, and bottom? Who will check his body for bumps and bruises? Who will tickle him and tuck him in and check on him? Who will smile at every single train he shows us with excitement? And understand every noise?

I don't care if he's seven or sixty. Even though he will look like a man, Cooper will still be a little boy. And his disability and vulnerability may not be as beautiful as it is now. Someday, to someone, he may be a burden. Wiping his bottom may be gross to someone. His hums, flapping, and squeals won't be smiled at. His obsessive, quirky behaviors won't bring a giggle and a hug.

My son has never been a burden to me. Not once. Not even during all the hardest parts of autism, the anxiety, the sleepless nights, and the behaviors. Keeping him safe, advocating, fighting, and loving him are my purpose. He is my world. But someday, I won't be in this world anymore.

Part of me wonders if Cooper should die a day before me. Can I say that? Am I allowed to? I want my baby to live a long, healthy, happy life. Obviously, that's what every mother wants. But can he live without me and his father? I had this overwhelming feeling that everything was not okay anymore. And now that I knew, now that I had opened up and acknowledged reality, I could never go back to being blissfully unaware.

My words continued to pour out of me into the camera on my phone. *"I try to adequately prepare myself. I think I know what I'm doing. I got this. I take all the precautions; I prepare for autism. We prepare for World War III, we're ready, we go, and then you're standing, waiting to meet Elmo, and you look to your left while holding your sixty-five-pound flailing, screaming, head-hitting child, and you see all the parents in line holding their adorable babies. And out of the corner of your eye, you can see them whispering to their spouses. And I know it's human nature. I would stare too. There's no anger.*

*"And you realize that this is not okay. It's not. I'm not gonna lie to you.*

*"You know, when Cooper was two and three, we could fake it. My son had severe autism. And I cried the whole way to work today because, somewhere in the last couple of months, I switched from praying that he would be a doctor or a lawyer, and now I just know that we are praying for quality of life. And that is such a hard switch. Because you hate yourself for giving up hope, but it is the fact of the matter.*

*"He could be the one in a million. But he's not. And I know that his joy is supposed to be enough, and it is a lot of the times, guys, it really is. But last night I lay in bed and I thought about his funeral. And if I'm gone, and what if no one goes? He's not going to have anyone.*

"*As a mom, to know that he's truly happy, and as I talked to Cooper's dad last night, I told him this isn't okay. And he's like, nope, it's not. And he told me he's afraid of when he's one hundred eighty pounds and kicking us, in line to see Elmo.*

"*I just feel like we're never going to be able to leave our home. The secret world of autism is unbelievable. I sat down last night after just a day of dysregulation and hitting and kicking, and I just thought about when I made that switch from being a blissful, happy parent to thinking about the future in a completely different light. It's brutal.*"

I stopped recording and wiped my tears. For a brief second, I thought about not sharing the video. I had never cried online before, and I wasn't sure if I was ready to share something quite so vulnerable. But I reminded myself that my following was so small that no one would actually see it. I pressed Upload and walked into work.

When I looked at my phone hours later, I had dozens of text messages from friends. The video had gone viral. In just a short period of time, my video had been viewed hundreds of thousands of times. As I scrolled through the comments from my desk, I was blown away by the love and support shining through from strangers. Thousands of other parents who felt the same way as me: alone, forgotten by the world and depleted of strength.

Still, I felt alone. I had hit my bottom. For me, depression was not something I had ever experienced before. Sadness, yes. But this time I was feeling bleak. I had failed my son and family.

That night, Jamie had the boys, so I went home, pulled the curtains shut, and opened a bottle of wine. I was not weak by any standard. I was strong and fiercely independent. So it was hard to admit that I was again hitting such a low point.

My six-year-old son had severe, nonverbal autism. It's the kind of autism that no one talks about. The kind that isolates families. The kind that doesn't sleep. The kind that forces a person to fight for every possible service and basic right. The kind that is completely and utterly depleting. The kind that feels hopeless at times.

As mothers, we're supposed to be invincible. As caregivers, it's even harder. Caregivers are expected to be strong. To be fighters. But caregiving for a special-needs child has given me a depression I don't want to admit is real. Because if I do, I'm showing a weakness, and mothers are expected to put their children first and stay strong. We're not allowed to succumb to the challenges. We're not allowed to show how hard it is.

There are days and weeks when I'm fine. There are days and weeks when it's hard for me to get out of bed. Thankfully I have two little boys who need me to get up, but it's not always easy. People often ask me about how I'm handling Cooper's diagnosis, and I honestly don't have an answer. I survive, mostly. Every few days, there's a new behavior, a new appointment, a new form to complete. I steel myself and do whatever I must, because I love my child with every breath. I would move mountains for him. But I'm not ashamed to admit that there are times when I need a break. There are times when I'm angry. Angry at myself. Angry at God. Times when I ask what I did to deserve this. Why my family?

Depression can make a person feel invisible and alone. I guess that's why I talk publicly about autism. It's why I posted that video of myself crying in my parked car. Some think I'm looking for a thank-you or a pat on the back. But I just need someone to know how hard it is to keep going every single day when all I want to do is give up. And I want others to know they're not alone.

You are not invisible.

The next morning, I sent Jamie a text and asked if he would meet me for lunch. In a crowded restaurant, over chips and salsa, I didn't waste any time. I told him I couldn't carry the weight of our son's disability alone anymore. I had pushed everyone in my life away to focus on autism. I built the wall around me so high and so strong that I was completely and utterly alone. I had made so many mistakes. I had tried to fill the hole in my heart by doing everything I could to help Cooper. Anyone who wasn't on board, I pushed away. I told myself alone was better.

And when I found the life I had thought I wanted, I was more alone than ever. I had completely given up my life to help Cooper, and at the end of the day, he was still severely autistic. And instead of getting better, he seemed to be slipping farther away. I felt like a fool. Because no one believed more than me that I would get him through all of this. That we would come out the other side, fine.

With tears streaming down my face, an action that I never let Jamie see, I waved my proverbial white flag.

And I apologized for everything I had done wrong. But mostly, I apologized for taking on the weight of autism alone, and not being able to fix it.

I told Jamie that for years I blamed him for our struggles and ultimately his reaction to our son's autism. I blamed him because he was the adult, and I couldn't blame a child. I told him I was wrong. And I cried the tears and said the apology that so needed to be said out loud. In a way I felt like everyone had trusted me to make Cooper better, and I had failed.

I told him that I truly believed I was meant to carry our son's disability alone. I wasn't meant to be happy, and I had finally accepted my fate. And the man who shows very little emotion reached across the table and put his hand on mine. Then he stood up and hugged me. And I lost it. I started sobbing in the middle of the restaurant.

For the first time in this journey, Jamie said the words I needed to hear. He thanked me for sacrificing myself for our child. He thanked me for stepping up and fighting when he couldn't. He apologized for not being the man I needed. And he told me that I saved our son.

"But I failed, Jamie. I did everything I could, and instead of getting better, he is getting worse."

"You saved him, Katie. You saved him."

I was at a loss for words. When I found my voice, I asked him why he didn't help me more. He had to have known I was drowning. His response was it was too hard. Too sad. Too scary.

And then it dawned on me that we were on the same roller coaster. He was just dealing with it in his own way. He had never left. I had been too clouded by my own grief to see that. No, he didn't cry as many tears as I did, and I think it's safe to say he didn't worry as much as I did either. But he was there. Through every appointment and every step of the way.

He loved our son. He figured out how to connect with him in a way I thought only I could. He sat with him and watched his trains endlessly. He wrestled him and tickled him. He kept his patience during the chaos. We each played our own roles as parents. I was the researcher and the decision-maker. And the emotional one. He was the one who showed up, calmed us down, and kept us moving forward.

And just like that, the weight was lifted. I let out the breath I had been holding for so many years. He told me he'd do whatever I needed him to do to help. He said I was no longer alone. We would do it together.

The words of validation that I wanted to hear so desperately were finally said out loud. From that moment, and that hug, we began healing, together. We walked back to my office hand in hand that day as different people. That night Jamie stayed at my house with the boys and me, and weeks later he moved in.

I won't say our relationship was fixed overnight. But it felt different this time. It felt like the pressure had been relieved, and finally we were on the same team.

Four months later, as spring settled into Minnesota, Jamie and I took a weekend to get our house ready to list for sale. We had found a bigger home, in a neighborhood full of families, and made an offer. It was dependent on our little home selling. Jamie had me sanding the day away while he visited the hardware store to get paint. The boys were at my mother's house for the weekend so we could get as much work done as possible.

While Jamie was away, I decided to take a little break on the couch and zone out on Facebook for a bit. When I opened up the app on my phone, a sentence jumped out at me.

Your son is better off dead than with a mother like you.

I couldn't possibly be reading that right.

I rubbed my eyes with a closed fist. My vision must have been blurry from the sanding, I thought to myself. I thought it was a mistake. The comment couldn't possibly be for me. Why would anyone wish my son dead? That made no sense. I scanned my eyes down to the comment below it, but it wasn't much better.

Why don't you drive off a bridge. The world would be a better place without you.

Suddenly I felt weak. I kept reading.

Time felt like it had stopped. My ears were ringing, and my cheeks were burning. I heard a hum all around me as if I was in the front of a crowded room in my underwear.

What was happening here? I clearly had made some people incredibly angry. I had been posting on *Finding Cooper's Voice* for a short time and had never received anything like this before. Sure, there was the occasional insult, like when I advocated at the state capitol to save Medicaid and someone called me a freeloader, or when I said we were using medical cannabis and was called a hippy dippy freak. This mama does not shy away from hard conversations and insults, and while there had always been naysayers, none of them ever wanted me dead before. Certainly, none of them wanted *my kids* dead.

People can be so brave behind a computer screen.

As I've gotten more into advocacy, and sharing our secret world, it seems like people don't want to hear about our realities. If I say autism is hard, I'm whining. If I say I worry about my autistic son, then I've lost hope. If I share our normal, I get called negative. And heaven forbid I talk about self-injuring or aggressive behaviors or lifelong care. Then I'm a monster.

Talking only about the positives of autism or parenting or motherhood in general isn't real. It's called toxic positivity, and to me it's doing a disservice. It's important for me to educate and advocate but just as important to not sugarcoat the struggles.

I had to figure out what post was causing this kind of hatred toward me. I thought back to the last few days. Yesterday I shared an adorable photo of the boys sitting in the backyard. The day before that, a video about assistive technology. Nothing controversial in the slightest.

I clicked on the comment telling me I was whining, and reality hit me like a train. These were all tagged comments. Some tagged my personal Facebook page, some my business. And they were all coming from a video of mine. A video on *The Today Show* Facebook page. I could not breathe for a second. Me. I love *The Today Show*! I knew that the *TODAY* Parenting Team was going to share my video but was told that only the very successful ones get shared by the actual *Today Show*. I guess I was successful.

I clicked on the video's still frame showing Cooper and me hugging. After a quick advertisement, the video started playing. There I was, sitting in my car. Gray coat. Bright blue nail polish. My words rang out in my quiet bathroom. "I want to talk about something that I think all my autism parents, um, will understand."

When was this posted? The date said just this morning. A quick glance down showed the video views well over a million already.

I let myself keep going, into the dark, ugly part of the internet. I let the hate wash over me. The threats, the slander. I suddenly felt helpless and small. But mostly vulnerable. Reading about yourself is such a weird feeling. I wanted to scream. These were all lies. I thought, *Do I defend myself?*

Being hated for the way I felt about my son had never crossed my mind throughout any of this. In fact, it never crossed my mind that someone could feel different than me. Because to me, it felt so simple. I loved my son so much. That was number one. I was also sad and heartbroken that he might never talk or live independently. I didn't know that could offend somebody.

When Jamie got home, he found me sprawled out on my bathroom floor, eyes glued to my phone, manically scrolling and refreshing comments. Tears were streaming down my face. He immediately dropped to the ground.

I could barely speak, his concern stirring up the violent sobs I had been holding back. Once I caught my breath, and he confirmed that I was physically fine, I went on to tell him that the video I had made in my car, well, it went viral.

"They shared my email, Jamie, my LinkedIn profile, my phone number, even our old address. If they want to find our current address..." I trailed off. He helped me up and eased me to the couch. He got me a drink of water, although I wished I could have had something stronger.

"Kate, you need to calm down. You need to explain what is really happening here, because you aren't making all that much sense. Who cares if people hate you on the internet? Just turn your phone off. It is that simple. Ignore it. Or take the video down." But it didn't feel simple to me. I thought that as parents, especially parents to kids like Cooper, we were all on the same team. It's not like I expected us to sing "Kumbaya" by any means, but this amount of hate felt unwarranted.

I thought about quitting my Facebook page and blog right then and there. I could shut it all down and never go on the internet again. But then I saw a comment from a woman who said that because of me, and my courage, she didn't feel so alone. In fact, she felt seen and heard for the first time in years.

I took a few moments to laugh about the irony of all of this. The video that people hated me for, that was causing me so much stress at this moment, had actually saved me, because it wasn't until that night that I truly accepted autism was forever and all the things that "may" never happen.

I expected to be depressed for days, even weeks after that trip to see Elmo. But I wasn't. I had spent the last five years fearing the unknown parts of my son's autism. And secretly thinking, *If I do more, it will go away.* I was living in this weird limbo that no one talked about. One where I told myself I'd be happy *when.* Happy when he started talking. Happy when he made a friend. Happy when it was all eventually okay. And because of that, I was missing out on his life.

And in those dark hours, I explored every fear I had ever had for Cooper. I let the unknowns be known. I thought about the worst-case scenarios. I thought about a life without I-love-you's. I thought about lifelong care and what that looked like for our future. I thought about retirement with three rocking chairs on the porch.

After I saw it all flash before me, like a movie of someone else's life, only then did I acknowledge that we would be okay. Because we would make it okay for our son. And suddenly I felt a rush of calm take over my body, one that I hadn't felt in years. Because I was enough. And he was enough. I was going to give him his best life. His autism didn't start one place and end in another. It was woven into him like pieces of light shining through. I vowed to stop trying to change him or fix him.

Instead, I was going to meet him exactly where he was and go from there. I was going to help him and see him and improve his quality of life. I was going to make him happy. Because if he is happy, then I am happy.

The worst day of my life saved me. It helped me to accept reality, allowed me to hope for the things that were within the realm of possibility and not focus on the things that were outside of our grasp. It only took me five years, a divorce, and a breakdown in my car to get there.

I read one more comment before I turned my phone off for the evening.

These martyr moms make it all about them. This isn't her story to tell. It's her son's.

I thought about that statement as I watched my boys play, Cooper lining up his favorite objects, and Sawyer building a spaceship with blue and orange Legos. They were my everything, each perfect in their own way. Neither one less than or more than. But one could speak for himself and one couldn't. One could tell his story and one couldn't.

Had I become a martyr? Jamie may have said yes at certain times. And maybe I would have too. But it was only because I felt like I was dropped into a war zone, fighting a battle I wasn't prepared for. I was fighting for Cooper to be happy and healthy. For him to have a seat at the table like every other child. And for him to have a voice, even if he couldn't speak. The world deserves to know Cooper and he deserves to know the world. Yeah, I suppose I could stop talking. But I refuse to silence severe autism. And my dream is that someday he is able to speak and advocate for himself and looks at me and says, "I got this, Mom."

Until then, I guess I'll just tell my story. The story of a mother to an amazing, misunderstood little boy. And if it inspires just one person, then, well, I served my purpose.

# ELEVEN

While Jamie and I were divorced, I spent many a late night on dating apps, swiping right or left, looking for the perfect man. Dating wasn't really an option because of the insanity of my life, but looking never hurt, and it provided entertainment.

I knew what I was looking for: someone with a good sense of humor, similar interests, a good job. Shared values. Obviously, someone I was sexually attracted to. And deep down, I was looking for something different from the marriage I had left. The stress and the struggles had taken their toll on me. I felt a hundred years old and needed to take back the spice in my life.

In hindsight, I was being ridiculous. I was looking for a fairy tale that didn't exist. A break from reality, as they say, and I was most likely having a midlife crisis and trying to escape. Thankfully, when it was all said and done, I had a man who loved me enough to agree to a do-over.

When Jamie moved into my house, a short time after our emotional lunch together, no one thought we were being impulsive. In fact, everyone was relieved. I was too. Our friends and family even said, "About time." Getting back together, as a family of four, felt like going home. There was no awkward adjustment period.

I smile at what I now think it means to be a good husband, after kids, a divorce, and getting back together. He's a man who puts gas in my car without telling me because he knows I am unable to stop and safely get gas when I have Cooper. A man who changes diapers, slathers butt cream on a rash, gives baths, puts a wiggly baby in jammies, does nighttime feedings, kisses boo-boos, and wipes boogers. I love seeing how he wipes Cooper's face when it's dirty and straightens his waistband and shirt, making sure he looks his best self. He plays trains endlessly and dances around the living room with him. He attends every IEP meeting, makes phone calls to therapists, completes evaluations, and never gives up hope.

He's a man who coaches hockey and baseball and who never misses a single practice. A man who sits in the trenches with me, through the self-injuring, the screaming, the sleepless nights and early mornings, the meltdowns, the hard days that turn into hard months and then years.

These traits may sound silly to some. But not to me. Not anymore. Marriage is hard. Parenting is hard. Choose the person who chooses your kids and family, the person who doesn't leave even when pushed away—even when life gets really hard.

In the weeks that followed, Jamie and I talked at length about what needed to change for us to be successful in our relationship long-term. When we stepped back and objectively looked at the breakdown of our marriage, what we needed from each other was obvious. I needed him to open up to me. He needed me to relax. I needed him to get on the roller-coaster ride of special-needs parenting with me. He needed me to give up some of my control. I needed him to do more. And we both needed to acknowledge our son's disability realistically. The answers to a successful relationship were right in front of us. We just had to act upon them.

We'd been through hell up until this point, and I was pretty sure it wasn't going to end anytime soon. It wasn't like Jamie moving in magically fixed our problems. Cooper's needs were still very significant and seemed to be increasing as he aged. By anyone's standards, our life was hard, and there was no way to snap our fingers and change that.

Every so often, I will see a photo of Jamie and me before we had children. Typically, this is because Cooper has found an old album and hoarded what he could under the couch or entertainment center. I will study our smiling faces, marveling at how young and innocent we looked.

It took us five years to figure out who we were going to be after autism. Some parts we figured out gracefully. Some not. When you have a child diagnosed with an illness or disability, it becomes all-consuming. The diagnosis doesn't just happen to the child. It happens to you and your partner and your other children as well—your whole family. Everything becomes about helping and caring for that child, and that's how it should be. But it's life-changing, and the pressure is immense. It takes time to figure out who you are going to be within that new reality.

Some days I'm amazed at how far Jamie and I have come. We are still standing. We are still smiling. Yeah, we have aged considerably. There is no doubt about that. But we are kinder and more patient. We take nothing for granted with Cooper, not a smile or a wave. We are stronger, and that strength has helped us to give back. We root for the underdogs. We advocate. We speak up about injustices and seek out disabled adults and children to make them feel welcome and seen.

We also know how hard kids like Cooper work to live in this world that wasn't designed for them. So we celebrate everything, no matter how small. Yeah, it's hard alright. I won't lie about that. But it brought so much good into our lives too.

Years ago, when we separated, I thought autism caused our divorce. I was wrong. But, thankfully, autism brought us back together. We just had to figure out how to get on the same team instead of being opponents. As Jamie and I worked on building our marriage up again, from the foundation first, it became obvious to me that he couldn't give me what I needed emotionally. He was a great husband and father in many ways, but anything emotional brought his walls right up. I was puzzled. He showed up, he stuck around, he dug in and never gave up. But worrying about Cooper wasn't in his wheelhouse. A friend of mine recommended I read *The 5 Love Languages* by Gary Chapman. She said it would help me understand the ways that Jamie and I experience and show love differently. She said it wasn't that Jamie didn't love me, but rather he was showing it the only way he knew how. I was fascinated.

After a quick trip to the library, I immersed myself in all things love language and understanding our differences. The five love languages are words of affirmation, physical touch, receiving gifts, quality time, and acts of service. In theory, these are the five different ways a person can give and receive love. That night, Jamie and I took the quiz and compared our answers. I was physical touch and quality time. He was receiving gifts and acts of service. Polar opposites, but very helpful to know. Jamie showed me love by doing the laundry and filling my car up with gas. He was a doer. A fixer. If I wanted this to work, I needed to meet him where he was.

I immediately started including Jamie on all communication related to Cooper. I call it the business side of autism. That included emails, letters, faxes, phone calls, and even texts with social workers, financial workers, teachers, doctors, and therapists. I once counted, and Cooper had over twenty people in his life who required something from us regularly. An evaluation here, a phone call there, and so on. The amount of work to keep the plates spinning was astronomical and very much interfering with my job. I was also frustrated that I was doing it all alone, but in the past, when I delegated to Jamie, he didn't seem to understand its importance. These were Cooper's services and his benefits. It had to be done perfectly or it would set us back. But it was time for me to pass the baton. Jamie started making appointments and phone calls, and he'd bring Cooper to appointments without me as well. There was a learning curve, no doubt, but I was so appreciative to have the help from him.

He came to me one day a few weeks later and threw his hands in the air in frustration. "I don't know how you managed this all by yourself," he said. "This is a full-time job on top of a full-time job." It felt good to be validated. It felt good to have him understand how all-consuming it was.

We also agreed to make big decisions together. One of my biggest frustrations had been that huge monumental decisions always seemed to fall to me. And while I was comfortable flying the plane, I sure wanted a copilot to help me with our directions. I explained that I needed to be able to run everything by him, so if and when it failed, it was a team decision. Having him more involved in decision-making sounds so simple, but it was life-changing for us. We were finally on the same team; we wanted the same things. After our divorce we understood that more than ever.

I have spoken about the isolation that comes with special-needs parenting, the silent killer of many families. Usually, I am referring to physical isolation—being locked in your home with the curtains closed. My girlfriend Jess refers to her house as a tomb, some days wondering if she will ever make it out alive. But there is another kind of isolation that can happen in a crowded room with girlfriends or over drinks with coworkers. It's the isolation of realizing you no longer fit in where you once did. Some women claim they were abandoned by friends after the diagnosis came. It wasn't necessarily like that for me. When

Cooper was born, I had a very tight-knit group of friends, many whom I had known since elementary school. And in a twist of fate, many of us had babies at the same time.

I believe, deep down, I pushed people away, because it was just too hard to accept that our babies weren't going to grow up together. As with my marriage, it was just easier that way.

Before I became a mother, my friends and I were all the same, nothing differentiating us. We graduated, went to college, got married, and got pregnant all on the same timeline. But within weeks of our babies being born, the differences started appearing. My baby didn't sleep. Theirs did. Mine never stopped crying. Their children cooed and smiled. Mine was chronically ill with ear infections and constipation. I never slept. They started going back to normal life. I never did.

I started to slip away, subtly at first. We still frequently got together, but instead of hitting the bars like we did pre-kids, we would get together with kids in tow. The shots turned to a glass or two of wine and somewhat early to bed knowing that our children would be up early. I have so many memories of staying at friends' houses, their kids sleeping, while my son cried all night, often keeping others awake. The morning would come, and I would lie, saying we slept great, ashamed to say what really happened.

Then the differences really started to show in my child. He was no longer just a bad sleeper or a difficult baby. This was more serious. The differences between our children hung in the air while our babies sat side by side on a blanket or crawled around the house. There was no pretending anymore.

We would talk at length about how Cooper was not autistic. We would trade stories of other mothers we knew who went through the same thing...and it turned out to be fine. They were fine. I was going to be fine. This was going to be fine.

But we were wrong. It was autism. And I was completely unaware of the hurricane that would soon consume my life.

My life quickly became doctors, therapies, and IEPs. I couldn't relate to friends anymore. And they most definitely couldn't relate to me. It was like I was in a movie. I watched myself turn invisible in a crowded room full of women I went to high school with. I felt out of place. I felt irrelevant. But most of all I felt jealous, which could not have been more conflicting, because I loved their babies like my own. But I didn't understand why Cooper was chosen.

And as time went on, and their children met milestones, said first words, and learned to use the toilet, I withdrew. I stopped calling. That is the blatant truth. I won't dance around it.

I didn't know how to be a good friend anymore. I ignored calls and texts. I stopped committing to plans because I knew I would just have to cancel.

My world became doctors' offices, therapy appointments, and autism. I once heard through the grapevine that a so-called friend said I gave up on life. I don't look at it that way. I saw it as committing to my son. The weight of Cooper's disability rested solely on my shoulders. It was bigger than me. And so I had to say goodbye to some of the people and things that mattered to me. Right or wrong, I didn't know how to live in both worlds.

I want to apologize to my friends that I unintentionally pushed away. It wasn't you; it was me. It just got to be too hard. By walking away, I let you off the hook in a way.

Thankfully, no amount of pushing worked for many of you. You stuck around. You understood that I was struggling. You kept calling and texting and offering invites. You will never know how much that meant to me.

I look at your kids on Facebook from time to time, celebrating their success from hours away. From a different world, really. I don't want you to ever downplay your child's victories for me. I just ask for compassion if I have to pull away from time to time. Our kids are still young, and the milestones seem small. But I know what the future holds. I know because I've immersed myself in it. And right now, I can't imagine the pain I will feel watching your babies holding their driver's license for the first time, getting dressed up for prom, and signing college acceptance papers. Give me time. I will always be a cheerleader for you and your kids, but I need grace to get there.

Cooper and I are trying so hard to navigate this world and to fit in. Please celebrate our successes too. Like the first time he put his own shoes on or buckled his seat belt, many years after he should have. To me, that was our college diploma.

I've never claimed to do any of this right. In fact, I know I've made a lot of mistakes. I pushed and I pulled. But I've learned a lot too. The good people in your life will stick around. They will never leave.

I am so thankful for the new friends too, ones who walk the same road as me daily. Women I send midnight texts to, who show up with coffee, who I don't have to pretend to be okay with. And sometimes the kindest gestures come from strangers, people we don't know at all, but who recognize themselves in us. The bond of special-needs parenting tying us together.

One of our favorite family pastimes when we were newly married was boating. In the early years we lived near Lake Superior and spent many a weekend on the water. I would fish at first with Jamie but always ended up catching a tan while reading a book.

After two boys, those boating trips changed. Sawyer was a rambunctious kid who wanted to bait every hook and catch every fish in the sea. Cooper, who also genuinely enjoyed being on the water, wanted to throw everything that wasn't tied down overboard. Oh, the things we lost in those days. Shoes, phones, bowls, iPads, fishing poles. You name it, and Cooper has most likely thrown it overboard. But we vowed to make it work, so thankful to have an activity that we could enjoy as a family of four.

On one particularly sunny day, as we were getting ready to dock the boat at a very busy marina, I could feel Cooper's anxiety rising. He was such a runner in those early days. He didn't walk. He didn't mosey. He sprinted to and from. And he was drawn to water, busy streets, even chaos. The hypervigilance needed to keep him safe was monumental.

As we docked that day, my hands reaching out to prevent the boat from smashing, Cooper saw his opportunity and dove onto the dock, sprawling out, his feet dangling over the edge.

My mama instinct kicked in and I dove after him, scraping my knees on the rough wood, and losing one shoe in the process. He was up and running before I even caught my breath. When I looked up, I saw two trucks backing their boats into the water, people everywhere.

I have never run so fast.

With one swift yet not athletic motion, I dove and caught him by an ankle. We both lay there for a second, stunned, sprawled out. As I felt the adrenaline rush through me, knowing I couldn't let go to even reposition myself, a woman walked by me and paused. I saw her shoes first, then her face as she bent down, putting her hand on my shoulder.

"You are doing a fantastic job, Mom. My son is autistic too," she whispered in my ear. "It gets easier, I promise."

I looked up at her kind eyes, tears in my own. She saw me. She knew how hard this all was. She understood.

I'll never forget that lady. While every other person seemed to shy away in the face of a meltdown, this woman walked right into mine. And her *me too* was perfectly timed.

# TWELVE

I was going to be the perfect mother. Well, maybe not entirely perfect, but close. I knew I wanted to be a super involved mom, one that brought her kids to and from activities, and hosted play-dates, and threw amazing birthday parties.

Even before I had kids, I knew what I didn't want to do. I babysat much of my teenage life and I loathed dirty car seats full of Goldfish and fruit snacks, which Jamie and I would affection-ately refer to as "now and laters." I also couldn't stand when kids had crusty noses or drool-soaked shirts. And I would never co-sleep. I remember before we had Cooper, a couple with much older children told us how they played musical beds all night long. That baffled me. Later I boasted how that would never be us. Our kids would sleep on their own, in their own rooms. I had these ideas. But that was before I had kids.

There is a day that is burned in my memory. I remember it like it was yesterday. I was at the park with a six-month-old Coo-per, my little meatball who was just barely sitting up. We were spread out on a blanket, soaking up the unseasonably warm day.

Next to us was a mother and her son. He looked to be around six or seven, in my mind the appropriate age to be well-behaved. The boy would run off and return every few minutes, only one time, the boy started to scream at his mother. I should have noticed that he wasn't saying words, just sounds, and that he was a little bit clumsy. But remember, this was before I knew anything about autism.

I couldn't make out what the boy was screaming about. I just remember his mother trying to calm him down. She seemed so unrattled by his high-pitched screams and his intensity in that moment. The other moms and children around the park had started to stare at her, but she seemed unfazed.

The boy then pounced, fast. He grabbed a handful of her hair, pulling hard. I had never seen anything like it. He was on her so fast, and the clump of hair he held was big.

The mother maintained a level of composure that seemed unbelievable. She continued to speak to him in a quiet yet stern voice about calm hands and taking deep breaths. I probably should have been impressed, but I didn't see it that way.

Instead, I was shocked and mortified. Maybe even a little bit scared. No child should ever behave that way, not ever.

I began internally judging that mother, that boy, no grace coming from me. I remember looking down at Cooper and thinking that I would never in all my days allow that type of behavior. My children would never act like that. I was a good mom. And as I fed Cooper little pieces of cut-up fresh strawberries instead of sugary fruit snacks, I felt confident in my mothering.

*Never* is a funny thing, though. A diagnosis of autism has a way of making you eat all the "nevers" you once thought.

Over time, my confidence started to waver. Cooper eventually didn't want to eat healthy food anymore. In fact, he only wanted to eat five different foods, all from the carb family. He didn't want to go to the park or play with me or engage with anyone.

He didn't learn his ABC's or nursery rhymes or participate in the mommy-and-me classes we joined. Instead, we were asked to not return, the teacher saying that there must be a better place for children like mine.

He hit his head in frustration with his hands and against the wall and floor. He cried and screamed for no reason.

His sleeping didn't get better like I told myself it would. Actually, it got worse. Then we found it was autism. And the curtain was lifted on my plans to be a perfect mother, exposing how much I didn't know and had to learn.

We were judged, and not silently, my mothering on display at all times. The tables were turned. I became the mom I silently judged years earlier, suddenly understanding the battles she was fighting daily, and the child she was trying to protect.

Years later, at a special-needs mom event, I saw the woman again. I recognized her immediately. The only difference was, there was no judgment from me. We were on the same team. As she told her story, she shared the long list of diagnoses given to her son over the years, like alphabet soup. Her son also happened to have ulcerative colitis, causing him to be in pain constantly, something they didn't know about until many years into it. She spoke of his chronic pain, his inability to communicate, and the struggle to get him help.

And she talked about how she blamed herself. I felt the tears roll down my cheeks as she spoke. I had judged a saint. I also thought about how foolish I had been, thinking that the perfect mother was someone who pureed vegetables into homemade baby food and joined the PTA. I learned that perfection comes in all shapes and sizes. We are all just doing the best we can, and in exchange we ask for grace. As special-needs parents, sometimes it feels like the world is against us, or that we're failures. But we have to ignore the stares, go home, cry, and then put ourselves back together so we can continue to be the badass parents who will fight to do everything possible for our children. *This* was the perfect mother, this brave woman, baring her soul. I wanted to be just like her. The bar she set was high.

Once kindergarten was behind us, Cooper made huge gains in full-time therapy. They say people are brought into your life for a reason, and the therapist who became Cooper's lead case manager was phenomenal. She sat me down, just one week after starting in-home therapy, and we made a plan. I told her I didn't care about education right now. I didn't care about teaching him how to read or throw a ball. I cared about making life easier.

We had to focus on safety. His aggressive behaviors were building, and as I watched him grow, I knew I would not be able to handle him much longer. Simple requests seemed to put him into hysterics. If I gave him the wrong food, he would throw chairs. If his video paused, he would throw the player. He developed a compulsive desire to run into the road, which would haunt me. I started having nightmares that I wasn't going to be able to keep him safe forever.

Together, we made a list of goals that included walking safely from the house to the car, requesting with his speech device instead of screaming and throwing, drinking from a cup, trying a piece of fruit, and so on. All things that would significantly improve our life and his.

She also taught me how to work with my son, something that often felt exasperating. Teaching Cooper and motivating him was night-and-day different than teaching and motivating a neurotypical child. She taught me to do first-then as a way to motivate him to do a nonpreferred activity first before then doing a preferred one. She taught me how to use visuals to help him understand what was coming next. She taught me to use timers and lists for everything we did. We practiced turning movies off and engaging in other ways. I focused intently on introducing Cooper to the world around him. I put picture labels, called PECS or a Picture Exchange Communication System, used to help kids communicate, on nearly every item in our house. I encouraged sounds and making choices. I dove in headfirst as a teacher and a therapist. And it paid off.

Within months, we saw huge improvements. I cried as Cooper drank water from a cup, put his shoes on, "spoke" three-word sentences with his speech device. But the safety goals, those were much harder. He wasn't seeming to have any breakthroughs, and I worried greatly he or someone else would get hurt. But I took the wins where I could and felt relief when a spot opened up at his center for in-person therapy.

I felt as if we had made it over the hump, and for a short period of time, I felt a calm that I hadn't felt for a long time.

For all of Cooper's life, I searched for ways to help him, but finding those who would listen, and take on his challenges, felt impossible. I wanted to know why he couldn't talk. I wanted to know why he couldn't sleep. I wanted to know why he hit his head and screamed in pain. I wanted to know if he had a genetic disorder. But getting anybody to listen to me was like pulling teeth. And if they did listen to me, getting them to talk to other doctors and look at Cooper's care holistically was impossible. Until I learned about the Mayo Clinic and their prestigious autism program. The head of the autism department visited the television station I worked for, and because of my affiliation with autism, my boss introduced us. I had been working there for some time now and was very thankful for yet another employer who understood how complicated my life could be. The flexibility they offered me allowed me to work, which continued to be a big part of my life. I quickly gave an overview of Cooper, and she invited us to visit the clinic.

The Mayo Clinic offered exactly what I was looking for. He'd have a lead doctor who would manage Cooper's case and seven appointments with other doctors that would roll up to her for case management. We would visit the clinic four separate times, having two appointments at each visit. The appointments would vary from genetics to neurology to gastroenterology to speech. The lead doctor would evaluate all the information and put together a plan to help my son. It was what I had dreamed of for so many years. I was putting all my eggs in one basket, or hope in one clinic, as they say. Finally, I would find out the answers to my questions. I felt like this was it. I so desperately wanted someone to tell me what to do, and I believed that I had found that. We just had to get through eight appointments first, which for any child is a lot, but for a child like Cooper, it is nearly impossible.

The day of the first appointment, I was practically giddy as Jamie, Cooper, and I packed up to go. We had to drive a little over an hour to get to the clinic, and while Jamie drove, I organized Cooper's paperwork, which would hopefully give their team a glimpse into the life of our son. I had pages upon pages of evaluations, reports, and notes—dead ends, reality, and hope all stacked high in a binder.

Our first appointment was with the doctor who would lead Cooper's team. She was an expert in autism. Only it seemed like she had never met a child with Cooper's kind of autism. As Cooper lined up the chairs in the room, over and over again, adjusting them to be just right, I could tell she was nervous. She didn't seem to know how to interact with him. Every so often he would scream out, upset by the chair configuration, and throw one or two on their backsides. She flinched at every sound he made.

She even seemed nervous to examine him. I watched her take out a light and run it up and down Cooper's body, looking for markers that would indicate a genetic syndrome. Examples are space between his eyes or curvature of his fingers. She found none.

At the two-hour mark in that tiny room, Cooper had had it.

He was trying to escape, beating on the walls. Jamie was trying to manage him, and I was trying to ask the important questions that I needed to know the answers to. I could tell that our time was limited.

"Can he get better? Can he improve? Will he ever learn to speak?"

They came off my tongue fast and quick. Typically, I am not so bold in my questioning, but I also had never been face-to-face with a doctor this important before. I was desperately looking for hope. Her answers were clinical. She didn't coddle me one bit.

"Yes, he can improve with therapy, but children this severe typically don't make much improvement. No, he will most likely never learn to speak. The benchmark is three words by age five. He has none at age seven. I don't see speech in his future."

As she rattled off statistics, I could feel myself withdrawing. This was not the first time I had heard this hopeless prediction of Cooper's future; countless professionals had said the same over the years. I seemed to be searching for an answer that wasn't out there. Maybe it was time to stop searching. To stop looking for those miracle fixes. But I had been searching for so long, I almost didn't know how to stop.

Our time was nearly up, but I had one final question for this doctor, one that Jamie and I had been going back and forth on for months. I wanted another baby. Of course, I was scared and nervous, but I also didn't want fear to rule my life. I wanted my boys to have another sibling. And I wanted to have another baby to love. Jamie was on the fence. We had spent many nights arguing, crying, and debating over whether we should or not.

In our late-night conversations, we went through every possible scenario, some uncomfortable to say out loud. Another sibling with autism, especially severe autism, would put a lot of pressure on our family and Sawyer. Cooper already required so much of our time, and multiplying that by two wouldn't be fair to either of our boys.

We asked ourselves if having another baby was careless. We even discussed what would happen if Cooper hurt a baby, as his biggest trigger at the time was a baby's cry. The discussions were endless and seemed to go in circles.

But I wanted a baby, and I refused to give up. I had done the research, and the odds of having another child with autism were one in five. Those odds did not provide us comfort, but I knew in my heart that no matter what, we would love our baby.

As our time with the doctor drew to an end, I looked at her and said, "We want to have another baby." I don't know why I told her this. Maybe I just wanted to say it out loud to someone besides my husband. I don't even know what I really expected her to say.

I noticed that she looked right at Jamie, not me, and said, "Do not have another baby without meeting with the geneticist first. If you do, this could happen again." She raised her finger and pointed at Jamie's face when she said it, as if scolding him. I thought back to many years earlier, when the audiologist told us Cooper was deaf and Jamie didn't want to get a second opinion because he believed that doctors are always right. Was this woman, with one sentence, ripping away the little chance I had at a third baby?

I reeled back. How could she say such a thing? It felt like she was implying that Cooper's life was not a life worth living, as if we shouldn't have had him either. Very few times in my life have I been at a loss for words. This was one of them.

We were supposed to make our way to the lobby and wait for the next appointment with neurology. We had seven more appointments to attend over the next couple of days. But Cooper was struggling. He was screaming and self-injuring. This had all been too much for him. Jamie and I made the decision right then and there to leave instead. I had come to this first appointment full of hope for answers about Cooper's future, and it was gone. I wanted to bring my son home instead. I didn't want to hear any more.

As we made our way through the never-ending halls of the Mayo Clinic, I felt drained. Cooper did not. He was running and screaming, pushing people, dropping to the ground, and rolling. Finally, Jamie picked him up and carried him the rest of the way through the hospital. Everyone stared at us, but we kept going, our faces made of stone. This was nothing new.

After what felt like an eternity, Cooper was buckled safely in his car seat. It was finally quiet. I had to say my piece.

"That was ridiculous, right? Her saying we shouldn't have another baby?"

Silence.

"I want to have another baby, Jamie. I think she was being dramatic. We aren't going to listen to her, are we?"

I don't know what I expected him to say, but it wasn't what came out of his mouth.

"Don't you force me to have another baby, Katie. If something is wrong with him or her, I will never forgive you. Don't force this on me."

His feelings and words hit me hard. I couldn't believe that I would never have another baby. I felt like autism had stolen Cooper from me, and now another child too. But deep down, I understood what he was saying. Although I would never force him into anything, especially having a baby, I couldn't imagine the guilt I would feel if we had another child with significant needs. He would blame me. And I didn't want that.

I cried the whole night. I grieved for what could have been, what probably should have been. I grieved it all. The next day, Jamie apologized profusely. He wasn't a mean man. I knew that. He was just scared, and I was too. And although his words were rash, I couldn't fault him for his honesty. That's what I had asked for years ago.

If we chose to have another baby, we were willingly choosing autism. We were no longer young, blissfully unaware parents. We were seasoned. And that was a hard decision to make.

Ultimately, after a few more months, we decided to try for a baby. I was pregnant thirty days later. As I watched the little heartbeat flicker on the screen of the ultrasound room, I made a promise to myself. I vowed to enjoy every second of this pregnancy and not worry about things that were out of my control. The next nine months were spent preparing Cooper for a new baby.

In April 2018, our family moved for the sixth and final time. We chose a house big enough for three growing boys in a neighborhood full of children. When we signed the paperwork, I told Jamie he would have to drag my dead body out of this house because I was never moving again.

The day after we closed, our doorbell rang at 8:00 a.m. Two little boys, who I learned were Cooper's age, stood on our porch smiling. "Do kids live here?" one said. Before I could answer, Sawyer ran around me and out the front door. I joke that we didn't see him again until winter. We learned that the neighborhood was bursting with children, enough on our cul-de-sac to fill up a whole school bus. In the home we owned before, the doors and windows were always triple-locked. But we knew right away that wasn't going to work with this house. The door felt as though it was constantly revolving as kids ran in and out, the rooms filled with little voices.

They were mostly there to play with Sawyer, as Cooper of course kept to himself. But they were very curious about Cooper. Their questions were endless.

"Why doesn't he talk?" "What is autism?" "Why doesn't he play?"

I waited for the grief that usually came with those questions, especially from boys the same age. But it didn't come. Something had changed. I welcomed the questions. I welcomed educating them about autism and Cooper. I appreciated the curiosity that came from kids. I learned over the years that adults don't ask questions because they don't want to offend anyone. What they don't realize is in their attempts to be polite, they actually alienate us and reinforce the idea that different is bad. It's okay to ask questions if the questions come from a place of kindness and a desire to learn.

In those first few months in our new home, I saw glimpses into my future, and I'll be honest, it scared me a bit. We had moved to this neighborhood for a sense of community for our family. And we got that. But we still had to keep Cooper safe, and how do you keep someone safe when they have no understanding of danger? We installed an alarm system, alarms on every window and door throughout the entire house, a bell ringing if any were opened. I hated that our house had to be locked up so tight, but the fear was real and we had to protect Cooper.

Jamie fell in love with his garage and spent much of his time building a man cave with a big-screen TV and his favorite beer signs. Jamie is an incredibly social guy and loved whenever a random neighbor would stop by for a chat. This was his dream, and I saw him enjoying it.

As for Cooper, we encouraged him as often as we could to go outside. Our neighborhood was full of trails and even had two parks. But instead of standing or playing near us, he would run in the opposite direction. This is called eloping, and it's very dangerous. He was drawn to the road, to moving cars, and ponds. And he was fast. Often, he would get so far away from our home that convincing him to make the walk back felt like pulling teeth. Eventually, staying inside was our only option. And it typically fell to me. I was his person.

I wish I could tell you that I took it in stride. It was hard watching through the window as Sawyer hit baseballs in a neighbor's backyard or seeing Jamie gathered at the end of the driveway with our new neighbors. I don't know if it was the pregnancy hormones, or the isolation in general, but I felt so lonely in those first few months in our new home. Cooper and I would sit in the living room, he on his iPad, me on my phone, the only sound being the characters on his shows. Glimpses of our future screamed at me. What would life look like after Sawyer and the baby in my belly were grown and living lives of their own? I wondered if Cooper and I would resemble a little old couple, spending our time in silence. Would we take solace in the words that didn't need to be said? I just didn't know.

In October of that same year, our third son, Harbor, named after the city we lived in when we were first married, was born after an easy delivery. So easy, in fact, that my seasoned doctor had to tell the intern that "they aren't all like this."

As I soaked up my last few minutes in the hospital, I was nervous about going home. Jamie and I had made contingency plans for life going forward, but I still didn't feel confident. We had made the tough decision that we would drive everywhere separately until Cooper could learn to be safer in the car. We knew that Cooper could never be alone with the baby, and we weren't sure if the baby would be safe in his crib with the door to his room open. But we were optimists too. I truly believed this would all be okay, because we would ultimately make it okay.

Our plan was to get discharged at 8:00 a.m., go home while the other two boys were in school, and get settled in. But life had other plans. Cooper woke up at Grandma's house with an ear infection, and we had to go straight from the hospital to bring him to the doctor. As we attempted to load him in the truck, he was over the moon when he saw the "It's a Boy" balloons but not as excited when he saw the baby carrier making noise. But we got home, me sitting in between my firstborn and my newborn.

It took over a month for Cooper to touch his baby brother. At first, he wouldn't come near me when I was holding him. But slowly, over time, he warmed up. I'll never forget the first time he walked up to him, and rubbed his fingers through Harbor's hair, laughing at how ticklish it was. And off he ran. For me, that was my sign. It was going to be okay.

Can a baby heal a family? When I was pregnant, and worried, I had no idea of the answer to that question. I was so terrified we were making a mistake, that another baby would be too much. Now I know the answer is yes. A baby can heal.

Harbor has brought so much joy to our lives. He's united our family in a way that I didn't even know we needed. He already looks at his brothers like they hung the moon. He is the brother that both Sawyer and Cooper needed. Sawyer spends so much time kissing him, holding him, and talking to him. He no longer feels lonely. And Cooper—he's been amazing. The aggression we feared never came. He sits near him and tickles him. He grabs Harbor's car seat for me when it's time for us to leave, as if to say, "The baby comes with us, Mama." Now I find our family gathered around the baby at night, cooing at him.

Harbor has added laughter to our home. He even fixed some of the heartbreak that we aren't supposed to talk about, the grief and the sadness that comes with the joy and the beauty of special needs.

Like almost everything else, I don't know what the future holds for these boys. I don't have a crystal ball. But I do know that long after I am gone, they will have each other to lean on. Again, I don't know what that looks like. I don't know if one of them will want to be Cooper's guardian, or maybe they both will be. I know the pressure won't come from Jamie or me, but I am so thankful that the three of them have each other, to be there when tough decisions need to be made. To love each other.

# THIRTEEN

I've heard stories of mothers having to choose between their children. Car accidents, drowning, fire—tragedies where they are put in the position to save only one. In the movie *Sophie's Choice*, Meryl Streep's character is a Polish immigrant after World War II who carries a dark secret: that in fleeing her country, German soldiers forced her to choose between her two children; only one could be saved. It's a choice no parent wants to have to make.

When Cooper was first diagnosed with autism, I decided to attend a support group for moms like me. I listened to stories of worry, sadness, hope, and reality. It was a world completely foreign to my own. I met a mother who told me she had four children. Her youngest, Jenna, had Down syndrome and autism. She was nonverbal like Cooper.

She told me about the choices she has had to make over the years, like the fact that she had to instruct her older three children to leave Jenna behind if there was a fire in the house. "Your sister is not your responsibility," she told them. "I need you three to save yourselves." She was so matter-of-fact in the way she described it to me.

I have never forgotten that conversation. I remember being dismayed. How could she say such a thing? At the time I didn't understand that way of thinking. I want my other children to always look out for Cooper. That's the hope of any mother.

Then I ran into her many years later at another event for our kids. We had both aged considerably. I was no longer the naive mother I was once. I asked her about our previous conversation. Why would she ever tell her other children to leave their sister behind?

Her answer came quickly and honestly.

"My Jenna would never go with her siblings. If there was a fire, she would freeze. She would refuse to move. She wouldn't listen. And they wouldn't leave her behind. And I would lose all my children. The responsibility to save her shouldn't be theirs."

That answer has stuck with me.

Choice.

What a thing.

I couldn't imagine having to protect one child over the other. Or having to make the choice to send a child away. For many families with a child with a disability, this kind of impossible choice is a reality. And it happens more often than you might think.

In some cases, the care of a child with special needs gets to be too much. It gets to be more than a parent can handle as their body ages and isn't as nimble as it once was. As the child grows into the body of an adult, they can be overpowering when they become aggressive or exhibit unsafe behavior. Or, quite simply, the adult child needs a level of care that the aging parent can no longer provide.

I've seen this in parenting groups in real life as well as on Facebook. Parents will choose to place their child in residential treatment for whatever reason. Maybe the child has become violent and they know that putting in the hard work now could bring their child home later. Or maybe, like I mentioned, the parent simply can't manage the care anymore.

These are terribly difficult choices that parents don't often speak publicly about. There is too much misinformation, judgment, and shame, but the experience is real and all too common. Can you even imagine being faced with the choice of dropping your child off somewhere and driving away? I certainly can't. I look at my son, and he is just too innocent and vulnerable. Nobody imagines something so awful until it's happening to them, which is why it's important never to judge a fellow parent who is put in this position. These parents need hope and support, not to be made to feel ashamed for giving up. In fact, their choice is the opposite of giving up; it's doing what they know is in the best interests of their children.

I know there will probably come a time when I'm forced to make this kind of choice. I've always told myself that I will keep Cooper forever. He will grow old with Jamie and me. He will be with us as long as we can keep him safe. That is our plan, and both Jamie and I agree on it. In fact, whenever I'm traveling, the last text I send to Jamie before turning my phone to airplane mode is always the same: "Take care of Cooper." He knows what that means. We should be visiting a lawyer's office soon to talk about forever and put it in writing, but I can't yet. I'm not ready.

When I think about the future, our future, I envision me, Jamie, and Cooper traveling in an RV, visiting every historic train station in the United States, and spreading autism awareness as we go. Two aging parents and an adult child, walking hand in hand. The other two boys will be in college and will visit when they can. At least I pray that they do.

I can envision those beautiful moments because my husband and I have had the agonizing conversations about what retirement looks like. We've discussed long-term care and then lifelong care. We've discussed the financial impacts as well as the housing impacts. We've learned that many retirement communities will allow disabled adult children. I was surprised to learn this—relieved too. But also heartbroken. It was like one of those pinch-me moments. *This isn't real. Cooper will be fine. I'm just being silly researching lifelong care. He won't need it.* I'm nine years in and I still have those moments when I doubt the severity or even reality of our life.

We've even discussed who will care for our sweet boy after we are gone, a boy who may not understand why Mom and Dad are gone. A boy who may not even be able to go to his own parents' funerals. It's so hard to think about. It took us years to be able to have these conversations constructively and without fighting. Neither of us had a crystal ball to see what the future held, so talking about long-term care when our son was only four or five or six felt like we were limiting his potential. One of us would be the voice of reason, saying, "Severe autism isn't going away." The other one would get mad and defensive. Or one of us would start crying because the thought of it was just too much. Talk about an emotional roller coaster.

Later, we'd try again, maybe over dishes, one of us tiptoeing cautiously into the loaded conversation. Only this time it would be from a financial standpoint. Jamie would bring up something he heard about the guardianship process, or I'd share something I saw on the news about a local day program. More arguing. Tears. Lifelong care. It's awful to think about. Those conversations were just too hard before our hearts and minds were on the same page and ready.

These are tough conversations, but they are very important. And if you haven't had them with your spouse yet, I suggest you do now. Set some time aside. Write down your greatest fears surrounding your child's future. There are no right or wrong answers. Then, start talking. Pro tip: sometimes it's best to start over a bottle of wine. It took many years, but now we can talk about almost all of it without crying or fighting.

When Cooper was younger, I would cling to the fact that he wasn't aggressive. He wasn't violent or mean. On our hardest days, Jamie and I would say to each other, "This could be so much worse." The stories I would hear from other parents would haunt me. Kids attacking their moms, dads, and siblings. A simple sound setting them off. A smell. A change in routine. Since I'm a blogger in the autism space, parents send me photos of their own battered and bruised bodies. Even videos of the abuse they receive on a daily basis, abuse they don't dare speak about out of fear, each a desperate plea for help. *"Tell me what to do. No one will listen. No one will help us. The doctors don't care. The schools don't care. I refuse to call the police. They don't understand my child. They will take him away."*

Their homes are on lockdown 24-7. No one is allowed in or out. Locks on the doors, alarms systems, cameras, and fences. I'd hear about siblings having to go stay with grandparents or friends during particularly hard times. *"I need to protect my children,"* the messages always say.

We didn't have that. Not yet anyway.

For many years I felt like we had hit the jackpot. Cooper didn't attack me or his father or his brother. In fact, he mostly just ignored everyone but me. In those early years I called him my little ghost. I knew he was there. I could hear him, but he was a blur. No interaction, just sound. My little blond-haired boy, continuously wandering around, feet paddling up and down the hallways, lining up pieces of construction paper like a treasure trail, all narrated by the sounds of Thomas the Train. Yes, he had meltdowns. What toddler doesn't? Yes, he had challenging behaviors, but those were mostly due to his inability to communicate and were short-lived. As long as I did everything I could to keep him happy, we were fine. I knew what every grunt and point meant, so we could avoid stress. At times I felt like a clown in costume, dancing around, trying to stay one step ahead of his demands and needs.

As he aged, though, it all got harder. He got bigger. He got louder. His intensity and anxiety would seem to flare up in an instant, the list of things setting him off growing by the day. And before we knew it, leaving the house was almost impossible. I felt like I was watching my world disappear. Visiting friends, eating at a restaurant, stopping by a park, or going for a walk... all activities I loved to do were no more. I felt the walls go up around our house. Around our family. The locks went on, the alarms were set, fences were constructed.

We chose safety and with it came isolation.

Some people think we should have kept going out, we should have kept trying—which may be true. But at the time, we were in crisis mode. It's easy to pick up a two-year-old who is upset and remove them from an unsafe situation. But a ninety-pound eight-year-old? That is a different story. Cooper had also gotten quicker to anger and easier to frustrate. The sound of his brother whining, stopping at a red light, turning left, leaving our house, riding in the car, having the lights on or off in our home. I could go on and on. We call them triggers. We tried everything we could to avoid them. But unfortunately, this parenting thing often feels like playing a game you don't know the instructions to. We could only control so much of our son's environment, and obviously it was easier at home.

My hardest parenting day, the day I realized that no one is free from choice, started off like every other.

It is a Saturday at 4:00 a.m. and pitch-black in my bedroom. Suddenly, Cooper is standing on my side of the bed. I always know he's near me before he makes a sound. I can sense him.

As Cooper does every single morning, he wakes me by touching my cheek. When my eyes open, he waves. He gasps and smiles like he hasn't seen me for ages. That's one of my favorite things about him. Every time he sees me after a period of being apart, whether it's thirty minutes or a day, he gasps. It's the best.

He clumsily grabs my glasses off my bedside table and attempts to put them on my face, only they are upside down. Then he picks up my phone and sets it in my hand. He waits.

"Give me a minute," I say, while thinking, *4:00 a.m. No one wakes up this early on a Saturday, dude.*

He waits. I curse my husband and my son and the lack of sleep and roll myself out of bed. I take a quick peek in Sawyer's room…sound asleep. He is my sleeper. I check on our three-month-old baby, perfectly snuggled up. Hopefully, he will be a sleeper too.

Cooper follows me from room to room, waiting impatiently. When we get to the stairs, Cooper bends down and grabs his stack of treasures, which he takes everywhere he goes. Books, papers, photos, mail, DVDs, postcards, usually a hundred treasures or more. Down the stairs we go, treasures falling from the stack.

Every step he drops another thing. Whenever this happens, I always think about Linus from Charlie Brown toddling along.

I just shake my head.

I start the coffee, pee, grab his snack and drink. Every single morning it's the same thing: a bowl of Froot Loops and a Fruit Punch Capri Sun. I set them next to him on the couch, where he is snuggled in with six or so fleece blankets and his treasures. If I don't do it just right, the exact same as yesterday and the day before, he will scream. I do everything I can to avoid the screaming because the other three are sleeping. I know it will start soon enough. The intensity that always seems to be brewing.

Before I can sit down, he is up. He starts his pacing. He winds a continuous path through our house. I used to think it was random, but after watching him one day, I realized it was a path that stopped in almost every room of our house, on repeat.

When I describe my son to new people, or doctors or therapists, I always say he is either sleeping or moving. There is no in-between. He doesn't sit down, rarely enough to classify as sitting. Sometimes people challenge me when I make that statement. They find it hard to believe that a child can go all day without sitting. But it's true. From 4:00 a.m. to 8:00 p.m., Cooper will maybe sit for five minutes two or three times…on a good day. He eats standing up. He watches his programs standing. He has trouble going to the bathroom because it requires sitting.

From the kitchen, I can hear him moving about the house like a little old man. Every light is suddenly on. He roams from couch to chair to office to bathroom to kitchen to living room, his feet padding on the hardwood floor. I hear Alec Baldwin blabbering about Thomas and Percy from his Kindle. I hear grunts and hums and squeals.

Don't believe for one second that nonverbal means quiet.

I can hear him dropping his body to the ground in my office. He loves my office. I hear him rolling across the carpet, banging his feet and hands in unison while humming, laughing, and screaming. I hear his beautiful giggle, which is one of my favorite sounds. I hear picture frames falling from my desk, the opening of drawers and rustling of paper. I know he is touching the carpet to his cheek and feeling the cool of the walls on his hands because I hear his gasp with the change of texture and temperature. I hear a grunt and he is up again. He runs past me, almost a blur. He is in rare form today.

He makes his rounds, a constant path throughout the house. When I finally sit down in my chair with my cup of coffee and grab my phone, I see it's 4:17 a.m. I am exhausted.

I can hear him in the bathroom. I know because I hear him tapping his fingers against the ceramic on the sink. He loves that sound. Tap, tap, tap. He quickly shuts the door. I know he is lying on the floor in the dark, marveling at the brightness of his Kindle screen against the darkness. He loves light and colors. I always say Cooper sees them brighter than we do, almost as if he is separating each one and studying them.

The door opens with a grunt, slamming against the wall. I hear him gathering up his treasures, hands full, I assume. I hear him wiggle the front doorknob, checking to see if we forgot to lock it. If we did, he'd be in the road by now. Of course, it's locked. It's always locked. It's locked in three different ways—the doorknob, a dead bolt, and a flip lock up high on the door—because I know he will figure out each lock eventually. Jamie and I also both wiggle the lock each time we walk by, dozens of times a day. And we remind Sawyer and any neighbor kid who comes by. We made a mistake once and the door was left open. Who knows who did it? Maybe me. Maybe Jamie. Maybe his younger brother. Anyhow, I was folding laundry one morning and looked out the window to see Cooper sitting cross-legged in the middle of the street. His Kindle was in front of him, his arms spread up to the sky. He loves clouds. He looked so calm. There was something eerily beautiful about it. I have never in my life run so fast. I reached him in seconds, although it felt like an eternity, and he smiled at me, gasped and waved, and pointed to the clouds. My sweet, innocent boy had no idea of the danger he was in.

I hear the toilet flush. He must have circled back.

I immediately jump up and run to the bathroom. He likes to plug the toilet with the whole roll of toilet paper. The toilet paper is supposed to be kept in the closet at all times, but sometimes we forget. Thankfully, there is no toilet paper. He was just flushing for fun. He grins at me, and he's off again. I dodged a bullet. We all have triggers, and my husband's is clogged toilets. I'd rather avoid that fight this morning. I sit down again, take a sip of coffee, open Facebook.

And suddenly he's in front of me, my little Casper. I steal a hug and a kiss. He tells me he wants paper and pictures by dramatically pointing to the basement and grunting. This is the part of the morning I wait for. I know it's coming. This is when it turns bad. He believes there is an endless amount of paper and photos in the basement. At one time there was, when we first moved in, but as his obsession grew, we had to rid the house of it. Anything paper, old photos, keepsakes, paperwork, or as we like to refer to it as, contraband, was now stored at my in-laws. Cooper could not take the stress of having it in the house. It upset him very much at the time, and now he remembers and believes it to be there still.

We only recently moved in, and our basement is a disaster zone of boxes and tubs, each one looking like a treasure chest to Cooper. Given the chance, he would spend all his time down there, rummaging through old boxes and bins filled with high school report cards, yearbooks, photo albums, love letters, and scrapbooking supplies. We honestly didn't know he was rummaging, hoarding, and eventually damaging all of our precious memories until I found an old fishing license from 2001 floating around my living room. Then it was a newspaper clipping of our engagement notice and finally a Valentine's Day card from a college boyfriend. Jamie found that one, which was awkward. Anything of value from that point was locked up, like contraband.

I take a sip of coffee calmly and ask Cooper if he would like some pancakes instead. Or juice. I am attempting redirecting. This is what the experts tell us to do. *"Offer something of value."*

He starts screaming.

I know what he wants. He knows I know what he wants. When I don't move, he starts hitting himself in the head. Sometimes he does this. He'll stand right in front of me and aggressively hit himself with a closed fist in his face. Self-injuring is my trigger. I can't take it. But I hold firm. I grab his hands and bring them to my cheeks to cup my face. "Should I put Barney on the big TV, buddy?"

Seeing that he isn't getting anywhere with me, he drops to the ground and puts his feet on my lap, purposefully trying to spill my coffee. Kick, kick, kick.

It's 4:24 a.m.

I set my coffee down and wait it out. I refuse to give him a reaction.

Then he's on the ground, in front of the basement door, his

feet banging on the wall. He knows this will get a reaction from me because his brothers are sleeping, as they should be. And the last thing I want is for them to wake up. He believes I will give in if he is loud enough. So I do what I have to do. I position myself on the ground between him and the door. My chest is now taking the kicks. Not hard, but enough to be frustrating.

This is anxiety. This is ADHD. This is autism. This is our world. From 4:00 a.m. to 8:00 p.m., every single day of the week, for the last however many years. And for however many in the future. This is why at times I feel like an open nerve, a shell of my former self.

I know that he will scream at that basement door on and off for the rest of the day until bedtime. And that wears me down in a way that I can't even explain. By the time my husband and the other two boys wake up, it is 8:30 a.m. I feel like I've run a marathon.

Now that the upstairs is awake, Cooper extends his pacing. Up the stairs, to each bedroom to strip the bed, to the bathrooms to put everything in the bathtubs.

We don't know why he does these things. Some experts say it's a sensory thing. Some say it's a way for him to gain control.

Bed stripping is the behavior that wears on me most as a mother. He will take off the blankets, sheets, mattress pad, and even remove the mattress from the box spring in every room if the doors aren't locked. When I hear the toilet flush from upstairs, I immediately run up and thank God that the toilet paper is hidden.

*Phew.*

I also stop him from putting everything he can find into the bathtub. The garbage, toothbrushes, soap, rugs, hand soap, shampoo, you name it—it all goes in the tub. Quickly and meticulously placed. If the door to a bathroom with a tub is left open, this will happen. Some days, I will admit, I am so worn down I just leave everything in the tub. And I will chuckle as

I bend down to get a squirt of soap to wash my hands or even set my contact case back down in the tub. In those moments I am pretty sure autism has won.

Then it's back downstairs.

Pancakes are made. Cartoons are watched. Little boys are dressed. Cooper is moving the whole time, never acknowledging his brothers. Then the doorbell rings. It's two of Sawyer's friends who have come to play in the backyard.

Bikes are taken out. Rocks are collected. Forts are built.

Jamie and I watch the world outside of our home from the window while Cooper paces inside. He is oblivious to the kids his age playing in the backyard. We rarely mention it anymore, but I know we both wonder at times what it would be like if it was different, if we could all be out there playing football or going on a family bike ride.

We take turns doing our chores and errands. One of us showers, one watches Cooper. One of us takes the garbage out, one watches Cooper. We trade off, the baby in tow. Each of us knows that Cooper needs constant one-to-one supervision.

Later that day, Sawyer and his friends come inside. They are full of mud, cheeks red from playing in the sun. They smell like little boys. They have grand plans. They want to ride their bikes over to the neighboring park.

They are so excited, but I say no this time. I'm too tired and worn down to deal with them going beyond our backyard. Sawyer looks at me and tells me he is going anyway. He marches to the door, puts his hat on, and opens the door to leave. He is acting tough because his friends are there. I recognize that right away, the courage of a little boy with an audience.

From the kitchen sink, I yell for him to get back inside and shut the door. Then I see the blur out of the corner of my eye. Cooper is running, iPad in hand. Barney is singing something about the alphabet. Cooper dives toward Sawyer. He pushes him and jabs him in the underside of his neck. Sawyer's head slams backward into the door.

For a second there is no sound.

Piercing wails immediately erupt from Sawyer, which is Cooper's trigger. He can't handle the sounds from his brother. I see Sawyer's friends standing on the front porch, staring.

I am frozen. Stunned. I have never seen my son attack like this before. Then I am running. I grab Cooper and pull him off Sawyer, holding the collar of his shirt. He has gotten so big that I can't really do much. I can't seem to tear him off his brother. I wedge my body in between them. I shield Sawyer the best I can.

Sawyer is screaming, and I can tell that he isn't badly hurt, but most definitely embarrassed. As I stand there between them, I scream for Jamie. I am thinking, *Where the hell is he?* He appears a few seconds later, and there's a look of shock on his face when he sees two screaming boys and me in between.

"Get him upstairs! Now!" I yell out.

Sawyer is Cooper's trigger, something I have heard from countless parents about their own children. Cooper cannot handle Sawyer screaming. If at any time in his life Sawyer cried or protested or disagreed with me, it would send Cooper over the edge. He would cover his ears and scream. If Sawyer screamed, Cooper screamed louder, which would scare baby Harbor and cause Cooper to scream even louder. Many years later I would learn a story about a family who decided to live separately, the mother taking one autistic son, the father taking the other autistic son. Their children could not be together. I just couldn't imagine that might have to be our life.

Today is different though. Cooper never before seemed to have the desire to hit or push. In fact, I would always say he simply didn't know how to be mean. He didn't have the hand-eye coordination either. Until today.

I am struggling to catch my breath. I am sitting on the floor of my entryway, door still open.

Sawyer is gone. I'm guessing he ran to hide. That's his thing. When he is embarrassed or in trouble, he hides. Cooper is gone too. I can hear him wailing from his room and the muffled sounds of Jamie's voice trying to calm him down.

I pull myself up and smile at the two boys standing in my doorway. I tell them it's okay and that they should go now. In my head I think, *Please don't tell your parents. Please don't be afraid to come over here.*

Once the door is shut, I collapse against it. A dozen more thoughts go through my head. *Why is this happening? Is Sawyer okay? Is Cooper okay? How could Cooper do that?*

The thoughts just keep coming. Until the final one. *What if I can't keep my other two children safe?* What if this keeps happening? What if I can't keep Cooper home? I am going to have to choose. It's happening. This is the moment I knew was coming since the beginning. The one that the other parents told me about.

I get up, walk to the kitchen, and find Sawyer hiding in the pantry. He is just sitting there, hunched over, knees up, with his head tucked inside folded arms. He looks so small wedged in between the giant Costco-sized boxes of fruit snacks and apple sauce pouches. I pick him up and set him on the corner of the kitchen sink. Five minutes ago, he looked like a teenager with his backward hat, asking to go to the park with his friends. Now his face is covered in tears.

As I begin to look him over, he starts screaming hysterically. I wet a washcloth and clean his face. I wait for him to catch his breath enough to get words out. "Why does he do that, Mama? Why? Why did he hit me in the face like that? I didn't do anything wrong." Before I can answer he says, "Make me go away, Mama. Send me away. I know he needs you more than I do. If I go away, then Cooper won't be mean anymore."

And with that, I lose it. I can't believe it, this sweet, selfless little boy. I am at a loss for words. I hug him as tight as I possibly can, the whole time thinking, *I am going to have to make a choice. I am going to have to choose.* And let me tell you right now, in this situation, there is no right choice.

Cooper is my firstborn, the one who made me a mom. He does not speak. He can't communicate pain or fear or wants. He needs constant care and love, attention, and patience. He is incredibly vulnerable and susceptible to abuse of all kinds.

And my other two boys? They are growing up in a world that most know nothing about. I call it the secret world of severe autism. A world where Jamie and I do everything in our power to make it right. And give them a good life.

I would never forgive myself if they grew up needing to recover from their childhood. A memory flashes in my mind, a memory from a party many years ago, long before I knew about the world of special needs and the choices we make. I was drinking a beer with a boy at some college party when he told me that his brother was disabled. He couldn't walk and needed constant surgeries. He told me he hated his parents for always choosing his brother. He spoke of one specific memory—his parents skipping his ski meet because his brother needed them. He said he was still angry about it. Holding my son in that moment, the foreshadowing is not lost on me.

I am suddenly angry. Seething. Angry at this situation. Angry that my child has autism. Angry that he can't communicate what is bothering him. Angry that he hurt my other son. Angry at God. Angry at the world. Angry that this is happening to my family. Angry that Sawyer has to go through this. Angry at the choice I may have to make.

Send Cooper away? Not an option. He's too vulnerable. Send my other boys away? Never. They have done nothing wrong. Nothing at all. I feel paralyzed. There is no right answer. No winning. And then Jamie appears. I ask where Cooper is. He says Cooper is exhausted in his room and resting. I hand Sawyer to Jamie and head upstairs.

As I walk by him, I whisper, "This is not okay, Jamie." I take one step at a time. Slowly. I feel so out of control and helpless. I think about what I want to say to this little eight-year-old boy, who has no words and who just attacked his brother. I have so many questions for him. I want to know why, and how I can help him so it won't happen again. I want to know how to fix it. But I know I won't get any answers. He simply isn't able to tell me, a hard thing to accept. With a typical child, with two brothers scuffling over something, you can reason with them. But this, this is different.

I climb the stairs slowly, flooded with so many different emotions. I walk into Cooper's room and sit down on the corner of his bed. He is huddled under what have to be a dozen blankets, all piled on top of him.

*"Cooper, Mommy needs to talk to you."*

A little tear-stained head pokes out from under the covers. The instant he sees my face, he bursts into tears and starts wailing. He reaches his arms out for a hug. I know him well enough to understand that if he asks for a hug, he really needs one.

This is a part of autism that is often not understood by the world. My son is not cold, or unlovable. He very, very much loves attention and affection. He craves it and needs it. He just can't regulate his emotions sometimes. He can't control his body. And he is trying to live in a world that doesn't make any sense to him.

I imagine what it's like to be him sometimes. Sounds, colors, smells and feelings a million times stronger than they should be, all coming at him at once. Overwhelming him. Now imagine you can't communicate. You have no way to verbally say, "TOO LOUD!" All you can do is scream, which hardly ever gets the reaction you need. And when that doesn't work, what do you do? You act out physically.

So often, we act out with aggression toward those who love us the most, because we know they will never give up on loving us. I will never, ever let another person label my child as a monster. He is trying. And it's my job to help him navigate and understand this world. But he can't attack his brother either.

I can tell that Cooper feels remorse. I wrap him up in my arms and hear him taking deep breaths, as he is taught to do in therapy when he gets upset.

*Deep breath. Deep breath. Deep breath.*

I smell his hair as I am consoling him, rocking him back and forth, like a much younger child. He smells like the wind. His big body is curled up in my lap. I breathe him in deep, to remind myself that this is my boy. My baby.

I feel empty and depleted, numb even. I feel like I don't know this little boy anymore. He reaches his hands up and puts one on each side of my face and presses his forehead to mine. This is one of the ways Cooper shows affection, something fairly new for us. Over the years, showing affection to others hasn't come naturally for Cooper, a very common trait of autism, but in this moment, he must know I need it.

The tough supermommy, who can take on autism and manage a household and have a job and be the perfect wife and mother, starts crying. I can't hold back anymore. Early on, I made a pact with myself that I would do my best to hide how hard this all is from him. My goal was to never cry in front of him, and while I have slipped here and there, today I couldn't hold it back.

What will he do? I wonder. I know I have to talk to him. I have to make him understand how very serious this situation is.

"Cooper, do you understand what just happened?"

Silence.

"I need you to listen to me, buddy. I need you to hear me. You don't have to answer, but you need to listen. You can't hit your brother. Because if you do, you are going to have to go and live somewhere else. And Mommy can't handle that. Do you understand? She can't lose you."

Silence.

"You need to be good. Or you won't be able to live here anymore. Please, buddy. I need you to understand. Because Mommy can't make the choice between you and your brother."

Silence.

I study his face, looking for any response. It is almost as if he is looking right through me. I wonder if he understands anything I am saying. The tears stream harder down my cheeks.

Suddenly, he brings his face right next to mine, our noses practically touching. I can see him studying my tears. He reaches a finger out, touches a tear on my cheek, and brings it to his mouth for a taste. Then he puts his finger back to my cheek, capturing another tear, and drags it up to my eye. Over and over again. He is trying to stop my tears.

Silence.

By this point I am practically hyperventilating. He sees my tears. He doesn't want me to be sad. "Do you understand, Cooper? Mommy can't lose you. Please, don't make me choose. Promise me, buddy, you won't hit again. Please."

Silence. I'm not sure what I am hoping for at this point. I know it will be almost impossible for him to acknowledge my words, but I have to say them out loud in the hope that he understands how important this is.

We sit there for a bit longer, his breathing slowing down, his body relaxing.

I then hug him and go downstairs. I ask Jamie for a moment away. I ask if I can leave. I need time. I back the car down the driveway, drenched in sweat, red-faced, heartbroken, and a little bruised. At thirtysomething years old, my body can't take a good brawl like it used to.

As I drive away, I wave to my neighbors. I smile at happy families in their yards. I wait until I turn the corner out of the neighborhood before I let the tears flow from behind my glasses. I crank the radio up. And I leave it all behind. The aggression, the fear, the choice that we may have to make. I drive, going nowhere really. I let myself feel out of control for a while, and let the dark, scary thoughts consume me.

I let myself wonder why and how. I think about full moons, changes in routine, medications, and the mystery of autism: all things that the professionals and other parents will say cause aggressions and none of which provide me any comfort. In fact, I feel exhausted trying to figure out why. Honestly, I don't want to do it anymore.

I let myself think about how we got here. Right here, to this very moment. I let myself cry, be angry and worried. I think about group homes. I think about my vulnerable, sweet boy. But mostly I think about Sawyer. He didn't ask for any of this. Hell, I'm the mom, and this is more than I know how to handle. How will he ever make it through?

I pick up the phone and call a friend. She is the only person I know who won't judge me and who will understand. And she does. She listens without judgment. She lets me cry. She lets me say that I can't do this anymore. That I can't choose. That this isn't fair. She shares her similar story. She sent her other children to stay with grandparents while her son had similar issues. She lived the same life. And suddenly I'm not alone.

As I pull back into my neighborhood, it is nearly dark. I see kids playing tag. Some are riding bikes. I roll my window down as a few wave and shout, "Hello!" I see people gathered at the park a block from our house, babies in strollers, dogs chasing balls. I live here, in this neighborhood. Suburbia. Every family is much like ours. We all work, mow our lawns, and barbecue on beautiful days. On the outside, our house looks like every other house on the block. On the inside, it's different.

As I turn the corner, I see a group of boys, Sawyer included, using up the last few minutes of sunlight to play catch in our driveway. He must feel better. I wonder if his friends asked him about his brother or if they pretended it never happened. I try to imagine what he'd say if they asked. Would he talk about autism like we've taught him to?

I study that very brave little six-year-old boy with the backward baseball cap on, the one who an hour before said he wished he could be gone so his brother wouldn't hurt us. I watch his peers too, all of whom are laughing. And I think about the secrets we keep behind closed doors. The choices that families like mine have to make.

This day was my hardest parenting day so far. It was so much more than two brothers fighting. Instead it was a glimpse of the future. It was a reminder that autism doesn't go away. That little boys become big men. And that I too am getting older. It was a realization that I may not be able to do this forever.

As I sat there in my driveway, not really wanting to go in, I let myself consider the fact that maybe I had been a little delusional up until this point. I know my son is growing up. I know he's getting bigger. I know it's only going to get harder. But I always thought I could manage it. I could do enough and be enough to make it work. If I was a good enough mother, the best mother, I could make this work. Love would be enough to overcome the hard parts of autism. Only, I was wrong. Sometimes love isn't enough. What am I going to do when he's twenty years old and two hundred pounds?

I think about my own mother now. She's almost seventy. She spends half her time in Minnesota and the other half at a retirement community in Texas. She does pool aerobics and golfs with my dad. They are living the second half of their lives. The golden years. When I am seventy, my son will be forty-three. He will be a grown man, but he will be living with us. I'll help him get dressed and feed him. I'll wash his hair and his feet. Jamie will shave him. I'm sure I'll take him to some sort of day program, but otherwise he will spend his time with us. I know it won't be easy. I gave up the hope of easy a long time ago. But I still believe I can do it. We can do it.

Is it so wrong to believe that? I spend my energy on social media sharing the beautiful parts of severe autism. I show our family—all three boys, my marriage, our home and how we integrate in the community. I show the real sides of severe autism. And let's be honest, it ain't all pretty.

I share because the word *autism* can be terrifying, especially when it's written on a piece of paper about your beautiful three-year-old child. I want to show the parent of a newly diagnosed child that it doesn't have to be quite so scary. Yes, there will be hard days. There will be so much good too. But I also don't lie or sugarcoat it, because what good would that do for anyone?

I talk about the future when I can, and I pray that I am doing the right things. I want to believe that we are going to be okay. That Cooper won't get aggressive and that he will be able to live with Jamie and me forever. He can watch his iPad while I do pool aerobics and ride in the golf cart while his dad golfs. I want to believe that the world will accept autism and people with differences. I want to believe that my son may talk someday. And make a friend. And graduate from high school. But most importantly, that I will always be able to care for him. I don't want to dwell on group homes or lifelong care or even nursing homes. I thoroughly enjoy my delusional life. It's pretty great here. But this day changed all of that.

It was silent when I walked back inside and for much of the rest of the night. Cooper slept the rest of the day and night, all snuggled up in his bed. Those episodes really exhaust him. Me too. I call it the post-meltdown hangover.

Jamie, Sawyer, the baby, and I sat on the patio for what felt like hours that night, watching the sun go down and talking about the day. It's something we wouldn't have been able to do if Cooper was awake. Too dangerous. But we were able to sit outside the walls of our house, as a family, minus one, and relax.

We talked about the realities of autism with Sawyer. But we also talked about how we would always keep him safe. And we reminded him that his feelings matter. He asked again why his brother hit him. He asked if it was going to happen again. We spoke with him about Cooper's triggers and how loud crying is really hard for him. We told him to imagine that every sound was at maximum volume. We asked him how that would feel.

We talked about scenarios and therapies and how hard we are working with Cooper.

A lot of families hide the realities of autism. They don't talk about it. I have a friend who whispers the word *autism* in front of her other children like it's a dirty word. We don't hide it here. We have talked about it since day one. We do that to normalize it. We do it to help Sawyer understand and because we don't want it to be a secret. Or shameful. Cooper is Cooper and his beautiful parts by far outweigh his hard parts. That's what we need to remember.

So we talk as a family about autism. I don't want autism to be whispered. I want it to be said out loud, with conviction.

After our boys went to bed, Jamie and I discussed what had happened. We both said we must do better. We need to recognize the triggers and signs faster because this is on us. We are the parents. We cannot allow Sawyer to be hit by his brother. Not now and especially not when he is older. We spoke about the choice we may have to make. It was strained and we felt terrible.

We spoke about a story that had been on the news recently of two significantly disabled adult women being sexually abused by a male caregiver in their group home. No one knew for months. It only came out because one of the women got pregnant. You could feel the stress in the air as we thought about Cooper in a similar situation.

How could we ever make the choice of sending our boy away? We spoke about living separately, maybe having two houses. We spoke about emptying our savings to pay someone to always be here with Cooper. We talked about loading Sawyer's schedule up with sports and camps and playdates—anything to keep him out of the house. We talked about counseling for him as well.

We mostly sat in silence, thinking about how we got here. We prayed it was a one-time thing. We prayed that it was over and that it would never happen again. It wasn't though. Cooper had another meltdown a few days later. A worse one. This time I was home alone with the three boys. Jamie had to run a quick errand, as he should be able to.

It was a weeknight, a good night. I had just finished cleaning the kitchen after dinner. The two younger boys were sitting at the counter. Cooper was pacing. I noticed he was carrying my mail with him. I always find that funny, him carrying his medical bills around. I tell him, "You touch them, you pay them." The joke is on me, though, because he always seems to lose them. Weeks later I find them mixed in with other treasures under the bed or behind the entertainment center.

Sawyer and I were chatting about homework and movies. He wanted popcorn first, then movie, then homework. We were going back and forth. He tried to negotiate a little too loudly and when I said no, he turned to protesting. He's six. He was doing what six-year-olds do. Cooper couldn't handle it. He can't handle his brother yelling. He got upset. I could see all the signs brewing, clenched fists, heavy breathing, screaming, ear covering.

I did what the therapists say to do. I told Sawyer to calm himself because I can reason with him. He did. Then I ignored Cooper's behaviors. I redirected. I negotiated. I even tried to bribe. I asked him if he wanted to do a few puzzles, or have a snack. Anything to stop the inevitable. But he was too far gone. I couldn't pull him out. Cooper's meltdowns are like a snowball rolling down a mountain. Slowly at first, then it picks up speed, then more speed. If it gets going too fast, there is no stopping it. The key is to stop it before it gets out of control.

For the next twenty-five minutes, he raged. And I chased. I

did everything I could possibly do while he destroyed my house. He threw chairs. He picked up the vacuum and threw it into the living room. He slammed cupboards. He swept everything off the counters onto the floor. I had a bouquet of flowers from my mother-in-law on the kitchen table. It was a gift for being such a good mom. He obliterated them. There were petals everywhere.

I couldn't stop him. I felt like I was just reacting and not getting ahead of him. It's a very frustrating position to be in, one step behind.

I tried to get him upstairs to his room, to remove him from the situation. But I couldn't. He was too big, too fast. I could not force him up the stairs. The two little boys sat at the counter, watching. Once he was in full rage mode, he went for Sawyer. He pushed him in the face, not physically hurting him, but antagonizing him.

So I wrapped him up in a bear hug, just like I was taught to do, right there on my kitchen floor. Sitting behind him, I wrapped my legs around his waist and held his arms and head safe with my body. And I whispered in his ear.

*"I love you. I love you. I love you."*

We do this so our children don't hurt themselves. We sacrifice our bodies for our children. That's motherhood. I would rather have him hurt me than himself. Even though I was holding him, his thrashing was scooting us along the slippery hardwood floor. His flailing legs sent the garbage can flying. Cupboard doors banging. Rugs sliding. All the while Cooper was screaming and I was whispering in his ear, "Breathe, buddy. Breathe." I tried to keep him safe, and to protect myself, my other boys, and my house. Only I couldn't contain him. I wasn't strong enough.

For a brief second, I thought I lost control. I made eye contact with my baby, Harbor, who Sawyer was holding in the living room, both crying. As my firstborn raged, head banging into my chest, I looked at these two little boys watching us. I was failing. I couldn't keep anyone safe. I thought, *Who lives like this?*

I sent Sawyer and the baby into the office while I waited for Jamie to return. I told them to lock the door. Sawyer didn't protest. When Jamie got home, it looked like our house had been vandalized. I was still holding Cooper's body with the little strength I had left. He was exhausted too, so we were basically lying in the middle of the kitchen floor. Every so often he'd throw his head back into me. But I never stopped whispering in his ear that I loved him. And for him to come back to me. I knew he was in there. I just had to wait.

Jamie took one look around at the garbage all over the floor, flower petals scattered around, knocked-over chairs, and me, holding his ninety-pound son.

Jamie picked up Cooper and carried him upstairs. I just sat there for a brief second, stunned. I looked around and thought about what just happened. I ran to my other babies. They were sitting on my office floor, playing and giggling. In that moment I felt like I was straddling two entirely different worlds. Only I couldn't figure out where I belonged. And I couldn't figure out how to bridge the two together.

That night I realized my worst fear had come true. We weren't spared. We weren't special. We didn't hit the jackpot. All the stories I had heard over the years, it was happening to us now. I felt paralyzed by it. There was no one to help us, no one to talk to about it, no parenting books or advice blogs. It was just us, figuring it out.

"Mama, how do we know that Cooper loves us?"

The question came seemingly out of nowhere. Such a heartfelt question from a little boy.

I pulled Sawyer onto my lap and held him tightly, breathing him in. As I snuggled my face into his hair, I tried to remember the last time I held him like this.

"How do you know he loves us? He can't even say it…and he sometimes gets so mad at us."

We were going through a hard time. There was no denying it.

I went on to explain all the ways one can show love without words.

"Sawyer, every night since we moved in, Cooper has slept in your room. He has his own, but he chooses to sleep on the trundle bed next to you. That is love."

Just a few feet away from us, tucked into the corner of the couch, were a hundred or so random items, Cooper's treasures. It was like a nest. I walked Sawyer over and asked him to look through it.

He separated the items into piles. Magazine pages, books, DVD cases, playing cards, pieces of our mail, and one photo. In it, two brothers were hugging each other tightly, both smiling huge grins.

I watched the realization wash over Sawyer's face as he studied it.

"Love doesn't have to be spoken, Sawyer."

And then I told him my own story of love for his older brother.

"I fell in love with Cooper the second he was born, just like I did with you and Harbor. But with you and the baby, you loved hugs and snuggles and kisses. You both want endless attention and affection. Cooper has always been different in that way. He likes his own space.

"In the beginning, I didn't know if he loved me. I worried he didn't. And then one day, at age four, he touched my face for the first time. I thought my heart was going to burst. And then, when he was six, he kissed me for the first time. Waiting for those things was hard on me. I won't lie. Even today, I can count on one hand the number of times your brother has independently shown me affection. So when he hugs you, Sawyer, know that he truly means it. His love is not thrown around. It is only given to the ones who really deserve it. Treasure it. And give him extra in return."

I'm not sure if that pep talk was more for me or for Sawyer. I think we both needed it. For all of Cooper's life, I have said

*I love you* every time he leaves for school, every night before bed, and at other times throughout the day. He has never once said it in return. He has never signed it or typed it to me either. But I know he loves me. I feel it when he looks at me, when he snuggles into me on the couch in a rare moment of wanting to be touched, and when he searches for me in the house or in a group of people. I know I am loved, and it is my job to make sure that he knows that he is loved too. That's why I say it to him so often. I say it so he knows without a doubt that he is treasured and safe. And I smile as I imagine the day he says it back to us.

# FOURTEEN

*"My son makes fun of the autistic kid in his class and it's hilarious."*
With those words, the entire table went quiet. You know that phrase, *You could hear a pin drop*? This was one of those moments. I was sitting with four of my coworkers in the lunchroom on a slow afternoon, enjoying a cup of coffee and conversation. All five of us were mothers, and we were laughing about the drama of little girls and the chaos of little boys.

At first, I thought I must have heard her wrong. No grown adult would ever say something like that publicly. Or be proud of it. I know bullying happens in children. I am not naive. I know kids get teased for all sorts of things—their clothes, weight, glasses, or braces. I can still remember standing in line in gym class, waiting to go to lunch, and being asked why my jeans were so short. I looked down, confused, never having noticed the length of my jeans before. For the next week I was known as Highwater Kate. I can laugh about it now, but I was humiliated at the time. Kids can be so cruel, that I know. But what I didn't know is that adults can be cruel too. Sometimes, they find the bullying funny. They promote it, they laugh about it, and they even brag about it over a cup of coffee with friends.

*"My son makes fun of the autistic kid in his class and it's hilarious. He has the whole act down. He covers his ears and repeats sounds and even does a hand twitch. He has the flap down perfectly."*

My stomach dropped. My son has autism. He covers his ears and repeats sounds and twitches his hands. He flaps too.

The other women at the table and I stared at her, speechless. I waited for her to backtrack. I had assumed that everyone in this group knew about Cooper, not that it should matter. "Oh, he doesn't do it in front of him," she added, as if sensing our disapproval. "He just does the routine at home for us. He'll put on quite the show in our living room. He'll climb on the coffee table."

She quickly clarified, "The boy doesn't even know he teases him."

I guess that was supposed to make it better. I could tell she wanted us to understand how funny it was, so she actually mimicked the hand motions that the boy made. Right there at the table. I watched, mouth hanging open, as she flapped her arms like Cooper does when he's happy and excited.

I have always loved Cooper's flapping. It's part of who he is. If he is flapping, it means he is happy. But watching this lady do it, I felt sad about it. I felt embarrassed. Then it dawned on me, not only does her son make fun of the autistic boy in class, she does too. A grown woman. A woman with children. A woman raising children who will in turn go out into the world and have children of their own.

I didn't know what to say in that moment. We always think we are going to educate in the face of cruelty or advocate in the face of bullying. But I was frozen.

Once she realized that her audience didn't find it funny, she excused herself and left the lunchroom. I sat there stunned, as did the other three women. Finally, one of them broke the silence. "I'm so sorry she said that, Kate. I don't think anyone will ever tease Cooper like that. He doesn't look autistic."

I mumbled a few words and excused myself as well.

That night I found myself studying my own son. At nearly six years old, he had thick blond hair, choppily cut from a home haircut. His skin was like porcelain, his eyes a ruddy hazel with bits of red. He sat in the middle of my living room, surrounded by hundreds of his treasures. Ten or so fuzzy fleece blankets made a nest closest to him, and pieces of paper, books, photos, and DVDs completed the next layer. I could hear Barney singing on his Kindle. We have been watching Barney since he was nine months old. I knew from watching my friends' kids that Cooper should be into *Star Wars* and Ninja Turtles by now. He should be loving Nerf guns and Legos. But instead it's pieces of paper and Elmo. We are frozen in time. If his pants weren't getting bigger, I would think maybe time forgot about us.

The words from my earlier conversation rang through my head. *"He doesn't look autistic."*

What does autistic look like? Does it have a look? When he was two and three, Cooper looked like every other toddler, and people would bestow on us the kindness that all toddlers receive—a smile, a wave of the hand. But as Cooper has aged, people aren't always so nice. A child melting down at six is a lot different than a child melting down at two. And Cooper is going to be exactly who he wants to be no matter where we are and who is watching.

At times on this journey, I have thanked God that Cooper looks like his peers. That he doesn't have a physical disability that would make life even harder. But as he has aged, it's become obvious that visible signs of differences can bring grace too. A friend of mine once told me that strangers were incredibly rude to her autistic teenage son until he started riding in a wheelchair. Once he had the chair, and the high need was visible, people were kinder. I don't know if that is true or not, but what I do know is that people expect Cooper to act his age. And when he doesn't, they can be cruel.

I didn't say it to the group of women, because, well, it wasn't worth it. But Cooper has been teased before. And like the boy in that woman's story, he had no idea. We were at a local park and he was running around, carefree. He loved to watch the swings go back and forth. Not so much get on them, just watch them. As the chains moved, they squeaked. With each squeak, Cooper would flap his arms in excitement. The sound coming from his mouth was that of pure joy. To others it might have sounded obnoxious, but not to me.

When he was younger, long before we knew it was a sign of autism, we would say, "One day he is going to flap right off the ground." Flapping also told us when he was happy.

As he jumped up and down, watching the swings, a group of boys, not much older than him, took notice. The apparent leader of the group got very close to Cooper and said, "Hey, boy." Cooper paid no attention whatsoever. He was totally committed to his swing-sound joy. The boy repeated his hey one more time, and then turned around to his friends and started flapping his arms like Cooper.

The group of boys burst into hysterics. I watched, frozen for a second, waiting to see if one of the boys would say something, like ask the kid to stop. It was total sheep mentality. Within seconds they were all flapping and pointing.

Cooper, suddenly aware of the laughter, turned around, saw his audience, and turned back flapping harder. He had no idea they were teasing him. He didn't care that they were teasing him.

I suddenly saw red. It took everything in my being to not charge those boys and plow them over, scoop up my Cooper and run away. I calmly began walking over, trying to compose myself, thinking of the right thing to say. Once the leader saw me approaching, all the boys ran off. They knew they were being jerks.

Once I reached my son, I bent down next to him, taking in the magic he was supposedly seeing. His face was full of wonder as I gave him a squeeze and whispered in his ear, "Hi, buddy!" I stood guard for the next hour as Cooper enjoyed the swings and the many kids who used them, letting his joy wash away the cruelties of the world.

On the ride home that day, Sawyer asked me why I was protecting his brother. I explained that because he had autism, he needed a little extra help. Sawyer knew what autism was. We have always spoken about it openly in our home.

"Mama, can I have autism too?" As the words filled the car, I gasped. I immediately pulled over and turned to face my four-year-old in his car seat.

"Mama, I want to have it too. Then you can watch me at the park. And I can play with Cooper because we'd both have it."

I cried in that moment for so many reasons. I cried for the little boy, Sawyer, who was jealous of his brother for having autism. I cried because they should be playing together. They should be running and jumping and swinging and sliding together. I cried because Cooper was teased by boys who might have been his friends under different circumstances. But mostly I cried because the world is such a cruel place to anyone who is different. And there was nothing I could do to change that.

That night, as I vented to an old friend about what had transpired, the boys teasing Cooper, she asked me a few questions. "But was Cooper happy playing with the swings?"

"Yes, but he was being teased," I responded.

"But did it affect his joy at all? Did he stop playing?"

Her point hit me like a freight train. She was right. Cooper doesn't care what others think of him. He doesn't lose sleep worrying that kids his age don't like him. Instead, he finds happiness where he can. There is a lesson to be learned in that.

I once heard a story about a man in government who adamantly voted against benefits and resources for people with disabilities. He was quoted saying, "Who cares if they learn to roll over or drink from a cup? What does it matter?" Before I had a child with a disability, I probably wouldn't have paid all that much attention to that senator's statements. I will even admit I probably judged people who needed help to raise their kids and used government funds to do so. I was ignorant. I didn't know because I had never lived it. That is, until Cooper. Having a child with significant needs humbled me. It stripped me bare. And the me that once refused to ask for help began doing so.

No one is safe from disability. It knows no gender, no race, no socioeconomic status. Anyone can get hurt at some point in their life. Anyone can have a baby who has special needs. I am not saying that to scare anyone, but instead to make a person think before judging others. According to a new report from the Centers for Disease Control and Prevention, one in six children age three to seventeen years have a developmental disability, including autism and ADHD. That number is astounding when you think about it. These children live in your neighborhood. Their parents are your coworkers and your friends. Yet many people claim not to know a person with a disability and therefore may wonder why parents like me speak out so passionately. I don't do it just for Cooper. Heck, half the things I advocate for—safe transportation, housing, fair wages—he may never even use. I advocate because when you advocate for one child, you are advocating for all of them.

I heard many years later, in a random twist of fate, that the senator's wife was in a car accident and lost the use of her legs. He left politics to help care for her. I assume that was hard for him, as it is for many parents with children with special needs. It's not only a loss of income but a loss of identity too. The shift from spouse, child, or parent to caregiver is a life-changing one that rarely gets the emotional support it deserves. I think about that man every so often, how maybe he would have felt different in the beginning about helping people with disabilities if he had heard the stories of people who live it every day. This is one of the reasons I tell our story.

★ ★ ★

A few years after Cooper was diagnosed, I went to my local grocery store, rushed after a long day of work, and anxious to pay for my groceries and get home to my boys. As I stood in the checkout line, I noticed a group of folks in bright orange shirts bagging groceries. I knew instantly that they were like my Cooper. I heard the sounds and I saw the mannerisms. I was no longer blind to this secret world because I now lived in it. I watched the young gentleman at the end of my line intently. He picked up each food item slowly, lifted it to his eye view, studied it, and eventually placed it in the bag. He was doing a wonderful job, but he also wouldn't have won any awards for speed. I broke out in the biggest smile as I watched him clap for himself. If my hands weren't full, I would have clapped for him too.

Suddenly I had flashes of Cooper working or volunteering at a grocery store just like this one. And I wished I could talk to this young gentleman's mom and tell her how proud I was of him. I was rudely pulled out of my daydream by a man behind me. He was muttering under his breath, but I wouldn't say it was quiet.

"Hurry up. I don't have all day to watch these retards."

I immediately spun around to face the man. Thankfully, others in the line were appalled too. Before I could speak, another woman beat me to it. I've never seen a face turn quite so red before as he took his verbal tongue lashing. I turned back quickly to make sure the young man didn't hear. He was whistling away, packing away groceries, oblivious to the hate that was just spewed his way.

In that moment, right then and there, I vowed to change the world for my son. I felt the flame inside me burn brighter. I had been blogging for years at this point, with some success, but it was time for more. I didn't necessarily know how. I didn't have some grand plan. I just knew I had to make the world a better place for him. Because someday, he would be out in the community just like this young man. And I needed people to understand, to open their eyes to differences, and ultimately to be kind.

I soon started public speaking on behalf of those with disabilities and their families. I visited the state capitol building in Saint Paul and spoke with our governor and senators. I made phone calls and wrote letters. I joined other groups advocating as well. I started conversations about autism whenever I could.

And I shared Cooper. I shared his wins and his struggles. I shared his sounds, his hoarding, his joy, his anxiety. I did everything I could to normalize his differences in hopes that I would reach that awful man from the grocery store, and every person like him.

For years I didn't know if it was working, until I received an email from a woman in her seventies who lived in the southern half of the country. She told me she knew nothing of autism before discovering *Finding Cooper's Voice*. She was fascinated and touched by my stories, the highs and the lows. But she admitted she was confused as to why Cooper acted the way he did sometimes. One day she saw a grown man at her local grocery store. He was covering his ears and flapping. He never spoke a word, but he also never stopped making a sound. She stated she knew he was like my son and felt a protectiveness for him. A few of the women in front of her started criticizing him, not so subtly, for being loud. And ultimately for being different. She told me she let them have it. She laid right into them.

As I read her words, I knew I was doing the right thing. I have never been so proud to receive an email before. We had touched a person who knew nothing of autism and brought kindness to their heart for people with differences. That had been my goal since day one. If I can educate one unknowing person, remove the stigma of the diagnosis, or lessen the fear that a parent feels when they hear the words, *"Your child has autism,"* then I am doing the right thing.

# FIFTEEN

In the days that followed Cooper's increase in aggression, Jamie's parents invited us over for a Sunday afternoon dinner. The time we spent at their house was very therapeutic for us, and I don't know if they will ever understand how thankful we were that we could go there and relax. Being around people who loved and accepted us was exactly what we needed during our hardest days.

When we arrived, we were pleasantly surprised to see that friends of Jamie's parents would be joining us, a delightful couple who had been in Jamie's life since birth. Only, this wasn't the couple he had known all those years ago. The husband, Thomas, a teacher by trade, had been diagnosed with early-onset dementia years before. His mind was drifting away. His wife, Anne, a strong, loving, positive woman, had stepped into her role of caregiving with grace. I can imagine a diagnosis of dementia, especially at such a young age, felt unfair, like they were being robbed of their future together. I wondered if Anne had gone through the same cycle of grief as me.

I spent much of the afternoon in the kitchen with the ladies, Cooper, and Tom. Jamie and my other two boys were outside enjoying the sunshine. As we sat and chatted, I mentally noted the similarities and differences between Cooper and this man, seventy years his senior. Tom was tethered with an invisible cord to Anne like Cooper was to me. If she moved, he looked for her. The same with Cooper.

Tom sat silently at the table next to his wife, never moving once. He seemed unaware of the conversation happening around him. Anne shared that every day he seemed to have fewer words than the day before. She knew they would soon be gone. Cooper, also oblivious to the conversation around him, was the exact opposite. He ran throughout the kitchen, from wall to wall, bouncing and rolling. He would run to me every few minutes, grab my arms, demanding something nonverbally, and scream. I would calm him down, reassure him that we would be going home soon, and then he would run off again, only to return minutes later. Cooper's anxiety was overtaking him lately. Before I had Cooper, I didn't know children could have anxiety, but I know now they can. And there is a fine line between happiness and anger when anxiety is involved. The things that should bring joy—seeing trains, going swimming, being with family—often caused him so much excitement that it would eventually consume him, the anticipation too much, bringing him and us to our knees. Watching him be robbed of joy killed me as a mom. I spent much of my time in these days riding the wave of his emotions and trying to keep him even. I mostly failed.

Anne spoke of similar struggles with her husband—his loss of skills, his increased anxiety. How he couldn't be alone for even a second. The parallels were there. And just like Anne was her husband's person, I was Cooper's. Jamie was a wonderful dad, I knew that, but Cooper came to me for his care. I understood him on a deeper level, and words weren't needed for us. In a way, I felt like I could read his mind. There is so much beauty in being someone's person, but there is also so much pressure. I wonder if Anne ever felt that way.

During dinner, I cut up Cooper's food. Anne cut up her husband's. I fed Cooper. She fed Tom. I wiped Cooper's face. She wiped her husband's. I took Cooper to the bathroom. She took Tom as well.

As the day came to an end, Anne pulled me aside and commented on the parallels between our lives. We were both caregivers, two women who never expected to be. I was thankful she saw it too.

"I will be caring for my husband for a few more years, but you, Kate, you will be doing this for the rest of your life. Your strength is unbelievable, and your love is undying, but you must be tired. I don't know how you do it." She laughed then and said, "But again, I could say the same for me." There was such a sadness, almost defeat in her voice. One that I knew all too well.

I watched her wipe her tears and go back to her husband with a smile. I stood there as her reality washed over me. She and her husband should have been enjoying their retirement. They should have been traveling. They worked their whole lives and should have been living their best years right now. For a brief second, I let myself think about a life without autism. Not a life without Cooper, but one where he was free from his struggles. I saw trips to Disney, brothers playing. I didn't know if we would ever get there.

I watched them for a while longer. She helped him with his shoes and his jacket and led him to their car. She buckled him in, smiled at me, and waved goodbye. I saw the sadness in her eyes, but I also saw the love and devotion she had for her husband.

At many points in my motherhood journey, I've felt like it's different than it was supposed to be. Of course, I was Cooper's mom, a blessing that I treasured from the second he was placed in my arms. A blessing that I did not take lightly. But over the years,

I have often felt more like a therapist, a teacher, and a nurse, instead of a mother. Was I a caregiver? If I posed that question on social media today, I would be met with mixed responses. I know, because I've done it before. Many think mothers can't be caregivers. But when I looked at Anne that day taking care of her husband, our roles were incredibly similar.

According to the American Association of Retired Persons (AARP), more than one in five Americans (21.3 percent) are caregivers, having provided care to an adult or child with special needs at some time in the past twelve months. While many caregivers feel their role has given them a sense of purpose or meaning (51 percent), these positive emotions often coexist with feelings of stress or strain. Caregivers report physical, emotional, and financial strain, with two in ten reporting they feel alone (21 percent).

I thought about Anne and Tom a lot that night. She had told me in confidence that she felt judged for not placing her husband in assisted living, but the judgment if she did could be worse. I knew exactly what she meant. As Cooper had aged, and his struggles were becoming greater, many people in my life were quick to share their thoughts on our future. My mother told me frequently that I could never place him in care, saying he was just too vulnerable. She wasn't wrong, but talk about pressure. Another person in my life told me that we should consider our options, that there are places for kids like Cooper.

When Cooper was younger, I lived in a place of denial when it came to thinking about the future. Accepting the reality of our day-to-day was one thing, but accepting the reality that my son might never grow up was another. Don't get me wrong, I tried. I tried to picture the future, but it would bring such a mixed bag of emotions when I did. I would feel guilt for limiting his possible achievements. I would feel negative for looking at the future realistically. I would focus on what I knew, or at least what I thought I knew.

I was fairly certain he would be living with us when he was a grown man. But would he be talking? Would he have any self-care? What about his life? Would it be full of friends? Would he have a job? With Sawyer, I could see the future. I could see him moving out, I could see him dating, working, driving. All the rites of passage that we as adults go through. But with Cooper, I couldn't. And no amount of hope felt right. It all felt wrong.

As Cooper aged, I knew I needed a glimpse into our future. I sought out parents who had adult children like Cooper. Adults who were nonverbal, who were still dressed by their moms, who still held their dad's hand in a crowded parking lot.

In the beginning, I wasn't ready. Maybe I tried too much too soon, because instead of seeing all of their many successes, and how hard they worked to get where they are, I saw all the things they would never do, like driving a car and living independently. And my mama heart couldn't take it. But over time, slowly at first, I was able to realistically look at our future and replace the sadness with joy. The hope with realistic hope.

Other parents used to preach to me, even scold me, for focusing on the future instead of taking it day by day. I think they scolded me to protect me. Because they knew it takes time. My advice is to tiptoe into the future when you are ready. But most importantly, give yourself grace. It's okay to have expectations for your child's future, however low or high they are. You are human. And for me, accepting our future took time.

So how did I know when I was ready for the future? When Cooper was eight years old, we brought him to see Thomas the Train for his fifth time. In the years before, Cooper had somewhat blended in. But at eight, he was no longer little, and I was nervous about having not only the oldest child at the event but also a child who was struggling.

This time it was different. The depot where the event was held had graciously accepted suggestions from parents like me to have a sensory-friendly event for kids like Cooper, kids who struggled with crowds and bright lights and loud sounds. They also didn't put an age limit on the event, understanding that the love of trains doesn't end at a certain age for some people.

When we arrived, I saw him right away, an adult man in a bright blue Thomas the Train T-shirt. He had to be at least twenty-five years old, maybe older. He was very tall and towered over his mother and the majority of the guests at the depot.

He was practically levitating, he was so excited. His joy, it radiated like an aura around him. He was loud, his arms moving wildly. He ran right up to Thomas and started chatting to himself, fingers stimming, head down. He twisted back and forth like my son does.

"I love trains. Trains are my favorite. I love Thomas. Hi, Thomas."

This boy, this man, he was happier than I have ever been in my whole entire life. In that moment, I saw my future and the joy that I had ahead of me. When most of us transition to adulthood, our lives become about jobs, money, and achieving our goals. But this young man, he still had that childlike innocence. I wanted to be near him. I wanted him and his mother in my life. I didn't see the awkwardness of a man attending a child's event. I didn't see sadness. I saw nothing but amazing joy. And I wanted every bit of it in my life. I didn't say hi—I was too shy—but I wish I had. I wish I had told that mom what a great job she was doing and let her know that she and her son inspired me to do better.

On that train platform, I vowed to never hide severe autism again. I would get my son into the community like this young man. I would show the joy, and people could decide for themselves if they wanted to see happy or sad. Because the world deserves to know Cooper, and he deserves to know the world.

I have immersed myself into the world of disability, a world that I never wanted to be a part of, a world that scared me, a world that I assumed was sad. Boy, was I wrong. It's a beautiful world. But to see it, you have to change your way of thinking.

This morning I saw a commercial for an insurance company. With cheesy music playing, it showed the perfect family and house. As the oldest son graduated from high school, the tagline said something like... *These are the moments we prepare for. The only moments that matter.*

I've been thinking about it all day. My mind keeps going back to it. The only moments that matter...

First day of school. Graduation. A college acceptance letter. First job. A promotion. Marriage. Babies. Retirement. But what if a person doesn't achieve those moments? Does their life not matter?

My son is on a different path. Where is the commercial for his life? For his moments? Would they be perceived as negative when really, they aren't?

Our commercial would be about the transition from therapy to adulthood, finding a day program, volunteering, becoming an uncle, guardianship, and someday transitioning to a group home. Those will be our big moments. And I'll tell you this... they are not sad. They matter.

Last night Cooper had his best night. Ever. He asked me to sing "Itsy Bitsy Spider" and moved his fingers up the imaginary web. He ate a whole plate of spaghetti with a fork. He drank water from a cup without spilling. He did a puzzle all by himself. He blew me a kiss when he went upstairs for bed. And when I went to tuck him in, he rubbed his finger across his teeth, reminding me that I forgot to brush his teeth. As if saying, *"Silly Mama."*

I sat down afterward and told him I loved him, and I thought... this is it. He's doing it. He's doing all the things I dreamed of. These are the moments I prayed for. Our moments matter too. Don't ever let anyone tell you they don't.

# SIXTEEN

The day after Cooper's hardest day, I called an emergency meeting with his team from his therapy center, hoping that they would have ideas about how to help us. I didn't want to admit that I was scared. I didn't want to admit that his aggressions were more than I could handle, but I reminded myself that parenting a unique child like Cooper is a humbling experience. And it's okay to ask for help.

His lead therapist informed me that they were experiencing aggression as well. He was exhibiting many unsafe behaviors every day. When I described my hardest night and holding my sweet boy's body as he tried to hurt me, his therapist said that happened to them daily with Cooper. I had no idea. Hurting me is one thing. I can take it. I am his mom. And I will handle it with the gentleness that is needed. But another person?

As she spoke about hitting and kicking, and upward of forty unsafe behaviors a day, I felt the need to apologize. I was saddened and even a little bit shocked that no one had informed me how challenging he was being. Maybe they were protecting me. I didn't know. But I had a feeling of dread as she went on to explain the levels of autism to me and how Cooper was attending a level three center, one for children with significant needs. But recently, his needs seemed to be increasing, and the next resort was an in-patient center. They weren't kicking him out, she quickly reassured me, but we as a team needed to get a handle on this quickly, before it escalated any further. We looked at the data of his behaviors and saw the uptick in October, the month his baby brother was born.

The plan focused immensely on Sawyer and Harbor and keeping them safe. They called it a contingency plan. We wrote down steps of what to do if Cooper became aggressive again. Sawyer would take the baby and lock himself in my office, and he would only come out when I said "all clear." We would get Sawyer into therapy as well to discuss what he was seeing and feeling. Last, we would arm our home with additional alarms, locks, and cameras. It was hard for me to accept that it had come to all this. Had we reached the end of the road at age eight? Was that possible? She assured me that no, we hadn't reached the end, and together we made a plan. She assured me that my family was not alone.

I reached out to other parents who had aggressive children. I found comfort in their understanding but was saddened to hear the choices many of them were forced to make. One woman shared that her two sons had to be split up twenty-four hours a day. They rented an apartment, and she and her husband took turns living there with their autistic son. Another woman told me their neurotypical children went to boarding school; it was the only way they could keep their autistic daughter home.

I reached out to an ER nurse, an old friend, and asked if she ever saw children with severe aggression. Her response was so sad. "All the time. Parents drop them off because they have nowhere to turn, and we hold them for five days, max, drugging them so they are compliant."

Another friend signed away her custodial rights when she brought her son to a residential treatment facility. The facility refused to take him when they learned he was nonverbal, saying they were not equipped to help a person like him. She told me of the desperation she felt when she realized there was no help. Parents told me about severe aggressions, hitting, kicking, even self-injuring. That alone was devastating. But they also spoke of their fear of speaking about it publicly. People judged, blamed the child, blamed the parent. So they stayed quiet. They lived in silence and fear.

I couldn't believe our life had come to this. We were living in survival mode, far from thriving. It felt like we were walking on eggshells, which is no way to live. And we had been doing it for quite some time. I never knew about this part of autism before it happened to us.

I am a true believer that everything happens for a reason. It's cliché, I know. But the universe has a way of giving us gentle nudges. That evening, my mother-in-law saw Cooper in rare form for the first time. I knew people didn't believe us when we told them about the dangerous, even scary, sides of disability. They probably thought we were exaggerating or embellishing. We weren't. As we sat there in her kitchen, I held my son's arms to keep him from hitting his own head in frustration. I rocked back and forth with him. I whispered in his ear. He was anxious about paper and a missing color and about the Wi-Fi not being fast enough and about going home.

Jamie was outside with our other two boys, and I was in the ring with Cooper. And for the first time I said the words out loud...

"I don't think I can do this anymore, Diane. I think I give up."

My mother-in-law, a retired nurse, said, "Kate, look at him. He doesn't feel good. You have to look at medicating. His brain hurts. He hurts. No one wants to feel like that. If he was a diabetic, you would give him insulin. This is no different."

At this point in Cooper's life, I will admit medicating had never crossed my mind. I didn't even know what they would medicate him for. I didn't want to drug my child. I didn't want him to be a zombie. I had always been against medicating. There is a stigma around it. A shame, even. Parents didn't openly talk about this sort of thing. To be honest, I was scared to even ask questions for fear of being judged. But she was right. It was like a light-bulb moment for me. Cooper didn't feel well. I couldn't remember the last time I had seen my son happy or smile or laugh.

And to be clear, I would never judge another parent for medicating their child. For me, though, it felt like giving up. It felt like admitting defeat. And failing as a parent. I would soon learn that medications can be a wonderful tool to add to your toolbox.

When I spoke with the people in our life about it, I was met with mixed feelings.

"Don't drug your child!" "Medications can be life-changing!" "He'll be like a zombie." "I wish we had started our child on meds years ago."

I heard stories of children suddenly being able to focus, sleep, even interact in the community. The children they described after being on medications seemed unattainable to me. I couldn't even imagine sitting with Cooper. Or going to a restaurant. Or even communicating back and forth.

The pros and cons weighed on my heart, but I found so much hope in the possible good that could come. This felt like our last option.

I made an appointment with a highly recommended doctor to discuss medication, but later canceled it. I then made a second appointment after we hosted a book club at our house and Cooper wouldn't let any of the guests sit on our chairs. He spent the three hours screaming at anyone who sat. We had to end the book club early, asking our guests to leave. It was just too hard for Cooper to have anyone in our home. It was time.

As I waited anxiously for his appointment, the phrase *oh, that's*

*just autism* ran through my head on repeat. It had been said to
me countless times over the years. But what did that mean, really? I dove into research, reading books and blogs and talking
to people who had older kids like mine. I began to think about
autism differently, breaking it down into the parts that made it
up. I found out there were many comorbidities that could ac-
company autism. Anxiety, depression, ADHD, sleep disorders,
intellectual disorders, and so on. The list seemed never-ending.
All the parts of Cooper that I had been lumping together for
years, and calling autism, actually weren't. And some were very
treatable with medications.

For years I hated the word *autism*. I was angry at it, even. It
had been an explanation that I couldn't understand, a word that
was thrown at every issue we were facing. It was something we
needed to overcome. After shifting my thinking, looking at autism as a composite of different parts versus a single whole, I no
longer feared the word. It was my son's anxiety that was debili-
tating. His ADHD that consumed him. His apraxia that stole his
words. And his intellectual disability that hindered his learning.
And his autism, that was who he was. I used to think it was just
a part of him, but really it was every part of him. And it's not a
negative thing. Cooper is autistic. He has autism. However you
want to say it. *Autism* isn't a dirty word to us. I know people
who whisper it. Some who even refuse to say it out loud in the
presence of their children. Not us.

Autism isn't an excuse. It's an explanation.

I wanted him to live with autism but without anxiety, ADHD,
and all the other parts that plagued him. I ultimately wanted
him to be happy. It was as simple as that. Happiness above all.

When we went to the appointment, I was ready to advocate,
armed with data, and even ready to beg for help. I was nervous
I would be judged, but as Cooper rolled on the ground, kicking his feet at my legs, the doctor put her hand on my back and
promised me that she would help us. I was blown away by the

compassion she offered us. In so many appointments before, I felt like I had to defend autism, explain it, even. But not this time. She asked me what the hardest parts of life were right now.

"His anxiety. Our whole family walks on eggshells around the beast that is his anxiety."

We left with a prescription and hope, but this hope felt different. It was laced with so much desperation and a ticking clock. This had to work because we were running out of time.

On January 23, two days after we started antianxiety medication, for the first time in his life, Cooper sat for longer than mere seconds. He was eight years old, and I had never seen him sit before. Not like that. Not peacefully. Not ever.

He was wearing a red thermal shirt and brightly colored leggings, his pants of choice those days, and he was sitting on the couch in our living room. I walked by to take a load of laundry upstairs, and I stopped in my tracks and waited. My mouth was open as Jamie joined me. Together, we stood there, tears streaming down both of our faces.

He wasn't a blur of movement and sound. He was still. After minutes of us standing there, he looked up and smiled, as if surprised that we were watching him so intently. I dropped my laundry and without saying a word, Jamie and I both joined him on the couch, each holding an arm as tightly as we could.

We sat there for nearly thirty minutes with Cooper. Something that had never happened before.

In the weeks that followed, Cooper's anxiety released its hold on him. I describe it as a weight being lifted off his back. He stood taller. He looked at us with his eyes, and they were alive and bright. He started smiling more, slowly at first. Then giggling. Then poking fun at his brothers, even teasing me and his dad.

The transformation was almost unbelievable but undeniable at the same time. As the weeks turned to months, we were able to unlock our doors, even open the windows. He stopped lining up chairs and putting everything in our bathtubs. He stopped stripping beds and hoarding photos. He stopped screaming. He stopped hurting himself and others.

We had our first family movie night. Our first family dinner. Cooper visited Target and the grocery store. He held his baby brother.

And he said his first word. It was *Mom*. Only he said it long and drawn out, each syllable pronounced: "MMM-OOO-MMM." It was perfect. Other words followed. The most important one was *Sawyer*. The first time he said it, Sawyer cried.

Our goal had been to help Cooper find peace, to calm the chaos in his brain. The words were an unexpected gift.

People ask me often about my steps toward acceptance. One of the biggest ones for me was when I realized communication can happen in many forms. It doesn't have to be words. Cooper could have a meaningful conversation with sounds, gestures, his iPad even. And that was enough. Knowing that he could request a drink of water by bringing me to the sink or tell me he wanted to go to the zoo by showing me an episode of Barney visiting animals...that was enough. I grieved the words and I moved on, and after the grief came so much beauty.

When he reached twenty words, I told myself that I didn't care if he ever learned another one. I was grateful for what we had. Every sound a blessing. No one knows if he will ever become conversational, but we don't care. When you move from hope to realistic hope, this beautiful thing happens. You relieve the pressure of waiting, and if and when it does happen, the joy is indescribable.

If you were a fly on our wall, before and after we tackled Cooper's anxiety, you would be amazed at the differences in our home. We lived in a prison of his anxiety, and while it might never go away fully, we felt free.

I will never say that medicating a child is a cure. Because it's not. Nor was it our goal. Instead, it was to help him feel better and to give him peace from his demons. And it did that.

He was still Cooper, of course, unapologetically. Cooper was and is still severely affected by autism, that part hasn't changed. But he was happy. And he was calm. And he was present. He was more himself than I had ever seen him be before.

I beat myself up sometimes for waiting so long to think about autism differently. I wonder how far along he would be if I had started years earlier. But hindsight is twenty-twenty. I had to try everything first. My advice to parents is to understand that helping a child with autism is not one-size-fits-all. There is rarely ever one thing that helps them. For Cooper, and our family, we had to fill his toolbox. For him, it was a combination of the right therapies, the right medications, and age.

The other day I read a comment on one of my Facebook posts that read, "For some families, there is no light at the end of the tunnel." I thought about it all night. And when my toddler woke up at midnight for a hug, and then again while I drank my coffee and watched the news.

I thought back to our hardest days, when there was no apparent light at the end of the tunnel. We lived like that for eight years while we battled to help our son. And I can say with certainty that when some old mom on the internet told me there was light at the end of the tunnel, I most likely plotted her demise in my mind. When someone is sinking, there is nothing more annoying than someone who's been there/done that telling you it will get better. Because you want a life raft. You want someone who understands exactly what you are going through.

I'm here to say that I do. I completely and entirely understand, because we lived it. Many days we still do. And at the risk of someone yelling at me, I will say it again, because there is someone who needs to read it.

There is light at the end of the tunnel…it just may not be the light that you imagined. The light might be finding the right services and supports. It might be finding the right medications or the right therapies. It might be acceptance and getting past the emotional parts that seem to destroy us in the beginning. The comparisons. The differences.

The light might be finding a support system that understands. Friends you can cry and laugh with. The light might be someday finding a group home. It might be finding a person you can trust who can help you in your home and find balance with your other children.

When my son was diagnosed at age three, the light was my son talking someday. And being mainstreamed. It was our family traveling to Disney World and not thinking twice about attending a family event. I still don't know if those things will ever happen for us.

My light is different now. It's my amazing son being truly happy with his life. He loves school. He can sit. He can communicate without words. He sleeps with his brother. He laughs. His body and mind can be at peace.

We've figured out what our light at the end of the tunnel looked like. And I think that's what I needed someone to tell me years ago. You have a choice. You can live in the angry, sad, woe-is-me place, one that I knew all too well. Or you can choose the light. Even on your darkest days. Once I realized I had a choice, everything changed for me. I stood straighter. I saw more clearly. But most importantly, I let out the breath that I had been holding, waiting for him to get better. Before, I thought getting better meant no more autism. I was wrong. Getting better was this. A smiling, silly boy dancing in my kitchen to "The Wheels on the Bus," stealing a hug as he runs by.

We made it. Him first. Then me.

# SEVENTEEN

Motherhood is a funny thing. One day you are walking along, completely confident in who you are, showered, rested, and carefree. Then wham. You become a mother. And suddenly you can't remember the last time you slept through the night, or had a shower, or what hobbies you used to like. You peek in the mirror one day and barely recognize the woman staring back at you. This one is clearly held together with dry shampoo and caffeine, two products that you used to be able to live without. But you don't really care all that much. Because you're a mama. You are raising tiny humans and it's the best job on earth.

Certain parts of motherhood came really easy to me. The love part for sure. I fell in love with each of my babies the second I found out I was pregnant with them. The mama bear part came easy as well. I knew the first moment I held each of them in my arms that I would protect them until my dying breath.

But I wasn't prepared to completely lose myself in the process. I wasn't prepared to turn into an entirely different person after three kids. I could say it was autism. It wasn't just that, although

I would be lying if I said that it didn't change me in the most profound ways. But my other boys changed me too. They each challenge me, exhaust me, and fill me up in their own ways.

My boys are now ten, eight, and two. I think back to the woman I was before them, before *autism* entered our vocabulary. I like to use the term *blissfully unaware*. Many people will stay in that place, naive about special children and differences for their whole lives, and if you ask them, they probably consider themselves lucky that they've never experienced what I have. They feel pity for families like mine. But I can say with unbelievable certainty that *we* are the lucky ones. We were given the gift of seeing the good, the bad, the hard, and the ugly in this world. And above all, kindness. There is so much kindness. Children like ours are angels put on this earth. And my Cooper, he has this way of bringing the good people into our lives and weeding out the ones that don't deserve his light.

At thirty-seven, I am surrounded by good. In a way, I like to think having Cooper cut the nonsense out of my life. I have no time for people or things that drag us down. Negativity and ugliness aren't an option in our world. Not anymore. We live a life of gratitude because we choose Cooper. And that means we choose joy.

To be clear, the hard parts of our life are not gone. Far from it. Our best days wouldn't register as wins for most people, and we don't know a day without challenges. But that doesn't matter. We take the wins when we can because we remember the days when there weren't any. Today, we celebrate everything.

If you are wondering whether I am past the grief I spoke about in almost every chapter of this book, the answer is tricky. Grief is a sneaky thing. It's not linear and it's not logical. For me, it lies dormant, under the surface, for periods of time. And then it reappears when I least expect it.

Yesterday, my doorbell rang. It was a little boy, nine years old, shaggy blond hair, and soft-spoken. He lives down the road.

He rides his mom's bike and wears a bright-colored helmet. He sticks out because he is built like a linebacker like his dad. Like my Cooper. He politely asked for Sawyer. And out of nowhere, I felt the sting in my stomach. The tears sprang to my eyes. I held my breath for a second. And I waited for the inevitable flashes before my eyes of what could have been. For a brief second, I saw my Cooper independently riding a bike to the neighbor's house and using his sweet voice to ask a child to play. After so many years of hoping and waiting for that type of independence and play to happen, it was hard to even picture it happening. I could hear the words, though: *"Mom, I'm going out to play!"* I could see me standing there from the door, watching him go.

Grief. She comes out of nowhere. I don't think it ever goes away. It couldn't possibly. But grief is love. Grief is hope. Grief is acceptance. And I will carry the weight of grief with me forever.

My friend who has a teenager with autism calls them paper cuts, the little things that our kids will never do, the differences that scream at us. Another autism mom that I know references them as pinpricks in your side. As we get stronger as parents, we get used to them. But they still sting. They still cause us to stop what we are doing, feel, and acknowledge the pain. I am no stranger to any of it. And while I choose joy every single day of my life, my body is covered in paper cuts. One for words. One for friends. One for kids his same age. One for the car he will never drive. But the paper cuts make you stronger. I like to think my cuts have turned to scars, and they give me character. They've toughened me over the years.

As Cooper and I have aged, and we both have settled into autism, I see things differently now. Where I once saw sadness, I now see beauty. For years I couldn't look into the future. It hurt too much. But now, I am ready. I saw an adult man at a water park a few months back. I was chasing kids, managing chaos, when he caught my eye. He had to be in his thirties, yet he sat in the toddler section of the pool. His face was pressed up against the waterfall coming from the slide above. And he was laughing. This huge, happy, deep laugh that only comes from a place of pure joy. I stopped in my tracks. Cooper actually did too. We stood there, staring and smiling. I can tell you with certainty that years ago, I would have seen sadness in that scene. Not anymore. I saw joy. And I wanted it for my son too.

If I let myself, I can still get caught up in the grief and wondering. They go hand in hand. I would give anything to know the mysteries inside my son's head. I wish I could step into his world and fully immerse myself for one day, one hour, one minute. But it doesn't work like that. I may never know what he is thinking, but I can't dwell on that. I have to focus on what I know. He is happy. And that is enough.

If you've never met anyone like my son, you're missing out. Discover the gift of knowing someone who has special needs, or who is different. Do it today. I promise you the word *pity* will vanish from your vocabulary. And it will be exchanged with *joy, resilience*, and *triumph*.

Sometimes, I think back to the friend who told me in my hardest days that it took her five years to get to acceptance. I remember thinking that couldn't be right. It would put my son at almost nine years old. She was right. It took me five years exactly to walk bravely and proudly into the land of acceptance. I wasn't pulled in. I didn't crawl in. I walked in happily.

Today, when grieving parents ask me how long it takes to reach acceptance, I answer differently than my friend did. She wasn't wrong, but I see it another way. My son is exactly who he is supposed to be. And he was from the day he was placed in my arms. But me, whew, I was a mess. I made mistakes. I stumbled. I fell. I lost my voice and then found it. I thought when I named my blog, *Finding Cooper's Voice*, I was on a journey to find his. I no longer think that. I was searching for mine. I found it. And he guided me every step of the way.

It didn't take me five years to get to acceptance. It took me five years to become the person I was meant to be. The person after autism.

Sometimes I wonder who I would have been if I didn't have Cooper in my life. Would I be the mom who sits leisurely by the pool? Would I arrange endless vacations? Would I host dinner parties and book clubs? The answer is maybe. But my life took a different turn. An unexpected one for sure. So instead, I am the mom who swims with her ten-year-old on her back, taking him in the women's restroom to dress him before and after. We never travel because Cooper can't fly, but we do host dinner parties, ones with guests we have carefully chosen, ones who take the time to say hi to our mostly silent son, and gasp at his trains, and don't bat an eye when he strips down at 8:00 p.m. because people have overstayed their welcome.

I like to say I was thrown into autism, and it was a sink-or-swim situation for sure. I swam.

If you follow me on Facebook, you've probably heard my tag line, *Find the Joy.* I get asked daily by parents who are beat down and exhausted how I found it during our darkest times. They see me now, this version of me, laughing about hoarding and celebrating nonverbal communication, and they wonder how I got here. They ask because they saw me crying in my car, years ago, in that viral video, talking about how this life is not okay.

It was a journey.

When Cooper was diagnosed with autism, I took off running, motivated to fix him. I raced from one thing to the next, manically, trying to obtain as much information as possible. Books, articles, blogs—whatever could help me figure out the mysteries of my son. I thought I was in a race against time, refusing to pause even for a second. If I stopped to catch my breath, the realities of his delays would consume me. I had to keep going. I had to keep researching, trying more and more. My goal was simple: to do everything possible so he would be "fine" by kindergarten.

And the options to supposedly help him were endless, until they weren't. Supplements, diets, specialists, therapies, programs, the more the better. I tried so many different things. My hope rising and falling. Before I knew it, I had become the hard parts of my son's disability. The diagnosis had taken over everything in my life. It had stolen my joy. I let the words of the so-called professionals crush my hope.

"Your child will never talk, ride a bike, or make a friend."

"Your child has the most severe case of autism I have ever seen."

"If a child doesn't speak by age four then game over."

When we reached the end of the road, which happened way earlier than I thought it ever would have, I said *no more*. The world, society, me...we were all trying to make Cooper into something he wasn't. It's hard for me to admit that out loud. But in my defense, from the day he was diagnosed, autism was presented to me as something to overcome. I was failed as a parent. I was given a death sentence when I should have been given a ticket to a new life.

When Cooper reached his hardest days, it was time for me to make a change. There was no more pretending that autism was going away. But the change needed was not for Cooper this time. It was for me. I was doing the same thing over and over and expecting different results. I was living in a land of hope, which can be a beautiful place. And to this day I tell parents to hold on to hope as tight as they can. But I was hoping for the wrong things. It was time for me to hope for happiness. For acceptance. For peace.

People often ask me to tell the story of when I realized it was time to make a change. I can't pinpoint it exactly. I can't tell you the one story that bridged me into acceptance. It was more like an evolution. I remember no longer caring what people thought about me or my son. I remember once sitting in the entryway of Target, holding Cooper in a bear hug. I heard snickers. I heard gasps of annoyance as if us being there was affecting them. But I didn't care. I wanted to teach my son how to go to the store, and I knew it was going to take a lot of practice before we had success. Those snickers, those comments and judgments, I let them fuel me. I let them thicken my skin and roll off my back.

Another time, I found myself mistakenly on the cancer floor at Children's Hospital. I was stretching my legs after managing one of Cooper's meltdowns in the hallway above. He was scared, and doctor's appointments were a lot for him. I was taking a break, and wandering, feeling sorry for myself, wondering why everything had to be so damn hard. Suddenly I heard voices coming from a room. People were singing "Happy Birthday." I peeked in as I strolled by and saw a family gathered around a bed, singing to a girl no older than my son. She had a scarf covering her head. I froze. It wasn't like me to stare like that. To intrude. I mumbled out an apology and ran to the elevator, where I fell to my knees. I dropped to the ground in gratitude. I got to leave the hospital with my son. My challenging, amazing, complicated son. I was humbled.

I remember no longer thinking of Cooper's life as a race against time. Before, I was so focused on his age and what he *should be* doing that I missed what he was *actually* doing. Today, Cooper isn't really an age or a grade to us. He is Cooper and his time is infinite.

I once received a message from a mama who had a son much older than Cooper but was no stranger to the world of nonverbal autism and aggression. She told me that when she and her husband realized her son's challenges were not going away, or even improving, they decided to travel the world. They bought an RV, and they took their son across the United States. She commented on his joy and how making him happy had become her one and only goal. In that moment I felt inspired to do better and to not waste one more second being sad.

At a certain point, I realized I was missing my son's life, waiting for it to get better. I was living in this perpetual place of grief, where I told myself, *I'll be happy when he talks, happy when he goes to school, happy when he starts sleeping.* There was always a *when.* Always an excuse why I wasn't happy. I had to let go of the life I had imagined. We all do. But it was more than that. I had to learn and accept that our life was going to be different. Sometimes harder, sometimes easier. We no longer get the luxury of walking the same path as others before us. I might have fought that reality, probably for too long. But once I recognized that we would be fine in this different life, I accepted it.

A friend of mine with a son like Cooper once said to me, "Everyone has something hard in their life, Kate. They may not tell you, but they do. No one is spared. Ours is autism. And we don't get to choose it. Life doesn't work like that. But we do get to choose how we respond to our hard."

She was so right. I could look at my life and be angry. I could have a chip on my shoulder. I could carry on and focus on what we were missing. But why? Life is about choice. And I choose joy. I choose to see the beauty and be thankful for what I have been given. Once you do that, you've made it through.

Over the years I wished for a glimpse into the future, a crystal ball that could tell me that this was all going to be okay. I wanted to know what our life would be like when Cooper was ten and fifteen and twenty. I wanted to know if he would be talking. I wanted to know if he would be happy. I wanted to know if we would get past the challenges that consumed us for so long. I wanted to know how this all ended. Because to me, the only success story was one where Cooper was fine.

I had so many questions and no answers. Was I doing enough? Had I done the right things? Had I missed something that could have changed Cooper's future for the better? For so long, helping him felt like walking down a never-ending hallway with hundreds of doors. In I would go, out I would come. Sometimes whatever was behind that door would help, but often not.

Special-needs parents live in a constant state of worrying and wondering. I think we actually get comfortable there. And if for one second it gets easy, we wonder if we are missing something. Some doctors will call it PTSD.

I wish I had answers to those questions, even today. The boy who was frozen in time for so long has come so far. He loves the alphabet, DVD cases, old train magazines, and mail. Every day is the best day of his life. He has never once woken up crabby, even during his hardest years. Every morning he woke up joyful and dancing. He asks me daily to visit fire trucks and to fly on airplanes and for a birthday party. Which we throw, all the time. Balloons, cake, and all.

His life looks nothing like his peers'. But he is happy, and that's all that matters. Cooper is a success story. He is amazing. Every day he lives in a world that makes no sense to him, and he teaches us how to be better.

I feel like I weathered the storm long enough that I can be a resource to others now. I often think about what I needed to hear when my son was diagnosed, or when I was at my lowest points. What pearls of wisdom would have helped me the most? So, I leave you with this:

Much of what the professionals predict about the future may be wrong. No one knows what the future holds for our kids. No one. Take it with a grain of salt and move on. Not one person on this planet can predict our kids' futures. And if predictions do turn out to be right, well, you will figure that part out too. But don't let someone's words weigh you down for years like I did. If I had the power to change one thing about our journey to this point, it would be to remove the negativity that comes after diagnosis. I think about the narrative that we were told countless times over the years. The focus was on what Cooper couldn't do.

But can you imagine if we were told positives instead? Think how much that would change a parent's perspective.

Our kids are lifelong learners. Development doesn't stop at age four or six, like I was told so many times over the years. Once I fully immersed myself in the autism world, and stopped fearing the future, I heard countless stories of children saying their first words at twelve, fifteen, even twenty-six! I've been told that our kids learn more in their twenties than in all the years before. How's that for hope?

Our children have limitations. Every person does. There is no use denying that. There are things that Cooper will never be able to do. Do not waste your time on those things. Instead, pour yourself into the things that are possible.

Feel the grief. Feel the pain. You had expectations as a parent, and they didn't come true. You are not a bad person for being sad about that. You don't love your child any less. This is hard stuff, but don't run from it. Don't avoid it or ignore it. Feel it. That is when healing happens. And then pick yourself up and keep fighting.

Give yourself grace. I have made so many mistakes as a mother, many of them publicly. I am not perfect. I am far from it. And I will never claim to be an expert in autism, but I am an expert in Cooper. You are the expert in your child. Remember that. And give yourself grace for the things you didn't know years before. When we know better, we do better.

Know when to push and when not to. It's a fine line even for me today. Cooper would be happy sitting on my couch twenty-four hours a day watching train videos for the rest of his life. But that won't help him grow. He needs to get out into the world. He needs to learn skills, whatever that may look like. I am learning to push when I can, ever so gently. That's how growth happens.

Choose your battles. As a special-needs parent, there is no phoning it in. If your child is like my son, he needs to be taught everything. When I think about that, I get overwhelmed. It's so much. Safety, education, self-care, and so on. Choose your battles. I don't care if my son ever learns to tie his shoes; he can rock a pair of slip-on Vans. But buckling his seat belt is huge. We've been practicing for years. And I won't give up because I know he can learn to do it. And someday, when I'm older, it will be hard for me to bend over and buckle him. Choose your battles because your energy is not endless.

The goal should always be independence for our children. That is one of the keys to happiness, in my opinion, being able to independently live your life. I know that may never happen fully for Cooper, but I want him to be as close to independence as he possibly can. That is my most important job as a mother, to prepare Cooper for the future.

Don't take advice from people who don't understand your life, or those you wouldn't trust to raise your children. Everyone and their neighbor will have an opinion on how you are living your life. You decide whose opinion matters. Do not let someone criticize your decisions who doesn't understand the challenges you face.

There will be people in your life that you love, and who love you, who simply cannot be what you need them to be when it comes to autism. It's just too hard for them. Too complicated. And they aren't necessarily bad people. They just can't be your person for this part. The earlier you accept that, the less heartache you will have.

Prioritize your spouse. Do whatever it takes to get time with your partner. This parenting thing for us is not a sprint. It's not eighteen summers like they say. It's a lifetime. Find someone who understands you and who accepts your weird, hard, almost unbelievable life. If you find that person, hold on to them.

Take the help. Your life is difficult and it's okay to acknowledge that it is hard. There, I said it. I validated you, something I so desperately needed many years ago. Take the help. Take respite, take the offer from a friend to make dinner. Take financial help. There are no medals given out at the end of this life for the person who suffered the most.

Find something that works for your family. We can't go to parks, or movie theaters, or zoos, or restaurants. In fact, the list of places we can go successfully is tiny. Years ago, Jamie and I made it our mission to find one family activity we could all do together. For us, that is boating. It is our escape from reality. Find your escape. It probably won't look like other people's version of that activity, but who cares? Do what works and bring joy to your family.

Always try one more thing. I can't even tell you how important that is. When I have been at my lowest, not knowing how to help Cooper, beat down by this world, I've often wanted to give up. And maybe for a few moments I did. But I have always picked myself up and tried one more thing to help him. I tell you this because no one else is going to fight for your kid like you will. They need you to be that person for them. To never give up and to fight tirelessly.

Celebrate everything. Every small, tiny, huge-to-you victory. Who cares if no one cares or no one gets it? You celebrate!

Speak your truth. Even if your voice shakes. Share your life. You don't have to be a blogger or write a book. Just start talking at the grocery store or the park. Tell your stories. Own them. And don't let anyone shame you for them. Our lives are different. We don't have to hide that.

And last, choose joy. Every morning, before my feet hit the ground, whether it's 3:00 a.m. or 6:00 a.m., I take a moment and pause. And I tell myself to choose joy all day long. I don't care if it sounds cheesy or ridiculous. I do it every single day. I am the only person who gets to decide how I feel. I get to choose. It's amazingly powerful once you realize it. I've had parents challenge me on this and tell me that they have days, weeks even, without joy. I don't argue with them because you can't tell someone how to feel. I just tell them my stories. We can have awful days full of aggression, self-injuring, and screaming. And I can go to bed angry and mad at the world. But when I wake up, in those few moments, I always reflect on the day before, and I can always find an ounce of joy. Try it. It will change your life.

A few weeks ago, I found myself at a local coffee shop, grabbing a quick coffee. As I was adding creamer to my cup, a table caught my eye. A woman, a bit older than me I would guess. And a man, possibly in his twenties. He had bright red, oversize headphones on. He was wearing a costume even though Halloween was still weeks away. A smile came to my lips. I knew. I could just tell. He was like my Cooper. Instead of rushing out, hiding from our future, I snuck into the booth just behind them. I embrace the future now, wanting nothing more than to know what my relationship with Cooper will look like. I watched her cut his food, and wipe his mouth, the conversation staying mostly one-sided. As she spoke about their day, listing out each event, the same way I do, he perked up every so often at certain words. *Library* was one. He gasped just like Cooper does, his excitement radiating at the fun they had ahead. He never spoke to her, not out loud, but they did have a conversation. Just like the ones I have with Cooper. The mother using words, the son using gestures, sounds, and expressions. I stayed a few minutes longer, in awe of how they were out in the community, together. And I set my next goal. That will be Cooper and me. We will get there, in time.

Years ago, when Cooper was little, I had an experience like this one, only it didn't make me feel good. It was a mother and son, but instead of a boy like Cooper, it was a mother and her neurotypical son, and me feeling robbed and slighted as I heard them speak about college applications and his part-time job. I felt grief and a loss for what could have been.

I didn't get here overnight. I didn't walk a straight line, and boy, did I make mistakes. Some that I may never live down. But, well, I got here. I made it.

I have a favor to ask you, too.

Once you make it through, help another parent. Text them. Call them or go to them. Sit with them in the dark. Be the person you needed in the beginning. You might be the only person in their life who understands what they are going through. Because you have been there too. You know the unique grief they are feeling may take months or years to work through, like it did for you. And it may even return when they least expect it. And don't rush them through. Grief is not linear, my friends. You know that. Be the friend you needed in the beginning.

And then, when it's time, show them the bright side, the beautiful side that emerges after the darkness. Show them the beauty in giving a vulnerable child their best life, the joy in celebrating every victory, no matter how small. We get to see success in a whole different way. The joy in a child reaching a milestone that they have worked on for months or years. Tell them about the precious little human that they get to protect and celebrate.

Tell them that we won the lottery, that people should be jealous of us because we get the children with the purest hearts who know no evil or greed or deception. We get children who will hold our hand forever and remind us what really matters in life. We are the lucky ones.

Remind them just how lucky they are to have this beautiful, amazing, perfect child to be their teacher. They'll get there. Just like you did. Just like all before us did.

I recently stumbled upon a definition of the word *autism*. It was different from the clinical one I was used to. The Māori word for *autism* is *takiwātanga*. Translated it means, "In one's own time and space." I fell in love with it. Cooper. Me. Our family. We all settled into autism in our own time and space.

I used to be scared of forever. I'm not anymore. Now I am thankful. Because I get forever, with my boy.

★ ★ ★ ★ ★

# RESOURCES

## Books

Colson, Emily. *Dancing with Max: A Mother and Son Who Broke Free*. Grand Rapids, Michigan: Zondervan, 2012.

Hague, Jason. *Aching Joy: Following God through the Land of Unanswered Prayer*. Colorado Spring: NavPress, 2018.

Hall, Valerie. *Immersed: Our Experience with Autism*. Visual Summit Media and Publishing, 2016.

Hampton, Kelle. *Bloom: Finding Beauty in the Unexpected*. New York: William Morrow Paperbacks, 2013.

TerKeurst, Lysa. *It's Not Supposed to Be This Way: Finding Unexpected Strength When Disappointments Leave You Shattered*. Tennessee: Thomas Nelson, 2018.

## Blogs

Cariello, Carrie. *What Color is Monday?* https://carriecariello.com.

Dunn, Jennifer. *Keeping Up With Kya—#OnWeGo*. https://keepingupwithkya.com.

Hoogerwerf, Leasa. *Cody Speaks*. Facebook.
https://www.facebook.com/cody.codyspeaks.

Magro, Kerry. Kerry Magro. http://kerrymagro.com.

Shaklee, Eileen Carmody. *Autism with a Side of Fries*.
https://autismwithasideoffries.blogspot.com.

## Essays

Bombeck, Erma. "The Special Mother." *Today*, September 4, 1993.

Kingsley, Emily Perl. "Welcome to Holland." Down Syndrome Association of Simcoe County. 1987.
http://www.dsasc.ca/uploads/8/5/3/9/8539131/welcome_to_holland.pdf.

## Video

Beckham, Ash. "We're all hiding something. Let's find the courage to open up." *TEDxBoulder*. 2013.
https://www.ted.com/talks/ash_beckham_we_re_all_hiding_something_let_s_find_the_courage_to_open_up/transcript?langua.

"Father and Son with Autism." *Upworthy*. 2016. Facebook.
https://www.facebook.com/Upworthy/videos/for-this-proud-father-and-his-son-with-autism-patience-love-and-compassion-can-o/1236055726435283/.

# ACKNOWLEDGMENTS

I am grateful to the many people who inspired, encouraged, and supported me in the effort to write this book. I for one wasn't expecting a global pandemic that would shut the world down, the demands of homeschooling, or the blessing of a fourth pregnancy all while trying to tell the story of our family, so I am very thankful to everyone who pitched in to give me the opportunities to write.

My heartfelt thank-you to Rosemarie Lieberman for falling in love with my family and not only encouraging me to write this book but helping me to do so.

Thank you to Jennifer Weis for believing in me from the very beginning.

Thank you, Erika Imranyi, for holding my hand through this whole entire process.

Thank you to the friends I have, old and new, for accepting our unique family and giving us grace when we need it.

Thank you to Cooper for patiently waiting for me to become the mom you needed me to be. And for giving me the gift of sight. You have taught me to see what really matters in this world and to let go of the rest.

Thank you to Sawyer for being everything and more and for being my constant in an upside-down, inside-out world. Your needing me saved me, buddy.

Thank you to Harbor, the boy who healed our family and brought so much joy to it. You became the bridge between two worlds and two brothers.

To my husband, Jamie. You know that feeling of wanting to be home. That is you. You feel like home to me. Thank you for always waiting for me with open arms.

Thank you to my family: Mom, Dad, Dad, and Doug and Diane for supporting our family along the way. This has often been a lonely journey, and being able to visit you, or call, even, saved us many times over.

Thank you to each and every person who sat with me in the dark and didn't force me to rush through the pain or feel one way or another. You have taught me the importance of simply listening and not trying to fix. Thank you for that.

And lastly, thank you to those who have the courage to share their story, whether it's about autism or not. Showing vulnerability honestly is a gift. You inspire me to be better and do better.

I could never have done this alone.

Thank you.